FATIMA:
The FULL Story

By
JOHN DE MARCHI, I.M.C.

Translated from the Portuguese by
I.M. Kingsbury

AMI Press, Inc.
Washington, NJ 07882

Imprimatur: Rev. Msgr. John R. Torney,
Administrator's Delegate
September 16, 1986

ISBN 0-911988-70-X

first edition, 1950
second edition, 1980
third edition, 1981
fourth edition, 1983
fifth edition, 1985

This edition under the exclusive rights of AMI Press, Inc. in the English language contains all the text of the 1985 fifth edition published by Consolata Missions of Fatima, Portugal. A new introduction written by John M. Haffert has been added and the contents page updated.

I thought that there was little or nothing further to be said about Fatima. But here comes a priest, who, by questioning the contemporaries of the apparitions, and interrogating the very air, the stones, the wells, the holm oaks, the goats and even the wolves of the Serra de Aire, by gathering up every sound and giving life to dead leaves fallen on the ground, by linking and binding together all the scattered pieces, gives us the complete panorama of the greatest event of our century.

Fatima is, in the course of history, the beginning of a new era.

And I, for my part, express my thanks to Father De Marchi, congratulating him on being numbered among the greatest Fatima writers.

+ John Evangelist
former Bishop of Aveiro
Portugal

(extract from the first edition)

CONTENTS

CONTENTS

FATIMA: THE FULL STORY

AN IMPORTANT EXPLANATION

by John M. Haffert

FATHER John DeMarchi had already been in Fatima three years when I met him there at the home of Maria de Freitas in 1946.

He was the first "foreign" priest associated with the Sanctuary of Fatima *and has written what is perhaps the most complete and authoritative book on the Fatima apparitions.*

This book is based not only on the Memoirs of Lucia (as are most such books) but also upon long, *personal conversations* with the families of the children, as well as Lucia herself.

First published in Portugal under the title *A Woman More Brilliant than the Sun,* it became (and still is) the most popular and widely read book about Fatima.

Father DeMarchi's Story

Father DeMarchi was a brilliant young priest of the Consolata Missionary Society with a gift for languages. In addition to his general studies he spent three years at the Pontifical Biblical Institute in Rome where he learned not only the languages of the Bible but also mastered Portuguese, Spanish, French and later Amharic (one of the languages of Ethiopia) besides his native Italian.

When the Archbishop of Mozambique sent a petition to Rome in 1943 asking to have a member of the Consolata Missions sent to Portugal to open a seminary there (so that missionaries for the Portuguese colonies of Africa could be trained in Portugal), the community chose Father DeMarchi.

Despite the difficulties of travel at the height of World War II in 1943, Father DeMarchi made his way to Portugal, arriving on June 13, Feast of St. Anthony of Padua.

"This seemed to be a loving sign," Father DeMarchi said, "because I was born in the Diocese of Padua and always had great devotion to St. Anthony whom most people honor as an Italian saint, but who in reality was born in Portugal

1

and had been ordained a priest in Portugal before he came to Italy."

When asked if he had actually planned to arrive in Portugal on the Feast of St. Anthony, Father DeMarchi replied: "To the contrary. I was supposed to arrive on a different date but the problems of travel during the war had delayed me. And to think now," he recalls, "I arrived on that great feast which is celebrated with almost as much enthusiasm and joy in Portugal as it is in Padua itself, *and it was on this very day that Our Lady appeared to the three children in Her second apparition, during which She promised to take them to Heaven.*"

Help in Portugal

In Portugal, at the request of an official in Rome and of the Archbishop of Mozambique and the help of the Bishop of Aveiro (a port city in the north of Portugal), Father DeMarchi was given permission to build a seminary in Portugal, *wherever he chose.*

Father DeMarchi's first thought was to go to Fatima. There was a great need for a priest who knew languages. And Father DeMarchi was the first "foreign" priest to present himself to the Sanctuary offering to hear confessions and to help in "any way I can."

He was received with open arms!

His lifelong devotion to Our Lady endeared him at once to this place where She had stooped to the world in what was to become perhaps the most critical moment in history. Everyone there was appalled at the extent to which the Second World War was spreading as predicted by the Virgin who had said (during World War I) that there would be a still "more terrible war" if Her requests were not heard.

The Families

Father DeMarchi was able to spend a great deal of time with the families of the three children to whom Our Lady of Fatima had appeared. He became particularly close to Lucia's oldest sister (who had become a sort of "second mother" to her) and to Mr. and Mrs. Marto, the parents of Francisco and Jacinta.

Indeed, the friendship between Father DeMarchi and Mr. Marto (father of Francisco and Jacinta) became so intimate *that shortly before he died, Mr. Marto expressed to all around him the desire to see Father DeMarchi before the* end. At that time Father DeMarchi had long since been recalled by his community and sent to new foundations in Africa, but yet Mr. Marto's wish was fulfilled.

"It seemed a wonderful coincidence to me," Father De-Marchi recalled, *"that without having any idea whatever that Mr. Marto was soon to die,* on a trip from Africa to America, I came to pass, almost by accident, through Portugal and went to Fatima for a visit and was able to spend a few loving hours with this gentle and wonderful man, who seemed at the time to be in the best of health, but who died not long afterwards."

Seminary Built at Fatima

During the time that Father DeMarchi was praying to know God's will as to *where* he should build the mission seminary, he met two other wonderful persons who greatly influenced him and whose names should be mentioned in connection with this book and perhaps whenever the history of Fatima is remembered: Maria de Freitas and her sister, Maria Rosa.

Maria de Freitas was an accomplished pianist, a gifted writer, fluent in English, French, German, Italian, Spanish, Portuguese, and even to some extent in Chinese. As a volunteer, she handled almost all the foreign correspondence for the Bishop of Fatima and, at the request of the Bishop, became the first International Secretary of the World Apostolate of Fatima (The Blue Army).

Maria de Freitas had come to Fatima because her sister, Maria Rosa, had a bone disease and was completely bedridden. They bought a cottage not far from the Cova and Maria supported them by teaching music and languages.

"Maria Rosa was a saint, " Father DeMarchi says. "*I never knew anyone like her.* To this day I feel closer to her than to any other saint in Heaven." Even as Father De-Marchi recalled this to me in the summer of 1985, his eyes filled with tears.

One day Maria Rosa said to him: "Father, why don't you found your seminary here in Fatima? I will pray for it." Shortly afterwards, the Salesians loaned Father DeMarchi a small house as a basis of operations. Maria de Freitas introduced him to a wealthy family from the north of Portugal who offered to help him with money to buy a large piece of land (part of which had belonged to the parish priest of Fatima).

It cost little then, but today it is one of the most valuable (and indeed one of the largest) pieces of land close to the Cova, actually adjoining the Sanctuary of Fatima.

Bishop Jose Correia da Silva, having witnessed the wonderful spirit of Father DeMarchi, embraced him and readily gave permission for the building of the seminary, *one of the very first important buildings erected in Fatima outside of the Sanctuary.* From the beginning the new seminary was blessed with an abundance of vocations. Hundreds of Portuguese young men studied there and were ordained not only for the Portuguese missions of Africa but also for the missions of the Consolata Fathers all over the world.

This Important Book

I went to Fatima the first time in July, 1946, when it was still primitive.

Maria de Freitas and Maria Rosa soon became my own close friends. Maria de Freitas helped Father DeMarchi with his book, and later helped me with the book *Meet the Witnesses.*[1] She always stayed in the background but did most of the work while insisting that her name should not appear.

When Maria de Freitas died, I flew to Portugal to attend her funeral. When she was buried, we uncovered the body of Maria Rosa, placing Maria de Freitas in the same grave where these two saintly sisters await the glorious day of resurrection.

I had gone to Fatima in 1946 with the intention of writing a book about the apparitions, but Father DeMarchi, with the help of Maria de Freitas, had done a better job of it than perhaps anyone else could do. And Dr. William Thomas Walsh was there at the same time, producing an excellent book based largely on Lucia's Memoirs.

I did write other books based on the Fatima Message[2], but Father De Marchi's book filled the need for a "history."

AMI Press, Inc., a subsidiary of the World Apostolate of Fatima (The Blue Army), was privileged in 1985 to obtain from the Consolata Fathers the exclusive rights to the English edition of this great classic, to which have been added the statements of two recent Popes: that of Paul VI (who went to Fatima on May 13, 1967), and of John Paul II (who went to Fatima on May 13, 1982).

The "bible" of Fatima is the book of Lucia's Memoirs. It deserves being read over and over. Our Lady Herself told

Lucia that she was to remain on earth and to learn to read and write. When we read the Memoirs we understand why Our Lady gave that instruction and kept Lucia on earth so many years after She took Francisco and Jacinta to Heaven.

Those of us (like Father DeMarchi) who have studied the Memoirs (seeing the original pages written by Lucia and knowing the difficult circumstances under which those pages where written), are astounded at the fluidity, at the exactness of detail, the clarity, the absence of even the slightest contradiction even though written at different times and without opportunity to compare one part with another. One is soon convinced that this is more than a purely human work.

But a book like this one by Father DeMarchi "fleshes out" *Lucia's Memoirs* with many other details of the marvelous story of the divine intervention of Fatima in the atomic age.

Perhaps there has not been a more important message to the world since biblical times.

It is most important to keep in mind as you read this book that it has not been "updated." It is as it was written while Mr. and Mrs. Marto were still living.

Note: Lucia's Memoirs is published by the Sanctuary of Fatima, with notes by Father Joaquim Alonso, C.M.F., as *Fatima in Lucia's Own Words*.[3] An annotated edition, with explanatory chapters based on the notes of Father Alonso and written by John Haffert, is published by AMI Press, Inc., under the title *Fatima and Nuclear Peace*.[4]

1   160 pp., copyright 1961, AMI Press, Inc., Washington, NJ 07882.
2   Other books written by John Haffert—in addition to *Meet the Witnesses*—and published by AMI Press are: *Sex and the Mysteries*, 282 pp, copyright 1970; *Queen's Promise*, 95 pp., copyright 1966; *Night of Love*, 176 pp., copyright 1967; *Russia Will Be Converted*, 270 pp., copyright 1952; *The Brother and I*, 213 pp., copyright 1970; *A Letter from Lisieux*, 120 pp., copyright 1965; *Sign of Her Heart*, 270 pp., new edition copyright 1971; *Explosion of the Supernatural*, 245 pp. copyright 1975; *Dear Bishop!*, 342 pp., copyright 1982.
3   Available as B3 from the Blue Army Supply Shop (Washington, NJ 07882).
4   AMI Press, Inc.; copyright 1985, 1986.

FOREWORD

Thirty years after its first appearance, *FATIMA THE FACTS* was published under a new title, *FATIMA FROM THE BEGINNING*. Now, once again, this book is being given a new name and released by AMI Press in the United States under the title of *FATIMA: THE FULL STORY*. The change is fully justified.

The events of Fatima are not outdated, but rather seem ever more living and actual. The charism of Fatima is truly universal. The Message that Our Lady addressed to the three little shepherds at the Cova da Iria is a genuine expression of the Gospel, for Penance and Prayer will always be, as they have been in the past, means that lead to conversion and holiness.

However, if it is true to say that the words Prayer and Penance have not always been exemplified in the lives of the faithful, the word Peace has the power of stirring the most rugged mind and restless heart in our age, which has seen the whole of humanity so greatly harassed by the scourge of war and violence, and the evils that flow therefrom.

Besides, to make known the Message of Our Lady of Fatima is to direct the attention of the faithful towards the renewal of Christian life, the aim of the Second Vatican Council.

Furthermore, the coming of Pope Paul VI to Fatima, as a Pilgrim of Peace, and Pope John Paul II fifteen years later, proclaims the abiding force of this Message, so simple and clear but yet so demanding, which points the way to reconciliation and concord among peoples.

The new title of the U.S. edition is better suited to the contents and the purpose of the author. Father John DeMarchi had the great privilege of living for years close to the spot where the Apparitions took place. He came to know, in the profoundest way, the environment, the customs and the characteristics of the people, gaining a firsthand account of the happenings during those memorable six months from May to October of 1917, from the parents and relatives of the three little shepherds, from those who knew them well and those who were eyewitnesses of these extraordinary events.

Father DeMarchi's great concern was to study the whole matter thoroughly and to set it down in writing with the greatest care and authenticity.

May this new edition help the reader to capture and comprehend ever more deeply the true meaning of the Message of Fatima.

THE EDITOR

INTRODUCTION

THE remarkable events which took place in the Cova da Iria in the months from May to October, 1917, have aroused unusual interest of late years, not only in Portugal but in the Catholic world at large. The spread of the cult of Our Lady of Fatima has been little less than prodigious, while books and publications on the Apparitions of the Blessed Virgin and on the seers themselves have poured from the printing presses in almost all languages.

The documents upon which the present work is based are in their chronological order the following:

(1) The newspapers of the period, especially the *Seculo*, the *Diario de Noticias*, the *Mundo*, all at the time anti-clerical in tone. They referred largely to the events which took place on the Serra de Aire and show clearly the religious strife which was the background of the Apparitions as well as the conflicting opinions on the events themselves. It is an interesting fact that the Catholic Press did not lag behind its secular contemporaries in scepticism.

(2) In 1921 appeared the first publication on the subject from the pen of Dr. Formigäo (Visconde de Montelo). It was entitled *Os Episodios Maravilhosos de Fatima* (*The Marvellous Events of Fatima*), and was the account of his interrogations of the children, together with his personal impressions.

(3) In October, 1922, the first number of the *Voz de Fatima* appeared. When, in 1919, Bishop José Alves Correia da Silva took possession of the newly-restored Diocese of Leiria, he at once proceeded to set up a canonical inquiry on the Apparitions. The most relevant testimonies were:

　(a) The interrogations of the seers by the Parish Priest of Fatima after each of the Apparitions from June to October, which he carefully set down.

　(b) The canonical interrogation of the only surviving seer Lucia, in 1924. Also notable was a letter* from Dr. Carlos Mendes written to his fiancée, dated September 8th, 1917, and the depositions of

* Appendix I.

various people who witnessed the events of that year, among them Baron Alvaiázere, who was not of the parish of Fatima.

(4) Meanwhile, Lucia had entered the College of Vilar (Oporto), directed by the Congregation of Dorothean Sisters, later joining their Community at Tuy (Spain) as a lay sister. It was there that she wrote her memoirs by the order of the Bishop of Leiria. These valuable documents are four in number and were written in 1936, 1937, 1941, and 1942. The first memoir is before anything else a biography of Jacinta with only scarce allusions to the Apparitions themselves.

In the second we find a more detailed account and, incidentally, a reference to the Apparitions of the Angel. After twenty years of silence on this subject the revelation came like a bombshell.

The third memoir is richer in detail and new facts emerge, among them the famous aurora borealis of January 25th, 1938, which was, in Lucia's view, the sign preceding the outbreak of the second World War, which had been foretold by Our Lady in the Apparition of June, 1917.

Finally, having been ordered by the Bishop to set down a definitive and complete account of everything that she remembered, Sister Lucia, on the Feast of the Immaculate Conception of the same year, after imploring the grace to write with precision and exactitude, began the fourth and most extensive of her memoirs, including all circumstances and details of the Apparitions of the Angel as well as of Our Lady.

(5) These alone would seem sufficient basis for the construction of a critical history of the Apparitions. However, some points still remained obscure and gave rise to varying interpretations, and there followed a series of interviews of the seer by serious students of Fatima. Among them we may mention:

Dr. Luis Fischer, Dr. Galamba de Oliveira, Fr. Yongen, Fr. McGlynn, O.P., William Walsh, the American writer, and Fr. Fonseca, who submitted his books for correction to Sister Lucia.

We also submitted the second edition of the book, *Era Uma Senhora mais Brilhante que o Sol*, for her revision and certain corrections and alterations were made. The third edition, therefore, from which the present translation has been prepared, can be said to be authenticated by the seer herself.

(6) Having had the incomparable privilege of living in Fatima since 1943, we had the opportunity to question at length and undisturbed the many reliable eye-witnesses of the epoch of the Apparitions. Among them the following are most notable:

Senhor Pedro Manuel Marto (Ti Marto), father of Jacinta and Francisco, and his wife Olimpia de Jesus (Ti Olimpia); Senhora Maria dos Anjos, Lucia's eldest sister, and her sisters Carolina and Gloria; lastly, Senhora Maria Carreira (Maria da Capelinha), who died in March, 1949, and her son John, sacristan of the Chapel of the Apparitions.

Every Sunday afternoon for six consecutive months, after the recitation of the Rosary at the Shrine, Ti Marto came and talked to us of his Jacinta and Francisco; of " his Reverence, who didn't believe and didn't let us believe either "; of the Mayor of Ourem, etc.; all this with a con- scientiousness and scrupulous care for truth remarkable in one already old and worn with work. But Senhor Marto is obsessed with a desire for truth. " We must not exag- gerate or squeeze more out of things than was there," he fre- quently remarked.

He rarely hears a chapter or passage read from a book on Fatima without correcting some detail or adding some missing fact.

" It wasn't exactly like that! " he would say. And then there followed a torrent of detail and reminiscence which often caused the subject under discussion to be completely forgotten.

Every now and again our Sunday interview failed to take place. Ti Marto, who never likes to refuse anything, excused himself on various grounds, of lack of time, visitors and so forth, making it clear that only necessity would have kept him away. When I asked him if he did not feel a certain pride in being the father of such privileged children he replied with the utmost simplicity:

" Our Lady chose this part of the world and she might have appeared to others. They just happened to be mine! "

It is possible that his narratives may contain some slight confusions or mistakes. It would be absurd to claim infallibility or absolute objectivity for this old man. But we can assure our readers that there is on his part a constant desire to be truthful and exact, and everything that we have been able to verify from independent witnesses bears out his statements.   In this respect, Dr. Fischer's book, *Die Botschaft unserer lieben Frau von Fatima,* was an excellent "control".   We did not find the smallest contradiction even in details, in the account which the distinguished Professor of Bamberg University wrote some fifteen years ago after visiting Fatima to investigate the facts.   We found the same hesitation over certain points, the same often insignificant details, often the same words.   Of Senhora Olimpia, Maria dos Anjos, Senhora Carreira, etc., much the same can be said.

Maria de Capelinha would often assert that she was "muddled", but, in fact, this is not so, because the events of Fatima are so engraved on her heart and memory that she never contradicts herself, even during a gruelling interrogation.

The surprising fact is that few of these people can read and a particular impression was made on us by the fact that none of them, even the older ones, made any confusion between their own personal experiences and what has recently come to light through the memoirs of Lucia.   When interrogated on one or another of these points, their invariable reply was: "I know nothing about that".   And yet it would be so natural for certain suggestive processes to have been set in motion by the constant talk of penance and prayer, the sanctity of the children, the Apparitions of the Angel, etc.

"We knew nothing," declares Ti Marto invariably. "Nothing about the cord, nor the fasts, nothing . . . nothing!   Even after the Apparitions I always thought the children very little different from others!"

The following facts emerge from a study of Lucia's valuable volume of documents.   That in 1916-1917 there occurred in Fatima a series of supernatural events.   That three children saw an Angel three times and that they received from his hands Eucharistic Communion.   That Our Lady also appeared to them several times, spoke to them and confided a secret of universal interest.

What historical value have these documents?   And, above all, how reliable are the affirmations of these three children?   Were they entirely free from hallucination, suggestion?   Most important of all, to what point do Lucia's memoirs, if the Apparitions are admitted, faithfully transmit

the message of Our Lady? Has there not been a certain
elaboration, psychological in origin, and a later supercon-
struction of events? Has not a religious embroidery been
superimposed upon the first, authentic matter of the
Apparitions?

If this were so, it would not be necessary to admit bad
faith. Such processes are commonly admitted in the lives
of the Saints, notably among the mystics (St. Teresa of
Avila, St. Gemma Galgani, St. Margaret Mary Alacocque).
That Lucia has not escaped the usual psychological laws
has been admitted, in recent years, by serious and conscientious theologians, chiefly in Belgium and France, who
have studied the matter.

Although we agree in principle that a certain
psychological evolution, due to her education in a religious
Congregation, may have exercised a certain influence on
Lucia's subsequent account of the Apparitions and message
of Fatima, yet a study of the documents in question, and
more especially of the personality of Lucia herself, leads us
to the conclusion that her declarations are trustworthy and
that we can accept without hesitation the facts and the
details which she sets forth in her memoirs.

Lucia has an absolutely normal personality. Nothing in
her suggests physical or mental unbalance. Every one who
has known her or spoken to her since the time of the
Apparitions is unanimous in this judgment. No one has
been able to detect in her the slightest indication of a morbid
temperament or one of excessive sensibility. Her daily life,
affirm her Superiors, presents nothing singular, nothing out
of the strictly ordinary.

"She is an eminently practical religious. The negation,
we may say, of poetic idealism." Such typical appraise-
ments are supported by a hundred authenticated details in
the history of the Apparitions.

It is true to say that the initial impression of almost every
one who sees the seer for the first time is one of disappointment, so ready are we to presuppose certain characteristics
in connection with the supernatural. In Lucia, the hypothesis
of pseudo-mysticism must be absolutely excluded.[1]

---

[1] My ministry in the priesthood has more than once afforded an
opportunity for the study of pseudo-mysticism and I can affirm, with
all confidence, that my impression of Sister Lucia is entirely contrary
to that received from false mystics.

Her manner of speech and of expression, whether by the written or the spoken word, her handwriting, which is commonplace, childish even, all denote perfect psychological balance and a healthy mentality free from any neurotic tendencies.

If we add to all this an especially acute memory—which we have ourselves had numerous occasions to test—we have every justification in placing our confidence in the last surviving seer of Fatima.

This, however, does not prevent our disagreement with Lucia in a few points which will be exposed in their proper places in the course of the story.

MY FIRST PILGRIMAGE

It was nearly half-past eight in the evening when we first entered the precincts of the Sanctuary by the road which leads directly to the Hospital and the Retreat House. As a matter of fact, it would have been impossible to penetrate through the main gate, so great were the crowds around it. In the refectory of the Retreat House we found the clergy of the Diocese of Leiria presided over by the Bishop. There was an atmosphere of cheerful comradeship which compensated in great part for the forced separation from so many of the members of our Congregation during those anguished days of war.

I was anxious to make the most of my pilgrimage and proposed to use the time before the start of the ceremonies in an extensive tour of the Sanctuary and, above all, to observe at close quarters the vast crowd of pilgrims about which I had heard so much in Italy. I did not at that time realise the ordeal which was before me.

Hardly had I emerged on to the stone parapet of the Hospital when an old man, cap-in-hand, and a woman muffled to the eyes, heading apparently a whole squadron of penitents, came up and asked me to hear their confessions.

" I will hear yours," I told the man, for night was falling and in Portugal women may not be confessed after sunset. He and I pushed our way through the crowds towards an open field, where we could feel more at our ease. In a few moments, I told myself, I shall be free to enjoy the fascinating spectacle unfolding before me. But as I sat on the stone, with the old man kneeling at my feet, I noticed with a pang of disappointment that a long line of people, looking like ants and rather reminding me of a cigarette queue, was forming as if by magic apparently from nowhere.

Struggling against my impatience, I strove to remember that Fatima is the place of sacrifice and penance and comforted myself with the thought that it must end some time.

Once more I was mistaken. The queue stretched interminably on, not only in front of me but also in front of other priests who were sitting on the stones which at that time, when building operations were not complete, strewed that part of the Sanctuary. From time to time deliverance seemed near; the queue dwindled and there were only two or three people in the line. With courage renewed, I bent to catch the rustic expressions which were not yet in my vocabulary. As the penitent murmured his Act of Contrition, I raised my eyes again to those other three. Alas for my optimism! There were now twenty, thirty, forty! I wondered why they could not join the crowd of well-to-do people who waited their turn in the various chapels. In any case, there was nothing to do now but swallow my impatience as best I could.

And as I saw the calloused hands clasped before me, the weather-beaten faces and the far-travelled feet, I knew that these people had every right to my consideration and to demand this sacrifice of me. Remain I must while the hours pass by. . . .

*   *   *   *

The Rosary is being recited in preparation for the candle-light procession and below me is a sea of gently waving light. Ten thousand . . . a hundred thousand? . . . more, perhaps many more. The lights twinkling like the stars symbolise those myriad souls. And then there is wafted to my ears the first verse of that haunting little hymn which is sung at Fatima and has been sung since the first pilgrimages were organised. The chorus rings out and the pilgrims measure their faith by the force of their lungs:

> *A treze de Maio, Na Cova da Iria,*
> *Apar'ceu brilhando, A Virgem Maria. Avé, Avé, Avé*
> *Maria!*

*   *   *   *

The Vigil

When the night was far gone I absolved the last of my penitents. I noticed that he was barefooted and had an air of extreme fatigue. He was quite young—twenty-five or thirty perhaps, but he rose to his feet with obvious difficulty.

I encouraged him as best I could and as I put out my hand to help him I asked:

"Have you come far?"

"From Tras-os-Montes, from beyond Mogadouro."

I made a swift mental picture of the map of Portugal. "Tras-os-Montes"—that was the most northerly province, level with the Minho.

"That's a long way. Two hundred, three hundred kilometres perhaps?"

"Fifty leagues at least," he replied, using the customary old-fashioned measurement.

"But you didn't come on foot?"

"Yes, to fulfil a promise. You see, my wife and I both promised to come here on foot if Our Lady would cure our little daughter, who was born blind. The doctors said she could not be cured, but now she sees!"

His eyes filled with tears as he continued:

"We made a novena and every night we put a few drops of Fatima water into her eyes. On the last day, just when we weren't thinking about it at all, I passed in front of her and she turned her head and followed me with her eyes. I nearly lost my head and shouted to my wife: 'Marie! come! Our prayers have been answered!' And so, Father, here we are. We waited a few days so as to be here on the twelfth. . . ."

"Did the journey take you long?"

"Eight days. We walked six leagues a day. Everywhere people were kind to us and we always had a mattress to sleep on. Once we were even offered supper and a bed! On the last night we had to sleep in the open in a pinewood near Leiria but it wasn't so bad."

"And your food? Did you bring it with you?"

"Food? Just our own barley bread, nothing more. We bought a few things for the little girl——"

The organ playing the *O Salutaris* for the second period of the Adoration interrupted our conversation. It was just 2 o'clock in the morning. As we walked towards the esplanade in front of the Basilica to take part in the Holy Hour that was just beginning I saw a woman, also bare-footed and carrying a child, come up to my companion.

"Here they are," he said by way of introduction.

Much moved, I put my hand on the head of the little *miraculada*. Two jet eyes shone from under a sort of hood and a little hand stretched out and pulled my beard. All three of us had tears in our eyes.

Lost in the singing, praying multitude, I passed that hour and a half of adoration in much spiritual consolation. The truths of our Holy Religion are so transparent here in Fatima! The supernatural can be felt and the nearness of Heaven is a matter of experience. Jesus, in the golden monstrance, hidden in the Eucharistic Species, is no longer a matter of faith, but living, real, merciful, and loving, as in the thirty-three years during which He lived among us a man among men.

The priest presiding spoke of the five Joyful Mysteries of the Rosary; the sublime mission of the Archangel; the hurrying of Mary over the hills of Judea; the humble cave of Bethlehem; the Temple ceremony which Our Lady, although purest of the pure, did not fail to fulfil; and, lastly, the Holy Child confounding the Doctors of the Law. Never had I lived those mysteries as on that night. I seemed to be enfolded in the love of Our Blessed Lady; to be living not in the year 1946 but in the time of Our Lord. The Cova da Iria was no longer a corner of Portugal but Nazareth, Bethlehem, Jerusalem, and even more—a corner of Paradise!

The second nocturnal period came to an end and was close followed by the third and so on until sunrise brought the Vigil before Our Lord in the Blessed Sacrament to a close. I longed to stay there the whole night, but I began to feel great fatigue and weariness. Sleep seemed to overcome me and I sought the little room which had been assigned to me in the Retreat House for an hour or two of rest. I felt ashamed to be sleeping in a bed when the vast majority of the pilgrims—hundreds of thousands of them— were stretched on the hard earth or dry grass wrapped up in their shawls and capes. The nights on these hills are really cold and I saw some of the well-to-do pilgrims who had miscalculated the temperature unashamedly walking about enveloped in car rugs. Here and there little fires lit up faces and lips which never ceased to murmur the prayers intoned by the voice at the loud speakers. In the distance came the braying of donkeys, the crowing of cocks, the horn of a lately arrived motor coach. Nothing more. I laid my head on the pillow and slept.

Penance and Prayer

At half-past seven I said Mass in the quiet chapel of the Retreat House. It was full. The last Mass had been said by the Missionary Bishop of Gurza, whose special devotion to Fatima brings him again and again to the Shrine. After breakfast I do as everyone else does and plunge into the crowd.

It must be about 9 o'clock. I wanted very much to visit the Chapel of the Apparitions, which I had not yet been able to do, and to see the famous Statue of Our Lady, but it was only with the greatest difficulty that I was able to come near it. Hundreds, thousands of people were pressing upon it, standing, kneeling, sitting on the ground, praying, thanking, supplicating. The thing which made most impression on me was the long line of pilgrims who were going round the chapel on their knees. It was explained to me that they were " paying " promises which they had made to Our Lady. I could hardly take my eyes off these men and women, who, at the cost of such sacrifice, were thanking the Mother of God for favours granted to them. It was really a most touching scene.

I saw a man with his rosary in one hand and his cap and staff in the other. Next a woman, thin and pale, upheld seemingly only by the flame of faith which burnt in her eyes; further back was a mother with a child in her arms, holding a lighted candle and supported by a young man who must have been her husband; and, lastly, young men and girls who, without the slightest human respect, repay the debts contracted in their moments of affliction. Dragging themselves over the stony ground, they tear not only their clothes and their stockings but also their flesh and leave stains of blood on the ground. Our Lady doubtless understands these simple hearts, in fact her preference is just for such heroic, uncomplicated souls.

I myself feel humiliated before these rustics. They have not only faith in the supernatural but know how to live their faith.

As I looked on at this moving spectacle, a woman, obviously in great pain, hardly able to walk, came up to me and said in tones of tormenting doubt:

" Father, I promised Our Lady to come on my knees from Fatima Church to the Chapel of Apparitions (two kilometres). I got as far as Lagoa da Carreira (500 metres from the Shrine) and then I couldn't do any more. My knees bled and bled. . . . I couldn't go any further and so I walked. It wasn't because I didn't want to but because I couldn't."

"Don't worry," I told her. "If you have done all you could, Our Lady will understand."

The woman waited anxiously for the verdict of God's representative and then with immense relief kissed my hand and knelt down as near as she could to the statue of Our Lady, while I, in my turn, approached the little Chapel. It is of extreme poverty and simplicity. My thoughts instantly turned to Loretto and the Holy House, which it so resembles. And here, too, during brief passages of time Our Lady stood.

The statue stands on a stone pedestal which marks the spot where the famous holm oak grew. It was ordered to be placed there by the Bishop of the Diocese in the hopes of saving any roots which might remain from the destructive piety of the faithful who tore them up as relics. At the base of the column there is an open grille through which any new shoots might have been able to breathe, but the little tree was quite dead and the people now think that the box-like opening at the bottom is a sort of heavenly pillar box in which they may place their petitions to Our Lady!

Mingling with the crowd, I, too, knelt before the beautiful image and tried to picture the " lovely young girl ", the " beautiful Lady ", shining in light. I almost brought myself to ask her to come again to earth and show herself to these people who seem to love her more and more.

All around me in whispers and murmurs the Blessed Virgin is being invoked with extraordinary confidence; they tell her that she is infinitely good, that never was it known that anyone that fled to her protection was left unaided. They call her by the tenderest names—Queen of Heaven, sweet Virgin, Helper and Comforter, but, above all, Mother. Virgin Mother, merciful Mother, Mother of God, Mother of Christ, my Mother, our Mother, Mother of men. Mary here is first and essentially Mother. And the prayers continue; for temporal necessities; for businesses which are not prospering; for fields which need the rain; for a sick child; a daughter's marriage; a husband's unemployment; those exams. which mean so much for the future. Spiritual needs too; a son gone astray; a husband against the Church; a father who never goes to the Sacraments; a threatened civil marriage. A religious asks for wings on the way of perfection and a seminarist for perseverance towards the altar. All is laid with the utmost simplicity and faith in Mary's maternal heart. I rose at last and gave my place to others waiting for their moment before Our Lady.

My next visit was to the Basilica, but I had not gone further than the Chapel of Penance[1] when a young woman dressed as a *Servita* came up and asked me if I could hear her confession. Replying in the affirmative, I went with her into the great building towards an empty confessional which was at once converted into the centre of a seething mass of women. The men were being more comfortably attended to in the sacristy or in various places in the Hospital and Retreat House, unless as during the night, they simply confessed in the open air.

It was high summer and even the size of the great church could not overcome the smell of that multitude which had travelled so far in heat and dust. But here there was no sign of difference of class. Gentlefolk and peasants mingled together and took their turns in strict fairness. While the *Servitas* patiently tried to marshal the people into some sort of order, a priest at the High Altar distributed Holy Communion almost incessantly—a distribution which would probably continue until the afternoon. Yet a few hours before, general Communion had been given in the open air by some twenty priests for more than two hours. Dozens of ciboriums had been emptied again and again to satisfy the great hunger for God. It was the re-enactment of the multiplication of the loaves but in an infinitely superior sense; not the five loaves which satisfied the 5,000 but the Redeemer Himself becoming the Food of souls destined one day for the blessedness of Heaven.

The Climax

The bell of the Sanctuary rang three times—the daily ringing of the Angelus which on the 13th of the month serves as a signal for the beginning of the procession of Our Lady. I shut the door of the Tabernacle and went to the tiny sacristy to take off my surplice. As I came out of the Basilica a glorious sight met my rather dazed vision. After the long weary hours in the confessional I felt new energy steal into me. From the steps of the Basilica to the farthest limit of sight there was a sea of people gently undulating to and fro. It looked as if the whole of Portugal were there. As a matter of fact this land of Our

[1] Since demolished.

Lady was largely represented, from the sunny dry Algarve
to the green Minho; from the Spanish frontier on the east
to the golden fringe of the Atlantic on the west.   There
were characteristic types from all these regions.   Women
from the Algarve with their semi-Moorish dress and their
great dark contemplative eyes fixed on Our Lady; the cow-
boys from the borders of the Tagus, dark-faced from life in
the open air.   They wear narrow trousers and a green cap
and hold their rosaries in wiry hands accustomed to the
control of wild bulls.   There were the people from the
coast, seafaring folk and fishermen whose clothes give out
a salt smell and whose faces are almost roasted with the
sun and sea.   They have left their oars and nets to pray to
the Star of the Sea.   The men wear thick plaid blouses and
the women pleated skirts and round black hats.   Everyone
knows them for they are the great producers of the mackerel
and the sardine.   I saw peasants from the region round
Cintra, the typical *saloio,* in short jacket and cummerbund;
Tricanas from Coimbra, barefooted or in clogs, moving
with a natural distinction; girls from the Minho saying their
Ave Marias as if enchanted, and lastly the folk from the far
provinces of Tras-os-Montes and the pastoral Alentejo.

Nearly everyone was kneeling as the Rosary was intoned
through the loud-speakers and the Ave Marias succeeded
one another with impressive devotion.   Kneeling on the
stony ground, the men with uncovered heads under the
blazing midday sun, the people appeared indifferent to discomfort and even seemed on the look-out for sacrifice,
choosing the most difficult positions, the most uncomfortable places the better to please her who had recommended
this place of penance.

At last the procession was organised—if one could call it
a procession.   The Scouts went first with their fluttering
standards and banners surrounding the statue which was
borne by the *Servitas.*   It passed slowly among the people,
and once more those thousand needs were presented, the
sighs and weepings in this vale of tears.   Petals fall like
snow against the purple and crimson vestments of the clergy;
snow against the snow of the surpliced seminarists.
Thousands of white handkerchiefs flutter in welcome.   Love,
tears, and tenderness greet God's Mother as she passes,
symbolised in her image, up the great stairway to the altar,
backwards so that the people may still see her face, to assist
once more at the renewal of the Sacrifice of Calvary.

Holy Mass was celebrated by a Bishop and the people followed the choir as they sang through the loud-speakers which could be heard in every corner of the vast arena. After Mass the Blessed Sacrament was solemnly exposed, and a few moments later "Hidden Jesus," as Jacinta used to call Him, was borne down the steps to bless the sick. There must have been 300 of them, grave cases for the most part. I saw some in the last stages of tuberculosis, in many cases with the pallor of the dying. Cases of Potts' disease, incapable of any movement, despaired of by science, hoping in the Divine Omnipotence. Wasted faces, skeleton-like limbs living a perpetual Calvary; the blind with dull and empty sockets; boys, girls, in the flower of youth: lives which should be a splendid vision and are instead spectres. Babies, monsters, deformities. They all wait with a suspense mingled with hope and confidence the hour of a stupendous miracle. The voice of the priest at the loud-speakers is vibrant with faith:

> "Lord, we love Thee!
> Lord, we put our trust in Thee!
> Lord, we believe, increase our faith!"

And at each invocation the voice of the people echoes over the *serras*, repeating the words:

> "Lord, we love thee!
> Lord, we put our trust in Thee!
> Lord, we believe, increase our faith!"

> "My Lord and My God!
> Thou art the Resurrection and the Life!"

cries the voice, and the words are repeated by the people. Again, with daring, almost importunate insistence:

> "Lord, if Thou wilt Thou canst cure me!
> Lord, say but a word and I shall be healed!"

and the people, like the crowds of Palestine, implore and importune the Saviour:

> "Lord, if Thou wilt Thou canst cure me!

> Lord, say but a word and I shall be healed!
> Lord, grant that I may see, that I may walk,
>   that I may hear!"

Nobody bothers to hide their tears. Christian charity unites this great multitude and all feel the same needs and suffer the same pains. The prayer of one is the prayer of all. And now with renewed fervour and faith the prayers are directed to her who at the Marriage of Cana had the power to hasten the hour of the miracle:

> " Mother of Our Saviour, pray for us!
>   Queen of the Holy Rosary, pray for us!
>   Comforter of the afflicted, pray for us!"

After moving along the benches with an individual blessing for each of the sick, the Blessed Sacrament again reaches the central aisle to move up the stairway to the altar. From all sides eyes follow it with an unspoken prayer, the prayer of the disciples at Emmaus. *Mane nobiscum Domine!*

The " Tantum Ergo " is majestic, full throated, and once again the blessing descends on the multitude, this time for one and all.

Everyone kneels or tries to kneel in the constricted space. Then the Blessed Sacrament is taken into the Basilica and the people's immense reverence for the Divine turns into an enthusiastic, human delight in Our Lady to whom they are going to give that impressive Fatima farewell. There is the charming good-bye hymn, " O Virgem do Rosario ".

The last words, the last confidences are whispered as she passes in a rain of flowers; again the myriad white handkerchiefs and we experience something in the depths of our souls which it is Fatima's alone to give. We must go. So must thousands of others. But they and we leave something of our hearts for ever at the feet of Our Lady of Fatima in the Cova da Iria.

$$* \qquad * \qquad * \qquad *$$

" Would you like to see the Basilica and go up to the top of the tower?" The question was put to us by the Rector of the shrine, and we four priests enthusiastically agreed that we would. We hurried after him almost at a run, for his time is strictly limited, and mounted the impressive esplanade and stairway which lead up to the Basilica.

" The first stone was laid fifteen years ago by the Archbishop of Evora," began the Rector, " and since then work has progressed rapidly considering that it has been paid for only by the spontaneous contributions of the pilgrims. We have never received any help from the Government."

" Could you not have launched a national or even international appeal for funds as was done at Lourdes?" I asked.

" Perhaps it was better not to do so. The Bishop thought that it should be built as a spontaneous gesture to Our Lady."

We entered the building which when complete will certainly be an imposing and impressive church. It is eighty-two metres long and fifty high. There are fourteen lateral chapels, which, with the High Altar, correspond with the fifteen mysteries of the Rosary.

We climbed to the vault of the roof, where the Rector explained some of the architectural details of the building and the difficulties which had to be overcome in supporting the great arch which weighs 350 tons.

Although the scaffolding in place at that time rather obscured the view, we were impressed with the size and beauty of this building of white stone which has been raised to the honour of the Mother of God.

We went up another dozen or so metres, riskily, by a shaky stairway, and found ourselves on the clock level which at that time was all there was of the tower. Another fifteen metres was to be added and the tower surmounted by a bronze crown, in the centre of which a glass sphere would hold an illuminated cross. The view from the top is magnificent.

Below lies the shell-like bowl of the Cova da Iria. The Chapel of the Apparitions looks like a toy, while to the left is the gilded statue of the Sacred Heart surmounting the water fountain, catching the last rays of the summer sun. To the right are the simple structures of the hospital and Retreat House, and to the left the still uncompleted corresponding block. Away beyond the main portico is a conglomeration of wooden shacks and huts which will be demolished under the new scheme of development and will give place to an imposing square which will greatly ease the traffic congestion on the days of pilgrimage. To the north-east we noticed a modern building too large for a private house, and the Rector at once satisfied our curiosity.

" It is the Carmel of St. Joseph," he said.

" Carmelites? How did they come here?"

" Just as so many people come here from all parts of the world! In a Belgian Carmel there happened to be some nuns learning Portuguese with the idea of a Brazilian foundation. They happened to be taught by a Portuguese Jesuit studying at Louvain and he, from the first lesson, conceived the idea of a Carmelite foundation in Portugal and never ceased to work for that end."

" He succeeded?"

" Months passed and everything was made ready for the departure of the nuns to Brazil, which in fact never took place. Authorities in Rome wanted a foundation in Uganda, but in the end the Superior and another religious arrived here in Portugal on August 20th, 1933."

We turned again to St. Joseph's Carmel and thought of those souls who in this materialistic age still hear the invitation of the Master to come apart into a desert place. . . .

" Is that Fatima over there?" we asked, pointing to a church and a slim white bell-tower away to the westward.

" Yes; the parish church of Fatima and the village."

" The place names of this region are curious! Cova da Iria, Ourem, Fatima. Until some five years ago the name of Fatima meant one thing to me—the sister of Mahomet!"

" This Fatima is also of muslim origin," explained the Rector. " It may not be strictly historical but this is the legend. The present Alcácer-do-Sal was the capital of the Moorish province of Al-Kasar. One night a group of knights and ladies left the city to celebrate the feast of St. John, who is to Mahometans a great prophet. They were amusing themselves on the banks of the River Sado when there fell upon them a band of Christian knights captained by the Terror of the Moors, Gonçalo Hermingues. The attack was so unexpected and so violent that most of the Moors were killed and the rest were taken prisoner to Santarem and handed over to the King, Affonso Henriques. The King asked the Terror what reward he desired for the exploit, and he replied that he asked only the hand of Fatima, daughter of the chief of Alcácer. The beautiful

Moorish girl became a Christian and was baptised with the name of Oureana, married to Gonçalo who received as a wedding gift from the King the village of Abdegas, which came to be called Oureana, and is now Ourem. The poor Terror, however, was widowed within a short time and could not bear to remain in the world without his Oureana. He retired to the monastery of Alcobaça while the body of his wife was taken to a place to the west of Ourem, where there was to be a new foundation of the Cistercian Order. Brother Gonçalo, abbot of the new monastery, ended his days in the place which is now Fatima."

" The name *Iria,* is that also of muslim origin ? "

" No. Cova da Iria, Ourem, Santarem, Leiria, all these names come from the name of a Portuguese saint, Irene or Iria. Here, too, we cannot take everything in a strictly historical sense. However, in the 7th century there lived in Tomar (then Nabância) Ermigio, and Eugénia, and their daughter Iria. Under the direction of an uncle, the Abbot Celio, Iria was educated by two aunts, Benedictine nuns, Julia and Casta. While still a child she made a vow of consecration to God and rejected the marriage proposals of young Britaldo. He, however, refused to despair of his suit, until there began to be calumnies against the girl's virtue. Then, mad with jealousy, and without troubling to verify the truth, he planned her death. His man-at-arms, obeying orders, ran her through with his sword and threw her body into the River Nabão which carried it into the Tagus. Tradition says the Abbot Celio in a dream or vision came to know of the fact, and went with his people to search for his niece's body. When he arrived at the spot near Santarem where his intuition led him, the Tagus receded leaving the river-bed dry, and there in a rich tomb lay the body of Iria, radiant and beautiful. All efforts to pull out the body were in vain and only a few relics were taken. Then the waters began to flow again, completely covering the tomb."

" For ever?"

" No. According to another tradition, when St. Elizabeth of Portugal was kneeling on the banks of the Tagus with great devotion and a desire to see the tomb of the martyr, the miracle of the waters again occurred, but no one succeeded in opening the tomb. Then King Denis

ordered the erection of the monument which still exists,
and later the Municipal Council of Santarém ordered it to
be covered with a dossel. The name Santarém, from the
Roman Scalabis, is derived from St. Irene or Iria. There
may have been a chapel dedicated to St. Iria round here or
perhaps the owner of this land in far-off times was simply
called *Iria*."

The Rector had been standing for a long time telling us
these interesting legends, although his eyes kept wandering
to where doubtless much work awaited him. Night was
falling and it was time to descend from our splendid view-
point, leaving the next excursion for the morrow.

*   *   *   *

"Would you like to meet the parents of Jacinta and
Francisco?"

Another question, put this time by Fr. Carlos de Azevedo,
Director of the "Voz da Fatima". Hardly believing in
my good fortune I gave an enthusiastic affirmative and
clung to Fr. Azevedo like a limpet in case he should change
his mind. We went along the macadam road which joins
Batalha and Vila Nova de Ourem and about three-quarters
of a mile from the Sanctuary turned off into a lane on the
right, which evidently led to Aljustrel.

The land looked poor and stony, but the hard work of
the local peasants has turned it into fertile fields. If God
sends them rain and saves them from tempest, June brings
its bushels of wheat and September the maize and the wine.
Olive oil, however, is the chief wealth of the *serra*.

The twenty or so houses of the hamlet of Aljustrel, all
built on one floor, are low and for the most part whitewashed. They are simple, homely and not without a
certain comfort. Some have a little roofed terrace.

Our first sight on entering the village was a group of
grubby barefooted children playing on the ground. We
passed a few more houses, and then Fr. Carlos stopped by
another group of little girls, some sitting on the ground,
others on the doorstep of the house. He addressed one of
them :

"Is Ti Marto at home?"

"Yes, Father."

A voice came from the house, cheerful and kindly:
" Do please come in!"

Then an old man about seventy opened the gate and showed us into the straw-strewn yard.

" Excuse my everyday clothes," he said, " but I was just going to the *serra* with the donkey to get firewood."

Taking off his cap he leaned over to kiss our hands according to Portuguese custom.

" This priest has come from Rome, where the Holy Father lives," said Fr. Carlos by way of introduction.

" To think of that! All that way!" exclaimed Ti Marto.

" I should like very much to hear something about your Jacinta and Francisco," I declared.

" Well, it's all in the books," said the old man, and then he called out to his wife, who was occupied in the kitchen:

" Come here, wife; Fr. Carlos is here and another priest from Rome."

At this point Senhora Olimpia appeared on the doorstep all wreathed in smiles.

" Sit down, sit down," said Senhor Marto busily. " There's no lack of logs anyway."

We sat on a pine chest in the little parlour. At the back there was a table covered with various holy objects. Above, were pictures, chief among them one of the Holy Father in a rough frame, giving his blessing to the couple.

Ti Marto talked with great enthusiasm about his surviving children. He got up frequently and gesticulated— typical gestures of his own—answered questions and made commentaries; talked of Africa where he had served in the army in his young days, and then with complete naturalness passed on to a eulogy of Baron Alvaiázere, a great friend of his. One could see that Jacinta had been the apple of his eye.

" She was a darling and no mistake," he said. " None of the others could compare with her!"

Senhora Olimpia tried to put in a word for Francisco here and there, whenever her husband would let her interrupt his almost constant flow of conversation. At one moment she discreetly left the room and came back with a basket full of great bunches of grapes as well as a basin and towel for handwashing, a measure of hygiene which surprised me at the time, in these very simple surroundings.

" Now, please have some to refresh yourselves! They were only gathered to-day. Now, please do, we don't need

them as neither my husband nor I touch wine. Sometimes
on Sundays he stays a bit in the village, but he never goes
into a tavern. . . ."

" Well, one gets prevented from getting home sometimes,"
began her husband, and would certainly have been set fair
for another long conversation if we had not been obliged
to cut him short. Time was getting on and we had still
a visit to pay to Lucia's house as well as to Valinhos and
Cabeço. Senhor Marto offered to accompany us.

Lucia's house is a short distance away. Everything is as
it was in the time of the Apparitions, down to the details
of the bedroom where Lucia was born and where her mother
died. The house is lived in at present by Maria dos Anjos,
the eldest daughter of Maria Rosa (Lucia's mother).
Although she is a busy working woman and a widow, everything is beautifully kept, and she is always ready to welcome
visitors.

She went with us to the well where the three children
spent long hours in the heavenly conversations which
alternated with childish play. One feels there a strong
sense of the supernatural and leaves it unwillingly.

On the way to Valinhos old Ti Marto never ceased telling us stories and detailed episodes of past events, and we,
it must be confessed, encouraged him to the utmost.

The place where Our Lady appeared for the fourth and
" extra " Apparition on 19th August, 1917, is indicated by
a little circle of stones whose centre must have been at one
time the oak tree. We knelt a few moments in prayer,
drinking in the scene which is set in deep peace. We
thought a little chapel there would be an excellent idea.
Following a stony path, we climbed to Cabeço where the
angel of Portugal appeared for the first and third times,
and taught the children those wonderful prayers which they
were afterwards to repeat countless times prostrated on the
ground. Rocks, trees and shrubs mark the place where
these extraordinary events took place. Here also we knelt
and repeated the words of the angel: " My God, I believe,
I adore, I hope, and I love You. I ask forgiveness for
those who do not believe, nor adore, nor hope, nor love. . . ."

In silence—and how sweet and necessary silence seems
here!—we returned to Aljustrel, to the house where Jacinta
and Francisco were born. In the tiny bedroom where
Francisco died, Ti Marto with evident emotion told of his
last hours.

" It was here that he received Our Lord for the first and the last time. He wanted to sit on the bed, but he was so ill that he couldn't manage it. Just before he died, he said to his mother, who was standing just there: ' Mother, look at that lovely light near the door! . . .' and later: ' Now I can't see it any more. . . .' And then he died, smiling. . . ."
Tears rolled down Ti Marto's cheeks as he told us this.

And so our pilgrimage ended. We left the old man at the door of his house.

" So you're going," he said, with a resigned air.

We left him, following us out of sight with his eyes and waving good-bye.

"What a dear old man he is!" said Fr. Carlos, as we strode along the lane. " Everyone loves to hear him talk, though they can't always follow his complicated stories and conversations!"

CHAPTER I

Tragic Hour

" It was a tragic hour of darkness and distress." Thus did the Holy Father in his allocution of 31st October, 1942, describe that historic moment when Portugal received the visits of the Blessed Virgin on the heights of the Serra de Aire.

Revolution succeeded revolution. There was continual party discord, religious persecution, general discontent, cowardice and wilful blindness of the people. Since the establishment of the Republican régime the country lived in a continual state of alarm. It seemed that the various Governments, one after another, were inspired by the sole purpose of furthering the powers of darkness. From 1910-1926, when the military coup d'état of 28th May, led by Marshal Gomes da Costa, inaugurated an era of stability and peace, there occurred sixteen revolutions, authentic revolts, not mere skirmishes. The worst and most to be feared occurred in October, 1921, and became known as the revolt of the " White Ants ", a Communist-anarchist party whose favourite weapon was the bomb.

The legislation of Pombal again came into force on 8th October, 1910, and one of the first acts of the Provisional Government of the Republic was to suppress all

Religious Congregations and to expel the Jesuits. All members of Orders who infringed the decree were considered as enemies of the State. The 18th of the same month saw a new decree abolishing the religious oath in the courts of justice, and on the 25th a traditional oath for professors and students, by which for more than two centuries they had sworn to defend the dogma of the Immaculate Conception, was likewise abolished.

Three days later it was decreed that days which had been considered holy days were henceforth to be days of work. On 3rd November divorce was recognised for the first time in Portuguese law, and on the 14th the Chair of Ecclesiastical Justice was suppressed in the University of Coimbra.

On Christmas Day marriage was declared to be a purely civil contract, and on the last day of that memorable year of 1910, yet another decree was promulgated which forbade priests and religious who had obtained permission to remain in Portugal to teach or wear religious dress or habit on pain of imprisonment which could be effected " by any member of the public ".

The Law of Separation (20th April, 1911) extorted incalculable sums from the Church. Many churches were used as barracks and stables, and convents and monasteries as Government buildings or other institutions according to the whim of the Party in power.

Freemasonry triumphed. Magalhães Lima, Grand Master, declared publicly that within a few years there would not exist in Portugal a single person who wished to be a priest. However, in the second international congress which took place in Paris and at which the Lusitanian Grand Orient Lodge was represented, these words escaped his lips: " The religious question agitates public opinion in Portugal more than ever."

For his part, the famous Minister of Justice, Afonso Costa, declared no less solemnly that by reason of the law which separated Church and State, the Catholic religion, the chief cause of the miserable condition of the people, could be eliminated in Portugal in two generations.

Protestantism, which had never found fertile soil in the Peninsula, succeeded in gaining the favour of the Republic for reasons easy to deduce. In January, 1911, the Methodist Bishop Hertzell, while passing through Lisbon, violently and openly attacked the Catholic Faith in a public lecture hall. The Foreign Minister promptly offered him a banquet at which, besides the Minister of Marine, Dr. Afonso Costa also took part.

With the outbreak and continuance of the First World War, the condition of the country became steadily worse. Things were in an unhappy condition when Salazar took over the helm of the ship of State. The financial situation was deplorable; there was a monstrous debt and payments were in arrears; there were obligations unfulfilled, debts unpaid and a chronic deficit. The country which in other times " had given worlds to the world ", had fallen into moral and material despair. " Portugal had forgotten God," said the Holy Father, " but God had not forgotten Portugal." Help was at hand.

CHAPTER II

LUCIA

THE three small people to whom Our Lady appeared were in every respect absolutely normal children differing not at all from their companions of the *serra* with whom they shared their games and their work of shepherding.

Lucia was the eldest. She was born on 22nd March, 1907, the last of the seven children of Antonio Santos (nick-named the Pumpkin)[1] and Maria Rosa, his wife. They lived in the hamlet of Aljustrel, a little green oasis on the arid rocky *serras* of Aire. Lucia was healthy and robust and could be trusted with the flocks, even at an age when most children cause nothing but trouble to their parents.

She was not a pretty child. The only attractions of her face—which was not on the whole repellent—were her two great black eyes which gazed out from under thick eyebrows. Her hair, thick and dark, was parted in the centre and peeped out from the kerchief which covered it and fell over her shoulders. Her nose was rather flat, her lips thick and her mouth large. A physiognomist might have put her down as gross, even perverse. But Lucia was not a bad girl. On the contrary she was very agreeable, and had a happy disposition.

---

[1] In a Portuguese village, people are more commonly known by their nicknames than by their real names.

We loved her because she was so intelligent and affectionate (Maria dos Anjos, her sister, told us). Even when she was older, when she came home with the flock, she used to run and sit on her mother's lap and be cuddled and kissed. We, the elder ones, used to tease her and say: "Here comes the cuddler!"—and we would even get cross with her. But she always did it again the next day. When my first baby was born you should have seen her! She came home from the *serra*, shut up the sheep and ran as fast as her legs would carry her to my house, which was just in front of my mother's. She clutched at the baby and covered it with kisses, not at all like the people round here.

She loved children and they adored her. Sometimes they would collect in our yard, a dozen or so, and she would be quite happy decorating the little ones with flowers and leaves. She would make little processions with saints, arranging flowers and thrones and sing hymns to Our Lady as if she were in church. I can still remember the ones she liked best. (Here Maria dos Anjos hummed a well-known Portuguese hymn to Our Lady.) And she would end up by giving the "blessing". She knew how to look after children and the mothers used to leave them in our house when they went out to work. When I was at my weaving and my sister Caroline at her dressmaking, we used to keep an eye on them but when Lucia was there, even when she was quite tiny, we didn't have to bother.

None of them could beat her at games. She was always the "He" at hide-and-seek. They used to hide under the fig trees and in the bushes or under the beds, anywhere where there was a hiding place. They would play many other games besides and when they were all tired they would sit in the shade of the fig-trees and Lucia would tell stories which never seemed to have an end. Some she had heard, and others she made up.

Lucia possessed, it can be said, an excellent memory which enabled her later to recount with exact detail the encounters with the Angel and Our Lady.

After twenty-five years of complete isolation from the world she was able to write—at the instance of the Bishop of Leiria—the scenes of her childhood, even to the dances at which she excelled among her companions.

She was a chatterbox, never still for a moment (said Ti Marto). She was very affectionate, too, even with me. It was "father do this, and father do that", all the time. She was full of mischief and I used to think at the time that she would either be very good or very bad.

Like all the other girls of the *serra* Lucia liked to dress up for *festas* and put on her gold chains and large ear-rings and her pretty shawl decorated with beads and coloured feathers.

In that neighbourhood (she confesses) there was no other girl so prettily dressed as I, and my sisters and godmother Teresa were surprised to see me looking so nice. The other children would crowd round me to admire all my pretty things. They all liked me except a little orphan girl whom my godmother Teresa had brought up after the death of her mother. She seemed to think that I would get part of the inheritance she hoped for and indeed she would have been right if Our Lord had not given me a far more precious one.

Another incident told by Maria dos Anjos:

One day, about nightfall, Lucia disappeared after she had shut up the sheep. Later when she came home our mother asked her where she had been. She said that they had been out begging, she and Jacinta and Francisco. They went to "Ti José", and "Ti Maria das Neves", and to godmother Teresa who gave them apples. They arrived at the door and pretended to be beggars imploring alms for the love of God and reciting the Our Father! Then Lucia asked for a knife and cut up the apples dividing them between us. She was most kindhearted and friendly with us all. It was only after the Apparitions that the trouble began in our family.

The family circle was the best place for the development of Lucia's natural dispositions. It is true that her father was not very religious. But her mother—and on the *serra* it is the mothers who educate the children—was a splendid woman and had a heart of gold. She also possessed tact and intelligence.

Senhora Maria Rosa, deeply conscious of the effect which the father's bad example might have on the children, redoubled her efforts to care for and educate them well. She tried to develop in them those Christian virtues which were to her as second nature. Maria dos Anjos describes her:

Our mother knew how to read printed letters but could not write. Every night during the winter she used to read us some part of the Old Testament or the Gospels, or some story of Our Lady of Nazaré or Lourdes. I clearly remember her saying crossly to Lucia at the time of the Apparitions: "Do you think that because Our Lady appeared in Nazaré and in Lourdes that she has to appear to you?"

In Lent we knew that the readings would be about the Passion of Our Lord. Afterwards Lucia would give her own account to the other children. Mother taught us doctrine and would not let us go and play till we knew it properly by heart. She did not want to feel ashamed, she said, when the parish priest examined us. And she had no need to be for the priest was very pleased with us and even when we were quite small

used to let us teach other children in church. I couldn't have
been more than nine when he made me a catechist. But
mother was never satisfied with our just saying the words and
explained everything so that we should understand it well. She
used to say that repeating catechism without knowing the
meaning of it was worse than useless. We used to ask her
all sorts of questions and she explained even better than the
priest in church. One day I asked her how it was that the
fire of hell did not destroy the damned like the wood in the
fire. She asked us if we had not seen a bone thrown into the
fire and how it seemed to burn without being destroyed. This
rather frightened us and we made firm resolutions not to sin
and fall into that terrible fire.

But it was not only to us that mother taught catechism.
Other children and even grown-up people used to come to
our house to have lessons.

In May, and in the month of the Holy Souls, also in Lent,
we used to say the Rosary every day at the fireside, and when
we went out with the flocks mother always used to remind
us to take a Rosary in our pockets. " Remember," she would
tell us, " to say your beads to Our Lady after lunch, and some
Our Fathers to St. Anthony to keep the sheep from getting
lost." We also used to say: *All honour and thanks to Our
Lord Jesus Christ, for the grace and blessing He has given us
and will give us.* We would always add some prayers for the
souls we knew in Purgatory. Night and morning we would
make an Act of Contrition and invoke our Guardian Angel as
well as saying several Our Fathers.

Lucia recounts the following:

Someone once asked my mother how it was that up to that
time dancing had not been considered a sin but with the
coming of a new priest it had become one? My mother
replied: " I don't know, but the Rev. Father does not want
dancing, that is clear, so my daughters will not go to dances.
They can dance a little at home because Rev. Father says that
in the family it is not wrong to dance."

For her the voice of the priest was the voice of God and
she obeyed without discussion his instructions from the
pulpit. This complete confidence in the parish priest who
doubted, or rather denied absolutely, the truth of the
Apparitions, and her own humility which placed her in her
own eyes on a level with all other ordinary women, go
some way to explain for us the reluctance of Maria Rosa
—a reluctance which lasted nearly to the end of her life—
to admit the stupendous grace which had been conceded to
her daughter. The priest told her that the Apparitions
might be of diabolic origin. How then should she believe
it to be otherwise?

Whatever happened (continues Maria dos Anjos) mother would have us all at home by nightfall. She would not let us stay out even on days of *festa*! The supper hour was sacred. She wanted us to be humble and hard working and it was the worse for us if any of us were caught out in a lie. It was one of the things about which she was most severe. The tiniest fib meant the broom handle for us!

From our first moments she instilled into us a love of the Church and specially for the Blessed Sacrament. In those days the First Holy Communion was not made until children were about ten years old and we had to know our doctrine well. But Lucia made her First Communion when she was six. It was when Father Cruz[2] came here. Our priest did not want to make an exception, but Father Cruz questioned her and gave his verdict: "The child knows quite enough, quite enough," and so she was allowed to receive Our Lord. I can still remember vividly how happy mother was on that occasion and what a *festa* we had at home!

Great mothers and other times!

CHAPTER III

FRANCISCO

FRANCISCO and Jacinta, first cousins of Lucia, were, as we have said, children of Manuel Pedro Marto and his wife Olimpia. They were respectively sixth and seventh children of their father and eighth and ninth of their mother, who had been married before and widowed. Francisco was born on 11th June, 1908, and Jacinta on 11th March, 1910.

"Seven months after the little girl was born," Ti Marto tells everyone, "Portugal came under the Republic, and after another period of seven—seven years—Our Lady appeared."

The little boy Francisco had not the rough, dark appearance which we have noted in his cousin Lucia. He had a round, plump face, skin slightly sallow, a small mouth and lips and a well-formed chin. In the colour of his eyes he resembled his mother. Ti Marto likes to ramble on about the colour of eyes intermingled with amusing stories of his military service—the connection comes from the physical description on his identity card—and consequently, of his experiences in Africa among lions and crocodiles. When we guided him back to the point he told us:

[2] Famous and saintly Portuguese Jesuit. *See* Appendix VI.

Francisco was a strong, healthy boy. We thought he would
live long and come to a good old age.   (Here Senhora
Olimpia interpolated):

It was a pity he died. He would have been a splendid man.
When we had the pneumonia in the house and it was nearly
turned into a hospital, Francisco was never any trouble taking
medicines. We thought he would certainly get well.

And so he did (put in Ti Marto). Didn't Our Lord take
him to Heaven?

The little boy had an exceptional character: " Very
affectionate," according to his father.

Lucia says that in contrast to Jacinta, who was vivacious
and sometimes capricious, Francisco was pacific and tranquil in temperament. Like all the children on this planet
he loved jokes and fun, but at the same time if during games
with others he was denied his rights he gave in without more
ado and did not seem to care even if his things were taken
away from him.

Every year godmother Teresa used to go to the coast
town and bring back presents for her godchildren, who
would run round and see her as soon as she arrived. On
one occasion Francisco's present was a handkerchief with
an image of Our Lady of Nazaré stamped on it and which
he showed with much satisfaction to his companions.
Now, at a certain moment the handkerchief disappeared.
Senhora Olimpia says that he treasured it very much and
was always talking about it, yet when he was told that the
handkerchief was in the possession of another small boy,
he said: " Let him keep it. I don't mind." Francisco gave
way easily and always with a smile. Lucia tells us this:

He would play with all the children without showing
preferences and he never quarrelled. But he would sometimes
leave the game if something happened which he didn't like.
If asked why he left he would say: " Because you're bad," or
simply " Because I want to." Although he tried his best at
games he was dull to play with because he nearly always lost.
I didn't get on with him very well myself, because his peaceful
temperament used to get on my nerves. If I ordered him to
sit on a stone or on the ground he would meekly do so as if
I had to be obeyed. Afterwards I used to be sorry and go and
find him and take him along with me. He would be as friendly
as if nothing had happened.

It must not be thought that Francisco was a boy without
energy or will-power. His father relates that at times he
stood up to his companions even more than his sister.

He was more courageous than she. He didn't always have as much patience and for some little thing would run about like a young bull calf. He was anything but a coward. He would go out at night, alone in the dark, without a sign of fear. He played with lizards and snakes and would roll them round a stick and make them drink out of holes in the rocks or milk from the ewes. He used to hunt hares and foxes and moles. He would catch lizards (put in his mother) and bring them into the house. I was frightened of them but not he. He was never afraid!

He liked to play practical jokes on his brothers and sisters. Ti Marto remembers one which he wanted to play on John one evening when he was snoring by the fire with his mouth open:

> He picked up a chip of wood and would have put it straight into his brother's mouth if I had not prevented him! Sometimes they would get cross with each other[1] and I had to give them a bit of my mind.

Indeed Ti Marto did not limit himself to rearing his children only, but tried to educate them wisely, and, to his way of thinking, reading and writing are not much missed. But, all the same, his manner of educating was serious if not severe. He himself tells us that the neighbours noticed it:

> They said that our house was always quiet. And yet we had eight youngsters! I liked things to be as they should be. I remember once that a certain person came to the house on some errand or another and the children would chatter and hinder me. I didn't say anything at the time but afterwards I gave them a scolding and it never happened again. After that when anyone came to the house they all went out into the street. A look was enough. That wasn't always necessary. If a donkey kicks you needn't cut off its leg!
>
> Once Francisco refused to say his prayers and hid in the out-kitchen. I went to him and when he saw me coming he cried out at once that he would pray! That was before Our Lady appeared. After that he never failed to say them. In fact he and Jacinta would almost force us to say the Rosary.

[1] The fact that Ti Marto differs from Lucia over Francisco's character, affirming a vivacity in him which Lucia seems to deny, can be psychologically explained. How often do active strong-willed children become subdued and even apathetic in the presence of a person who exercises a special domination over them, as was obviously the case with Lucia and Francisco? In her presence, which exerted a fascination over him, the little boy could never have exposed all the sides of his personality. Such facts can be verified almost daily and come within the personal experience of the present writer in the days of his childhood. The intimate character and reactions of each one are as an unknown sea, at times unchartable.

This and the incident of the chip of wood which he wanted to put in his brother's mouth were the two worst things I ever saw him do.

His parents, in fact, never had occasion to be seriously angry with him, for Francisco was a model of obedience. In this matter too, Ti Marto was intransigent.

I remember one time when another man and I sent the boy to do something or other and he tried to argue. I felt something boil up inside me and shouted to him: "Get out of here at once!" And he was off like a streak of lightning.

Fortunately the family were friendly with each other and alas! for them if they were not! Says Ti Marto:

When I saw things weren't going well I didn't let them go too far! And when two were quarrelling and I couldn't tell where the right lay I gave them both a box on the ear for their pains. To put sense into them (he concluded solemnly) I had to be a bit strict.

But to return more particularly to our Francisco. As a proof of the delicacy of his conscience and the rectitude with which he had been educated we may cite the following:

One day (the story is told by Olimpia) as he was going out with the sheep, I told him to take them to Teresa's ground which isn't here but near the village. And he said at once: "No, I don't want to do that!" I was just going to give him a slap when he turned to me and said very seriously: "Mother, are you teaching me to steal? . . ." I felt mad with anger and took him by the arm and pushed him outside. But he didn't go to Oiteiro! Not till the next day, after asking permission from his godmother, who said that he and Lucia might always go there. He was a clever little boy and it always surprised me how well he did the little jobs I set him.

He was as truthful as the sun. Ti Marto attests it:

I always trusted those two (the "two" were, of course, Jacinta and Francisco). Jacinta used to rebuke anyone telling an untruth even if it was her mother. But the others were not so careful.

Francisco had poetry in him. He loved music and would pass hours at a time with his reed pipe, accompanied often by Lucia and Jacinta, who would sing and dance. He liked to imitate the song of the birds and could not bear them to be taken from their nests. Lucia relates that one day he saw a boy with a bird in his hand and induced him to release it after the payment of a precious penny. Like Jacinta, Francisco adored flowers. One of his characteristics was the contemplative tendency which he certainly inherited from his father. Ti Marto is still the dreamer, the thinker, walking to and from the work which his seventy years still allow him to perform, not absorbed in vain thoughts and the world around but with downcast eyes as if in meditation.

Francisco had a soul particularly open to the beauties spread out by the Creator around him on the *serra*. He never ceased to wonder at the immensity of the sky and the stars, " lamps of Our Lady and the Angels ", lit to dispel the darkness of the night. He marvelled at the sun which rose behind Urtiga and Montelo and he would spend long hours contemplating it, above all at evening, when it set behind Cabeço in a fantastic sea of flame.

" Our Lord's own lamp is the most beautiful of all ", were his own words. The rays of the sun through glass enchanted him and drops of dew in the sunlight were to him as precious as jewels.

What excellent clay for the potter's skill!

CHAPTER IV

JACINTA

JACINTA was very different from her brother in temperament although very like him in appearance. She had the same round little face and regular features, the small mouth, fine lips and well-proportioned body. Describing her, Senhora Olimpia told us:

> She wasn't as plump as Francisco. Her eyes were light in colour, and brighter than mine when I was young. (As a matter of fact Olimpia is extraordinarily vivacious and animated for her age.) She liked to have her hair tidy and I used to do it for her every day. A little jacket and a cotton skirt and shoes, for I was always able to keep my children shod, were what she wore every day.

Such was the exterior appearance of Jacinta. Interiorly she possessed a remarkably sensitive soul, as we can see from the following words of Lucia:

> When she was only five years old or less, she would melt into tears on hearing the story of the Passion of Our Lord. "Poor Jesus," she would say; "I must never sin and make Him suffer more."

The friendship which bound her to her cousin Lucia was of a kind rare among children. The usual characteristics of childish friendships, such as envy and emulation, did not exist between them. Jacinta loved being with Lucia above all things and a day spent away from her was a day lost in her opinion. She wanted the elder girl all to herself and when the latter was obliged to stay with the small children whom the mothers left in her care, instead of going to the well which was the favourite playground of the three cousins, only then did Jacinta resign herself to the situation and join in the general play.

So deeply did she love Lucia that when at ten years old —which is the age when these little *serra* children begin to do a grown-up's work—her cousin had to leave her games for the serious work of shepherding, Jacinta was so inconsolable that her mother gave her a few sheep to take out to pasture at the same time.

Jacinta's warm nature was often shown in touching ways. Lucia recounts an example:

> My cousin went one day with her mother to a First Communion ceremony at which tiny " angels " strewed flowers before the Blessed Sacrament. After that she would often leave us at our play and gather armfuls of flowers which she would throw at me in the same way. When I asked her why she did it she said that she was doing what the angels did.
>
> She was always a sweet little girl (was Ti Marto's verdict). And she was like that from the beginning. If she wanted anything she would let us know in her own way or just give a tiny cry and then give no more trouble. When we went out to some place or to Mass, she didn't mind at all. We never had to make a fuss with her. She was naturally good and was the sweetest among our children.

Love of truth was one of her qualities says her father:

> When her mother told her some little fib such as that she was only going to the cabbage-patch when she was really going much further, Jacinta would always notice it and scold my wife! I myself never used to deceive them like that.

Her sincerity is attested to by Maria dos Anjos:

> One day, the children were playing a game of " forfeits " in the sitting-room. Jacinta was sentenced to give a kiss to my brother Manuel who was writing at a table. She protested, saying that she would rather kiss the crucifix on the wall. As the others agreed she took down the crucifix and did so. When I came in I saw the crucifix on the ground and the children gathered round it. I scolded them all, telling them that if they

could not leave things alone they had better go and play outside. Jacinta owned up at once and said that it had been her
fault and promised not to touch anything again.

Like her brother Francisco, and perhaps in an even more
marked degree, Jacinta had a delicate and sensitive soul.
She particularly loved her sheep and had a special name
for each one. There was "Dove" and "Star" and
"Beauty" and "Snow"—the choicest words from her
vocabulary. The white lambs were her chief delight. Lucia
describes a charming scene:

> She used to sit with them on her lap kissing and hugging
> them. At night she used to carry them home on her shoulders
> so that they wouldn't get tired, as in the picture she had been
> given of the Good Shepherd.

Flowers, too, were her special joy. By the house there
was a bed with white flowers which attracted her very
much, but on the *serra,* especially in spring, what riches
and beauty were to be found! Jacinta used to gather them
and put them in her hair and wreathe them into garlands
for Lucia. The discovery of the first wild peony was a
great occasion. The open flower resembles a cockscomb,
and Jacinta, enchanted, would run home crying:
Adivinha, adivinha, quantos galos tem a minha galinha.
(Guess, guess, how many cocks has my hen!) She loved,
too, the "Angels' lanterns" (stars) and would challenge
her brother to count them with her. She would watch the
sun gilding the hills with its splendid golden light, and the
moon, "Our Lady's Lamp", would enchant her because
she could look at it without hurting her eyes and when it
rose full and round she would run with the good news to
her mother. She loved the beauty of the mountains, everything, in fact, which the hand of the Creator had made so
beautiful. Jacinta was also gifted musically and her sweet
singing voice would break the absolute silence of the *serra*
during the long hours with the sheep. Sitting on some high
tor, she liked to hear her voice echoing up from the valley.

> The name which echoed best, says Lucia, was Maria.
> Jacinta sometimes said a whole Ave Maria, but only beginning
> the second part of the prayer when "Maria" had ceased
> echoing.

They would sing the well-known Portuguese hymns whose
repetitive choruses were splendid for playing at echoes.

Dancing, too, was one of Jacinta's passions. Lucia admits this both of herself and her cousin:

> We loved dancing and any instrument we heard being played by other shepherds was enough to set us off. Jacinta, although so small, had a special talent for it.

This passion for dancing is enough to show that the children were not little plaster saints. Jacinta was very much a child of this earth, with many of the failings of the children of Eve. We may here insert a description of her from the pen of Lucia which shows her disagreeable side.

> The least little quarrel which arose when she was playing with other children was enough to put her into a fit of the sulks. To make her return to the game it was not enough to plead and pet; she had to choose both game and partner!

Possessiveness was sometimes a fault in her. Lucia continues:

> Sometimes I was very upset with her because after a game of " buttons " I would have none on my dress when I was called to meals. She nearly always used to win them from me and this meant a scolding from my mother. But what was I to do when, as well as sulking, I knew she wouldn't give them to me so that she would have them ready for the next game instead of using her own! It was only by threatening not to play again that I managed to get them.

Prayer was not so popular as play, according to Lucia.

> We were told we must say our Rosaries after our lunch on the *serra* ; but as the whole day seemed too short for our play we thought of a good way of getting it done quickly. We just said: " Hail, Mary, Hail, Mary " on each bead and then at the end of the decade, " Our Father ", with a longish pause, so that in a very few moments the Rosary was off our minds.

So here are our three children on the eve of the great events, normal children, with their good qualities and their defects.

Our Lady used them to give her message to the world. She might have chosen others, but this story is the story of grace, transforming these children, rude, unlettered, but of an angelic simplicity, into passionate heroic lovers of the Cross.

CHAPTER V

SHEPHERDS

BEFORE sunrise, Olimpia used to wake the two children and with sleepy eyes they would murmur the first prayer of the day. " Bendito e Louvado. . ." "Praised be the ever Holy Sacrament of the Eucharist, blessed fruit of the most pure Virgin Mary ". Olimpia says understandingly:

> They used to make the Sign of the Cross and then say as much as they could. Children of that age soon get tired of praying.

While they dressed, their mother prepared their breakfast, which was a plate of vegetable or rice soup with a little olive oil and a piece of home-made bread. After loosing the sheep from the corral she returned to the house to prepare the simple picnic lunch for the children. This would consist of bread with olives, sardines or dried fish, or anything which was at hand. The children would hastily swallow their soup, thinking of freedom, fresh air and the hills. They left in high spirits, knowing that they would shortly find Lucia and her flock waiting for them on the way to pasture.

It must not be thought that they did not like the company of other children. On the contrary, before the Apparitions, the three used to join large groups of other shepherds and they would all go together the better to dance and play and make merry.

After the meeting with their flocks, Lucia chose the day's pasture, which would either be the waste land common to everyone or a property belonging to some member of the family. Sometimes she would go near Fatima, at others to Moita; nearest of all was a place called Cabeço, a hill overlooking the village, rich in trees and bushes and food for the flocks. Here the family owned a little olive grove, where the olive and pine trees and the great stones afforded a pleasant shade to the children in the heat of summer, as well as being an excellent place for games. The Cabeço was, in fact, their favourite place and they often persuaded their companions to go there. All together they would give themselves over to uninterrupted play, leaving the sheep for the most part to fend for themselves, for here the various herbs, flowers, and grasses, which the spring rains had caused to spring up between the rocks and stones afforded excellent pasture for them.

Lucia was always the games organiser-in-chief. Her character and qualities put her naturally at the head of her companions. One of these, Teresa Matias tells us about this:

> Lucia was very amusing. She had a way of getting the best out of us so that we liked to be with her. She was also very intelligent and could dance and sing and taught us to do the same. We always obeyed her. We spent hours and hours dancing and singing and sometimes forgot to eat.
>
> As well as the hymns we used to sing in church I remember one to Our Lady of Mount Carmel which I still sing as I go about my work and which my children have already learned.[1] (Here Senhora Teresa sang the hymn—four verses and chorus— in a voice prematurely cracked and tuneless from her years of laborious work and childbearing.) We sang folk-songs, too, which I can't remember now, and the little boys used to play their pipes while we danced.

When the position of the sun announced the hour of mid-day or the sound of the " Angelus " came over the hills, play ceased and a hasty inspection of the sheep followed in case they should have strayed into forbidden territory. Everyone sat down to the frugal meal and, after the recitation of the Rosary, play began all over again.

At last when the sun began to sink below the hills and mysterious shadows advanced and lengthened through the trees, it was time to gather the flocks together and bring the radiant day to an end. Next came supper; grace murmured over folded hands, a last Rosary, and then bed on the fragrant crackly mattresses of maize straw, and the sleep of tired happy children beneath the wings of their Guardian Angel.

---

[1] Senhora Teresa has nine children, the eldest nineteen years old. This is not an exceptional family in these parts for Fatima is one of the parishes, not only in the Diocese of Leiria, but perhaps in the whole country, where families are most numerous. It is no exaggeration to say that it is rare to find a family there with less than four or five children. Might Our Lady not have chosen this place for her new manifestation on earth as a reward for healthy normal family life, and as a basis for the resurrection of our society vitiated by the profanation of marriage?

CHAPTER VI

GUARDIAN ANGEL

THE first Apparition of an angel to the principal character in the divine drama of Fatima must have occurred when Lucia was for once, not in the company of her cousins.

At the time of this first Apparition, in which it might be said that the angel did not dare or choose to manifest himself fully, Lucia must have been very small, possibly eight years old. She did not then know how to count the years nor the months nor even the days of the week. It must have been one of the first days on which her mother confided the flock to her and before Ti Marto and Olimpia conceded the longed-for privilege to the other two. Lucia thinks that it must have been about the middle of the year 1915, sometime between April and October.

The fortunate companions on this occasion were three little girls about her own age who still remember, though rather confusedly, what happened on that day some twenty-eight years ago in the slopes of the Cabeço. They were Maria Matias, Teresa Matias—already referred to—and also Maria Justino. Lucia tells the story:

> We had had our lunch and were beginning the Rosary when we suddenly saw over the trees in the valley before us a sort of cloud, whiter than snow, transparent and in human form.

One of the children when she arrived home told her mother that she had seen something white on a tree looking like a woman without a head. The affair caused a good deal of speculation but nobody could think of an answer to the riddle. During the succeeding days the strange figure appeared twice more, leaving in the children's souls, especially that of Lucia, an impression which she could not describe or explain.

> The impression slowly disappeared (she says), and I fully believe that if it had not been for the events that followed we should have forgotten all about it.

It was only after another year had passed and the two younger children had received permission to go with the flocks that the angel appeared clearly to the three for the first time at the Loca do Cabeço.

As if by a special dispensation of Providence, of which they themselves were unconscious, the three children began to isolate themselves more and more from their companions. Lucia relates what happened on that spring day of 1916:

> We went on that occasion to my parents' property, which is at the bottom of the Cabeço, facing eastwards. It is called Chousa Velha.
>
> About the middle of the morning it began to drizzle and we climbed up the hill, followed by our flocks, in search of a rock to shelter under. And so it was that we entered for the first time into that blessed place. It is in the middle of an olive grove belonging to my godfather, Anastacio. From there one can see the little village where I was born, my father's house, and also Casa Velha and Eira da Pedra. The olive grove, which really belongs to several people, extends as far as these places.
>
> We spent the day there, in spite of the fact that the rain had stopped and the sun was shining in a clear sky. We ate our lunch and began to say the Rosary. After that we began to play a game with pebbles. We had only been at it a few moments when a strong wind began to shake the trees and we looked up to see what was happening as it was such a calm day. And then we began to see, in the distance, above the trees which stretched away to the eastward, a light whiter than snow in the form of a young man, quite transparent and as brilliant as crystal in the rays of the sun.
>
> As we came near we began to be able to see his features. We were astonished and absorbed and we said nothing to each other. When he came near us he said:
>
> "Do not be afraid. I am the Angel of Peace. Pray with me."
>
> And he knelt and bent his forehead to the ground. With a supernatural impulse we did the same and repeated the words we heard him say:
>
> "*My God, I believe, I adore, I hope, and I love You. I ask forgiveness for those who do not believe, nor adore, nor hope, nor love You.*"
>
> After repeating this prayer three times he rose and said:
>
> "Pray in this way. The Hearts of Jesus and Mary are ready to listen to you."
>
> And he disappeared.
>
> The atmosphere of the supernatural which surrounded us was so intense that we hardly noticed our own existence for a long period of time. We stayed in the same position in which he had left us and repeated the prayer again and again. The presence of God was so intense and intimate to us that even between ourselves we could not say a word. On the next day we were still surrounded by the same atmosphere and it only disappeared very gradually. Of this apparition none of us thought of speaking nor even of promising secrecy. Silence

imposed itself upon us. It was all so intimate that it was not easy to say a single word on the subject. It made more impression on us being the first clear manifestation.

Such was the first contact of the children with the supernatural. Heavenly things had touched them, but they were far from understanding the true meaning of the events which had held them spellbound for days and it was inevitable that they should return to their normal lives in which such things had no more reality than a dream.

Games, songs, and dances were begun again with increased vigour, but the wish for isolation from other children remained and grew stronger with time. Undoubtedly this wish had a supernatural origin in preparation for the events which were to follow.

And so summer came, scorching in the aridity of the *serra*.

In the half light of dawn the flocks were loosed in order to make the most of the early hours when the pasture was freshest and before the great heat drove flocks and shepherds to shelter from the sun until the evening freshness enabled them to go out once again. During this period the children used to rest and play under the deep shade of the fig trees or by the well if by chance a less intense sun shone through the lacy branches of olive and almond.

It was in this place, still so lovingly remembered by Lucia, that one day, during the time of *siesta*, the angelic messenger appeared for the second time. This is her account:

> Suddenly we saw the same angel near us.
> "What are you doing," he said. "Pray! Pray! The Hearts of Jesus and Mary have meriful designs for you. Offer your prayers and sacrifices to the Most High."
> "How are we to sacrifice?" I asked him.
> "In every way you can offer a sacrifice to the Lord, in reparation for the sins by which He is offended and in supplication for sinners. Thus you will bring peace to our country. I am its guardian angel, the Angel of Portugal. Above all accept and bear with patience the sufferings which the Lord will send you."

As later, in the Apparitions of Our Lady, Francisco heard nothing. In the evening therefore, when they had begun to play again, he asked Lucia what the angel had said. The little girl, however, who was still deeply under the influence

of the supernatural, asked him to wait until the next day or
to ask Jacinta. So he ran to his younger cousin:
" Jacinta, tell me what the Angel said."

But Jacinta, too, found it impossible to pronounce a word
about what had happened:
" To-morrow I'll tell you. I can't talk to-day."

> On the following day, relates Lucia, the first thing Francisco
> did was to ask me: " Did you sleep last night? I was think-
> ing all the time of the Angel and what he could have said."
> I then told him everything that the Angel had said in the two
> Apparitions. It seemed that he did not understand all that the
> words meant, for he asked: " What is the Most High? What
> does it mean that the Hearts of Jesus and Mary are attentive
> to your supplications?" And when I gave him the answer he
> remained thoughtful for a while before asking other questions.
> But my own spirit was not free yet and I told him to wait till
> the following day because I couldn't talk any more at the
> moment. He seemed content to wait a little but on the first
> possible occasion he began to ask questions again which made
> Jacinta cry out: " Be careful; one shouldn't talk about these
> things!"
> When we talked about the Angel (Lucia says), I can't explain
> how we felt. Jacinta said: " I don't know what it is that I
> feel. I can't talk or play or sing or anything." " Nor I,"
> replied Francisco. " But it doesn't matter, the Angel is better
> than anything, let's think of him."

" Pray, Pray, . . . offer your prayers and sacrifices to the
Most High." These words of the Angel, repeated to
Francisco, became deeply engraved on their hearts. Lucia
explains how this was so:

> These words were like a light which made us understand
> Who is God. How He loves us and wishes to be loved, the
> value of sacrifice and how pleasing it is to Him and how it can
> convert sinners. So from that moment we began to offer to
> God everything which mortified us, without however, seeking
> out new mortifications or penances, except that we passed hours
> on end prostrated on the ground repeating the prayer which
> the Angel had taught us.

Penance and Prayer. The great revelation of Fatima,
and the special message of the Mother of God.

Summer passed into autumn. The vintage on the *serra*
is soon over for the vines are small. The time of *siestas*
was over too and the children spent whole days with their
flocks and received another visit from the Angel. Lucia
describes it in these words:

> We went from Pregueira to Lapa, going round the slope of
> the mountain on the side of Aljustrel and Casa Velha. There

we said our Rosary and the prayer which the Angel had taught us in the first apparition. While we were there he appeared to us for the third time, holding in his hand a chalice and above it a Host, from which a few drops of blood flowed into the chalice. Leaving the chalice and the Host suspended in the air, he prostrated himself on the ground and repeated three times the prayer:

" *Most Holy Trinity, Father, Son and Holy Ghost, I adore You profoundly and I offer You the Most Precious Body, Blood, Soul and Divinity of Jesus Christ, present in all the tabernacles of the world, in reparation for the outrages, sacrileges and indifference by which he is offended. And by the infinite merits of His Most Sacred Heart and through the Immaculate Heart of Mary, I beg the conversion of poor sinners.*"

Afterwards, he rose and took again the chalice and the Host and gave the Host to me and the contents of the chalice to Jacinta and Francisco to drink, saying at the same time: " Take and drink the Body and Blood of Jesus Christ, horribly outraged by ungrateful men. Repair their crimes and console your God."

Once more he prostrated himself and repeated with us three times more the prayer, " Most Holy Trinity, etc." Then he disappeared.

As with the two first Apparitions, the necessity of silence imposed itself on all three. Only Francisco, who lacked the impression of the actual voice of the Angel, risked a question:

" Lucia, the Angel gave you Holy Communion, but what did he give Jacinta and me?" And she replied:

" It was Holy Communion too; didn't you see that it was the Blood which was dropping from the Host?"

" I knew God was in me, but I didn't know how!" said Francisco as if waking from a dream. And he knelt on the ground and spent a long time repeating the prayer of the Angel: " Most Holy Trinity, etc."

For some time the children seemed to be deprived of their corporal senses and were in a state of physical prostration, although absorbed by interior peace and happiness, with their souls completely centred in God. Lucia analyses the effects of the Apparitions:

I don't know why, but the apparitions of Our Lady produced quite different effects on us. We felt the same intimate happiness, the same peace and joy, but instead of physical prostration, an expansion of movement; instead of this annihilation in the Divine Presence, a desire to exult in joy; there was no difficulty of speech but rather a desire of communication. However, in spite of these feelings, we also felt the need for silence, especially about certain things.

Having fulfilled his mission, the Angel of Portugal returned to Heaven, which would open again six months later for the Mother of God to pass through and place her feet upon a humble oak tree growing on the Serra of Aire.

CHAPTER VII

BRIGHTER THAN THE SUN

DURING the winter months which followed it might have seemed as if the children had forgotten, almost completely, the Apparitions of the Angel and his recommendations. They lived again their simple carefree life and the seed which had been sown seemed dead.   But in the warm spring sunshine it began to germinate and produce fair fruits of grace.

After the cold, windy days of winter, the April rains bring forth an abundance of growing things which feed alike both flocks and shepherds.   Over the *serra* comes a stirring of life as nature wakes from her sleep and raises her song of praise to Him Who scatters flowers as lovely jewels over the rocky hillsides.   The month of May is the month of flowers and the Month of Mary.   It was on a beautiful 13th of May that the most lovely flower of all came to beautify the desolate earth.

It was the Sunday before the Feast of the Ascension.   As usual, the three children went to hear Mass before leaving with their flocks.   Then, as now, no one let a Sunday pass without hearing Mass.

> God preserve us (said Senhora Olimpia vehemently) from letting Sunday go by without Mass. We always went, children and all as soon as they were of an age to understand. Sometimes we had to go to other villages quite a distance off, but whatever the weather, rain or fine, I never remember missing Mass even when I had the children at the breast. I used to get up early and leave everything to my husband, who went to the later Mass. We never took the toddlers to church because they don't hear Mass or allow you to either. You think you're taking a little angel and it turns out to be a little devil!

After Mass the children went back home, collected their lunch bags and, with the flocks, took the road to the pasture which was Lucia's choice that day—a small property which belonged to her parents in the Cova da Iria.   They went happily along without haste so that the sheep could pick up what they could on the way. The path was stony and the sheep leisurely, so that it was nearly midday before they arrived at the place of pasture. The bells of Fatima ringing for midday Mass announced the hour and the children lost no time in opening their lunch packets, which were likely to contain some special treat in honour of the day. They made the sign of the Cross, recited an Our Father for the souls in Purgatory and began to eat, carefully keeping something for their refreshment later, before setting out once more for home. After grace, they pulled their rosaries out of their pockets as usual, and began to pray. We can imagine that Our Lady must have heard their innocent prayer with special pleasure on that day.

Afterwards they took the sheep higher up the slope to a fresh feeding place and began to build a playhouse. Francisco, the man, was the architect and mason and the little girls his assistants. In a very few minutes a wall was raised round a shrub and, no doubt, the house would soon have been finished by the clever little master-builder and his helpers had not a strange thing happened.

At that moment there was a flash of light which the children for want of a better word called lightning. They dropped their stones in alarm, knowing well that lightning was the herald of a thunderstorm. They looked up and around to see where it was coming from. But neither from the east nor the west was there the least sign of a storm, nor any cloud staining the deep blue of the sky. There was not a breath of wind, only splendid sunlight shimmering in calm clear air. Lucia, as usual, took command:

" We had better go home. The lightning may mean a storm." The others agreed and at that moment another flash rooted them to the spot. Almost automatically they began to move forward a few steps and then, spontaneously, without knowing why, they turned their heads to the right.

On the top of a little oak tree a vision cleft the horizon in two. The children remained immovable, astounded, bathed in the light which came from the Apparition. Lucia's well-known description is as follows:

> It was a lady, clothed in white, brighter than the sun, radiating a light more clear and intense than a crystal cup filled with sparkling water, lit by burning sunlight.

The children, as if enchanted, fixed their eyes ecstatically upon the beautiful Lady who comforted them in a tender motherly voice.

" Do not be afraid. I will not harm you."

She smiled a little sadly as if reproaching them for a lack of confidence in her. Lucia took her courage in both hands and asked:

" Where do you come from?" (Where does your Worship come from, in the politer Portuguese form).

" I come from Heaven."

And the Lady raised her hand and pointed to the blue firmament.

" What do you want of me?" asked Lucia with raising courage.

" I have come to ask you to come here for six months on the 13th day of the month, at this same hour. Later I shall say who I am and what I desire. And I shall return here yet a seventh time."

From Heaven, thought Lucia, she came from Heaven. It must be beautiful too.

" And shall I go to Heaven?"

" Yes, you will," came the answer.

Lucia was content, but at the same time remembered that she did not want to go to Heaven alone.

" And Jacinta?"

" She will go too."

" And Francisco?"

" Francisco too, but he will have to say many Rosaries first."

At this point the eyes of the Lady rested on the little boy with something of censure and disapproval the reason for which it is not given to us to know. It may have been for some small hidden fault. Accustomed as we are to looking at things with our carnal eyes, which can only discern the obvious, we forget that God in an ocean of light sees the lightest shadows.

Although bathed in the same light as Lucia and Jacinta, Francisco could not yet see the Apparition. He heard Lucia speak but could not hear the replies of the Lady.

The thought of Heaven was what most absorbed Lucia's attention. She was now sure of going there one day in the company of her little cousins. That was good. But at the same time a doubt tormented her. In Aljustrel recently, two girls who had come to the house to learn cooking and weaving had died. The anxious question came:

" Is Maria Neves in Heaven?"

" Yes, she is."

" And Amelia?"

" She is in Purgatory."

Lucia's eyes filled with tears. And then the Lady said:

" Will you offer yourselves to God, and bear all the sufferings which He sends you, in reparation for the sins which offend Him, and in supplication for the conversion of sinners?"

Lucia spoke for them all:

" Yes, we will," she said, in a decided voice.

" Then you will have much to suffer, but the grace of God will be your strength."

> As she pronounced these words (says Lucia in a well-known passage) she opened her hands and bathed us in a very intense light, which was like a reflection coming from them, and which penetrated our hearts and our intimate souls so that we saw ourselves in God, Who was this light, more clearly than in a mirror. Then by an impulse which was also interiorly given, we fell on our knees and repeated inwardly: " *O Holy Trinity, I adore You. My God, My God, I love you in the Blessed Sacrament."*

They remained a short time in that sea of light until the Lady said:

" Say the Rosary every day, to bring peace to the world and the end of the war."

War? Peace? What were these? The children did not know, but the Lady, reading their hearts, knew that her behest would be obeyed.

So ended the first discourse of the Mother of God with the three Portuguese shepherd children. Lucia describes her going:

> "She began to rise serenely, moving towards the eastward, until she disappeared in the immensity of space, surrounded by a vivid light which seemed to open a way for her. . . ."

The children remained spellbound for some little time with their eyes fixed on the sky at the point where the vision had disappeared. When, at last they came to themselves and remembered the sheep, what relief to find that they were tranquilly munching grass in the shade of the oak trees nearby!

Without further fear of storms they passed the rest of the day in that holy spot, remembering and savouring the smallest details of the astonishing events of the afternoon.

Unmixed happiness filled Jacinta's heart to overflowing; joy mingled with sadness made Lucia pensive and silent. The younger girl, fascinated above all by the indescribable beauty which she had seen, kept on exclaiming:

"What a lovely, lovely Lady!"

But Lucia kept in her heart the bitterness of the words which she had heard: "Will you offer yourselves to God and bear all the sufferings which He sends you in reparation for the sins by which He is offended . . .?" Amelia, her little friend, was in Purgatory, in that terrible fire which burns the impurity from those souls who cannot yet enter Heaven.

"What a lovely Lady!" sighed Jacinta again.

"I can see you'll be telling everyone about this," said her cousin.

"No, I won't," promised the other. "Trust me, Lucia."

Meanwhile, Francisco for his part, thought . . . and thought. All three talked of nothing but the beautiful Lady and of what she had said to them, until suddenly realising that the sun was already low in the sky, they gathered the flock hastily together and set out for home.

On the way Lucia never ceased reminding the other two of their promise of silence:

"I won't even tell mother," said Jacinta with her hand on her heart.

But even as she said it, her happy expansive manner betrayed the fragility of her promise.

At her father's gate she breathed again her ecstatic praise of the Lady, and Lucia, finger on lip, warned her:

"Remember, not even to your mother."

"I promise!"

The gate softly closed behind the last, laggard sheep.

CHAPTER VIII

THE BROKEN PROMISE

LUCIA, who was already a little woman, both serious and sensible, managed to keep her resolution not to say anything about the events of the afternoon to her mother and brothers and sisters. They had supper and the usual reading from the Old Testament and then went to bed.

But Jacinta, with her heart overflowing with what had happened, found it impossible to keep silence, above all with her mother, to whom she was accustomed to tell everything that happened in her daily life. She saw no reason for keeping this particular joy to herself and seemed to forget completely the solemn promises which she had made to her cousin. While Francisco was occupied in the yard she ran to the kitchen to find Olimpia.

Senhor and Senhora Marto, however, had not returned from the Sunday market-fair at Batalha, where they had gone to buy a pig. The little girl, therefore, took up her position near the gate to wait for them, determined not to waste a moment in telling her thrilling news. They appeared at last, Olimpia a little in front and her husband following, leading the animal which he had bought. Senhora Marto relates their homecoming on that 13th of May as follows:

My little daughter ran to meet me and clutched me round the knees in a way she had never done before. " Mother," she cried excitedly, " I saw Our Lady to-day, in the Cova da Iria!" "That's likely, isn't it!" said I. " I suppose you're a saint to be seeing Our Lady!" Jacinta seemed downcast at what I said, but she came into the house with me, saying again: " But I saw her!"

Then she told me what had happened, of the lightning and their fear because of it . . . of the light . . . and the beautiful lady surrounded by light so dazzling you could hardly look at it . . . of the Rosary which they were to say every day. But I didn't believe anything she was saying and hardly listened to her. I told her she must have taken leave of her senses to think that Our Lady had appeared to her!

After that I went to get some food for the pig. My husband had stayed in the corral to see if it was getting on with the other animals. When we had finished seeing to the animals we went back to the house. My Manuel sat down by the hearth and began to eat his supper. His brother-in-law, Antonio da Silva, happened to be there too, and all my chil-

dren—as far as I can remember, all eight of them. Then I
said to Jacinta:
"Tell us that story about Our Lady in the Cova da Iria."
And she told us what happened with the greatest simplicity.
There had been a most beautiful lady . . . dressed in white
with a gold cord hanging from her neck to her waist. Her
head was covered with a mantle, whiter than milk, and fell to
her feet. It was edged with gold and was so beautiful . . .
her hands had been joined, so . . . And my little girl got up
off the stool and stood with her hands folded on the level of
her chest in imitation of the vision.
She said (continues Olimpia): "The lady held a Rosary in
her hand; a beautiful Rosary shining like the stars, and a
crucifix that shone. . . . She spoke with Lucia a great deal
but not with me, or Francisco. I heard all that she said. Oh,
mother, we must say the Rosary every day; the lady said this
to Lucia. She said too, that she would take us all to Heaven,
and other things which I can't remember, but which Lucia
knows. When she went back into Heaven the doors seemed to
shut so quickly that I thought her feet would get caught. . . ."

Francisco confirmed these declarations. The girls were
much interested in the story, but the boys inclined to tease.
Olimpia says that she too, kept on telling Jacinta that she
supposed she was a saint, etc. Ti Marto's brother-in-law
opined that if the children had seen a Lady dressed in white,
who else could it be but the Blessed Virgin.

Ti Marto, the thinker, meditated and ruminated and
analysed his theological knowledge:

From the beginning of the world, Our Lady has been appear-
ing, at different times and in different ways. These have been
the important things. If there had not been such things the
world would be even worse than it is. The power of God is
very great. We do not understand everything, but let God's
Will be done.

To-day he concludes:

From the beginning I somehow felt that the children were
speaking the truth. Yes, I think I believed from the first. It
seemed to me extraordinary because the children had no
instruction whatever about such things, at least hardly anything. If they had not been helped by Providence how could
they have said such things! And if they were lying? But I
knew so well that Francisco and Jacinta never lied.

And so it happened that Ti Marto was the first believer
in the Apparitions of Fatima. From his somewhat
apocalyptic sayings it is easy to deduce his arguments and
a process of reasoning of first-rate value in the appraisement
of these supernatural events.

It is perfectly true that God can make revelations and has, in fact, done so during the course of history for the benefit of sinful humanity. Otherwise " the world would be even worse than it is ". For the rest, Ti Marto knew his own children and Lucia well enough to exclude the least probability of lying or deception. They were so obviously simple and sincere. He could read their thoughts in their transparent looks.

When later the Bishop of Leiria published his Pastoral letter on the cult of Our Lady of Fatima, declaring the visions of the children in the Cova da Iria, to be " worthy of belief ", he did no less than to develop in precise theological language, the same considerations which the illiterate Ti Marto had made on that 13th of May while eating his bowl of potato soup by the light of an oil lamp.

Upstairs the children slept, dreaming perhaps of the beautiful Lady. . . .

With the new day, the talkative Olimpia could not refrain from telling the neighbours the interesting confidences of her daughter. The facts were so sensational that it was natural that they should travel from mouth to mouth in the little village. In this way, they came to the ears of Lucia's family. Her elder sister, Maria dos Anjos, here takes up the story:

> First thing in the morning, a neighbour came and told me that Jacinta's mother had said that the child had told her a most extraordinary thing. When I heard it, it gave me rather a shock, and I went straight to Lucia who was sitting under a fig-tree doing I forget what.
> " Lucia," I said to her, " I heard that you saw Our Lady in the Cova da Iria. Is it true?"
> " Who told you?" she almost gasped.
> " The neighbours are saying that Jacinta came out with it to Olimpia." Lucia thought for a while and then said to me:
> " And I told her so many times not to tell anyone!"
> I asked her why, and she said it was because she didn't know if it was really Our Lady, though it was a beautiful lady.
> " What did she say to you?"
> " That she wanted us to go for six months running to the Cova da Iria and that she would tell us later what she wanted."
> " Didn't you ask who she was?"
> " I asked her where she came from and she said: ' I come from Heaven.' "
> It seemed as if she didn't want to tell me any more but I almost forced her to. I don't think I ever saw Lucia so sad. Then Francisco arrived and said that Jacinta had not been able to hold her tongue and that at home everyone knew what had happened in the Cova da Iria.

Other people began telling my mother, who from the first refused to take it seriously, but when I told her what Lucia had told me she began to take more notice and went to ask her. Lucia told her exactly what she had told me.

By that time there could be no doubt at all of the declaration of the three children that they had seen Our Lady, or a Lady in the Cova da Iria. And from that moment a terrible doubt began to take hold of Maria Rosa, a doubt that was shortly to become a certainty, that her youngest daughter had become a liar.

CHAPTER IX

SACRIFICE

LATER in the day the children went as usual to pasture their flocks. Lucia, who felt the threatening attitude of her mother, was silent and thoughtful, while Jacinta felt embarrassed because of her talkativeness which had caused so much trouble. The delight of the vision was spoiled and the sadness which followed prepared the ground in Jacinta's heart for a deeper meditation on the words of the Lady.

In the Cova da Iria she sat down on a stone and remained for some time deep in thought. Lucia was sad to see this unusual depression in her cousin, and with a forced smile which hid her own interior bitterness, she said:

" Jacinta, come and play."

" I don't want to play to-day."

" Why?"

" Because I am thinking how the Lady told us to say the Rosary and make sacrifices for the conversion of sinners. Now when we say the Rosary we must say the whole thing and not shorten it like we used to. And how shall we make sacrifices?"

"We might give our lunch to the sheep," suggested Francisco.

The proposal was accepted and at midday the children, with empty stomachs and watering mouths, watched the sheep nibble at the bread and cheese which their mothers had carefully put in their bags. Later the idea came to them that it would be more pleasing to the Lady if instead of wasting the food on the sheep they gave it to some poor children from Moita who begged their bread from door to door.

When towards the end of the day hunger became unbearable, Francisco climbed a holm oak to gather some green acorns to eat while Jacinta remembered that disagreeable as these might be those from the cork oak were even more bitter in taste and that the sacrifice would be greater in eating them.

> And so on that day (recalls Lucia) our food consisted of acorns. At other times we eat pine needles or roots, blackberries, mushrooms and some other things we gathered at the roots of pine trees whose names I can't remember. Sometimes we had a little fruit if we were near our parents' land.

The day passed rather heavily and seemed long. There was no more singing, nor the lightheartedness which had helped to pass the hours. Grace had begun its mysterious working in the hearts of the children.

The greatest trials, however, came at home. Lucia more than the other two passed through a sort of martyrdom. The only one who did not take much notice of the affair was her father who, with folded arms, would say scornfully:

"Women's nonsense!"

But this very indifference and incredulity caused acute pain to Lucia. Maria dos Anjos tells us something of the attitude of Maria Rosa:

> Mother was very upset about it all, and said to us: "Why should such things happen to me at my time of life? I have always been so careful about the children not lying and now they have to come with a lie of this sort!"

Maria Rosa did not content herself with verbal lamentations alone; she took practical steps. Lucia describes them:

> One day, before I went out with the flock, she tried to force me to say I was lying. She tried pleading, threats and even the broom handle. To all this she only received stubborn silence or confirmation of all that I had already said. She told me to go and get the sheep and to think well during the day that she had never allowed her children to tell lies, let alone lies like this! She said, too, that in the evening she would force me to go to those people to whom I had told the story and confess that I had lied and ask their pardon. I went to get the sheep and that day my cousins were waiting for me. When they saw me crying they ran up and asked me what was the matter. I told them all that had happened and added:

"What am I to do? Mother says that I am to say that I am lying. How can I?" Then Francisco said to Jacinta: "You see, it was all your fault because you told!" My little cousin begged our forgiveness on her knees and said: "I did very wrong but I will never tell anything to anybody again!"

When Maria Rosa realised that she could not drag the confession that she desired from her daughter she decided to have recourse to the Parish Priest, whose authority might yet put things to rights. And so one morning she went to the presbytery taking Lucia with her.

"When you get there," said the good woman earnestly, " go down on your knees and confess that you have lied and ask pardon, do you understand? You can explain it how you like; either you undeceive all these people or else I'll shut you in a dark room! My children have never told lies, and now I have this sort of thing with the youngest of you. If it was some little thing it wouldn't matter so much, but a lie of this sort, taking in all those people!"

Yet even to the Reverend Father Ferreira Lucia could not be brought to confess that she had lied. The words of the Lady were beginning to be verified: *You will have much to suffer.* The eyes which had contemplated her beauty were often to swim with tears, but the Lady's promise was fulfilled at the same time: *The grace of God will be your strength.*

CHAPTER X

The Thirteenth of June

THE 13th of June, the day marked by the Lady for her second interview with the children, drew near.

The news had by now spread through the whole parish, and even further afield, giving rise to the most varied speculations. In Aljustrel, no one believed the children. They were criticised and accused of deception; the parents were blamed for their weakness or incapacity to bring up their children properly. The usual self-righteous remarks were made:

" If it were my daughter now. . . !"

" A good dose of castor-oil would soon bring them to their senses, etc."

A woman standing in a doorway hands on hips, shouted to Lucia:

" Do you think I believe your visions?" and the boys would taunt: "Look, Lucia, there's Our Lady on the roof!"

These were the least of the affronts.

The Curate of Fatima, Fr. Manuel Marques Ferreira, a zealous, prudent priest, was far from defending the children, and maintained an absolute reserve on the subject. He thereby took the only attitude possible in the circumstances.

However, outside their birthplace the children found more sympathy. *The prophet is without honour in his own country,* were the words of the Redeemer.

Of the fifty people who went to the Cova da Iria on that 13th of June, one in particular merits our attention on account of the part she played in the sequence of the Apparitions and in the subsequent life of the Sanctuary. She is Senhora Maria dos Santos Carreira,[1] who for a long time has borne the nickname, *Maria da Capelinha* (Maria of the Chapel).

In her house by the Hospital, she told us, in various interviews, everything that she knew about the extraordinary events of the Cova da Iria, of which she had the good fortune to be an eye-witness from the very beginning. It is certain that in this woman Our Lady found a soul of good-will and especially well disposed to believe her revelations. Although now old and weary, Senhora Maria gave us several hours of intense spiritual recreation, making us live again in her company those impressions which can never be effaced from her mind. We transcribe her words exactly as they came from her lips, spoken with enchanting simplicity, slowly and carefully delivered so that we could set them down on paper.

> I have always had poor health, and seven years ago was given up by the doctors and told I had only a few years to live.
> It was two or three days after the first apparitions when my husband, who had been with Lucia's father, said: " Have you heard, wife, that Antonio Abobora says that Our Lady appeared in the Cova da Iria to one of his children—the youngest—and also to two of his sister Olimpia's children, the one who's married to Ti Marto, and that Our Lady spoke to them and promised to go back there every month till October?" And I said to him: " Yes, and I have got to find out whether it's true or not. And if it is I want to go there and see. But

Who died in March, 1949.

where is the Cova da Iria?" I asked him. As a matter of
fact it's very near where we lived at Moita, hardly ten minutes'
walk from our house, but I had never been there and had
never even heard the name. In those days it had no importance at all and now people talk about it all over the world!

My man told me whereabouts it was; and then said: "Do
you want to go? Don't be silly! Do you think you'll see her,
too?" Then he said nothing more so I knew he'd let me go,
and I myself was quite determined to go there on the thirteenth
of June.

To compensate the children for so much incredulity and
to console them in part for the hostility which they encoun-
tered everywhere and which grieved them so deeply, it
seems that Providence sent them this woman who with
others, knelt devoutly believing, on that memorable Feast
of St. Anthony in 1917.

So dawned the 13th of June. In Fatima the festive spirit
proper to the annual patronal Feast reigned in the parish.
Mass was sung in honour of the great patron, and there was
also a sermon and a procession. Youths and girls, then
as now prepared for the festivities which the saint was
expected to patronise. The bells rang and alms and food
were distributed. Fathers of families drove ox-carts decorated with branches of trees, flowers, flags and bedspreads,
carrying wife and children to the *festa* where some 500
people would be regaled with free meals.

They passed round the church several times and then
stopped in front of the verandah where the priest gave his
blessing. A barrier of poles was then erected round the
wagons, leaving spaces through which the people could
come to receive their meals.

Our mother knew well (says Maria dos Anjos) that Lucia
adored the *festa*, and hoped that the whole story of the Cova
da Iria would pass away with it. "It's a good thing we're
having St. Anthony to-morrow," she said. "We mustn't say
anything to her about the Cova da Iria, but only talk about
the *festa*, and then to-morrow she'll have forgotten all about
the other thing. Perhaps it's our fault for talking about it so
much."

We were very careful to do as she said, but Lucia hardly
said anything and took no notice at all of our plans. From
time to time she reminded us: "But to-morrow I'm going to
the Cova da Iria; that is what the Lady said."

Like Lucia, Jacinta and Francisco were both determined
to sacrifice the *festa* of St. Anthony for the sake of the
beautiful Lady, and they waited impatiently for the hour
of departure for the Cova da Iria.

Both children talked of what they hoped to see and of the joy which would shortly be theirs. Jacinta wanted her mother to share her happiness, and in her simplicity was quite unable to understand why Olimpia should be so reluctant to admit what was to her such an obvious reality.

" Oh, mother," she cried, " do come with us to-morrow to the Cova da Iria to see Our Lady!"

" What Lady, you silly girl? . . . To-morrow we're going to St. Anthony. Don't you want to see the Feast? And hear the music and the sermon, and the fireworks?"

Music and feasting! Magic words for a child! Irresistible, thought Olimpia. Little did she know that for a month past her little girl had renounced singing and dancing and even her frugal meals for the conversion of sinners as the heavenly vision had desired.

" But, mother," insisted Jacinta, " Our Lady comes to the Cova da Iria!"

" I'm certainly not going there; it isn't true that Our Lady appears to you."

" But she does, and she said she'd come again, and so she will!"

" Don't you want to go to St. Anthony?"

" St. Anthony's no good."

" Why?"

" Because that Lady is much, much nicer. I'm going to the Cova and so are the others, although we would go to St. Anthony if the Lady told us to." Describing the occasion, Ti Marto tells us:

" What an idea," I thought to myself. Going to the Cova da Iria with the children. And if nothing happened? Or let them go there alone while we went to the *festa*? Hum! . . . I didn't like the idea of that either. Then I had an idea. There was a fair next day at Pedreira and I'd go there and buy some oxen. " Look, wife," I said to my Olimpia, " to-morrow we won't have any *festas* or anything else either. We'll go to the fair to buy oxen and when we get back this affair of the children will be finished with. What a business it is to be sure!"

Jacinta had hardly opened her eyes on the 13th when she jumped out of bed and ran to her mother's room to invite her once more to go to the Cova da Iria. When she went in, however, she had a surprise. The room was empty. At that moment her eldest brother came in and explained that their parents had gone out and would only be back in the evening. Jacinta's first feeling was one of disappointment:

" Then mother won't see Our Lady!" And then with
relief: " At any rate we'll be free to go."

She ran to wake up her brother, and while he was dress-
ing went to loose the sheep so as to have everything ready
to leave punctually for the Cova da Iria. Munching their
bread and cheese on the way, they hurried along. In the
lane they met Lucia who awaited them with anxiety.

" To-day we'll go to Valinhos. There's plenty of grass
there, and we can get everything done more quickly."

And the three, as happy as little birds, led their sheep in
the direction of the Cabeço.

An hour and a half went by and the flocks were replete.
The children went home, shut them in the corral and went
to put on their best clothes.

" I won't wait for you," said Lucia, " I'm going to Fatima
to see some children who made their First Communion with
me."

And so it was arranged. Lucia, shawl fetchingly thrown
over her shoulders, new shoes, and a white kerchief on her
head, was ready in a few moments. Her mother watched
her with attention though she said nothing, satisfied that
St. Anthony had performed another miracle.

" We shall soon see," said Maria dos Anjos, " if she goes
back to Fatima or to the Cova da Iria."

Duty, however, obliged them to keep an eye on events.
So it was arranged that if the children went to the Cova,
Maria Rosa was to follow them, hide, and see what happened. If nothing extraordinary occurred and anyone
attacked them she would intervene especially as the parents
of the younger two had gone off for the day. One was
likely to make a fool of oneself, but what else could one
do?

" I'll start for the church," whispered Maria Rosa to her
daughter, " and you stay here and tell me what happens."

The good woman went out alone in a state of depression
deeper than she had ever experienced during her uneventful
years of life as wife and mother. About half-way to the
village she met a group of people whom she did not know
and whom she supposed to be going to the *festa*. Thinking
that they had mistaken the way (they were coming away
from Fatima) and in spite of her own preoccupation, she
said to them:

" If you're going to Fatima it's in the other direction."

" We've come from there," was the reply. " We're looking for the house of the children who saw Our Lady."

" Where do you come from?" stammered Maria Rosa.

" From Carrascos. Could you tell us where the children
live?"

" They live in Aljustrel, but they'll soon be coming to
the Festa of St. Anthony," replied Maria Rosa, concealing
her relationship with them. And to herself: " Then
people are going to the Cova da Iria. I shan't be able to
get there without their seeing me. Somebody is sure to
notice. These people look respectable. Well, we must
see . . . and may God's will be done. I shan't leave here."

To the surprise and satisfaction of the family Lucia also
went off in the direction of Fatima and mingled with the
other girls. After all, she's just like the rest. . . .

Lucia's *festa* on that day was, however, of a very different
kind. The following was told us by Senhora Leopoldina
Reis, who is about Lucia's age:

> About fourteen of us who had been Lucia's companions in
> her First Communion, joined together and decided to go with
> her to the Cova da Iria. As usual, when Lucia proposed a
> thing no one contradicted her.
> We were in a group ready to go, when Lucia's brother,
> Antonio, appeared and said: " Don't go to the Cova. If you
> don't I'll give you some money." And she answered: " I don't
> care about the money. What I want is to go." We then went
> to that house (indicating a building some 100 metres from the
> church) with the boy at our heels trying to stop us. But we
> just went on.

On the way other people joined the group of girls, among
them some who had come from as far away as Torres
Novas. When they arrived at the place where the main
gate of the Sanctuary now is, they met a group of women
who were awaiting the arrival of the little seers. There with
her cripple son aged seventeen, was our friend Maria da
Capela, who takes up the story:

> I had decided once and for all to go to the Cova da Iria on
> the thirteenth of June. On the evening before I said to my
> children: " What if we don't go to the *festa* of St. Anthony
> to-morrow but to the Cova da Iria instead?" " What for?"
> they answered. " No, we'd rather go to the *festa*." Then I
> turned to my cripple boy, John. " Do you want to go to the
> *festa* or with me?" " With you, mother," he said.
> So on the following day, before the others started for the
> *festa*, I came here with my John, who hobbled along on a stick.
> When we got here there wasn't a soul about, and we went to
> the roadside where the children would come along. After a

while a woman from Loureira arrived and was very surprised to see me there as she thought I was ill in bed. She asked me: "What are you doing here?"

"The same as you!"

She sat beside me and shortly after a man from Lomba da Egua arrived and the conversation we had was much the same as before. Then came some women from Boleiros and I asked them if they had come away from the *festa*. "People laughed at us," they said, "but we didn't take much notice. We've come to see what happens here and on whose side the laugh will be."

Then more people came and at last, about 11 o'clock, the children to whom Our Lady had appeared, with some little friends and people from quite far away, Torres Novas or Outeiro, I can't remember which. We all went to the holm oak and Lucia stopped about three yards in front of it and looked towards the east. It was very quiet, and then I asked her: "Which is the oak tree where Our Lady appeared?" "This one," she said, putting her hand on it.

It was a bush about a metre high, a nice strong sapling. It was very well shaped with regular branches. Lucia went a little further away and began looking again in the direction of Fatima and then went again into the shade of a big tree. It was very calm and still. Lucia sat down near the trunk and Jacinta and Francisco sat on either side.

At this point we insert the words of Senhora Leopoldina, already referred to:

We other children began to play and eat things we had brought, and as the time passed by Lucia became more serious and thoughtful. Jacinta, however, was playing all the time and Lucia told her to be quiet as Our Lady would be arriving.

Those who had come a long way (continues Maria da Capela) began to eat lunch and to offer some to the children, who each accepted an orange which, however, they didn't eat. I can still see the three of them with the oranges in their hands. Then a girl from Boleiros began to read aloud from a book of prayers which she had brought. As I was ill and feeling weak and tired I asked Lucia if she thought Our Lady would be long in coming. "She won't be long now," was her reply and she watched for the signs of the arrival. We said the Rosary meanwhile and when the girl from Boleiros was beginning the Litany, Lucia interrupted, saying that there would not be time. She got up immediately and cried out: "Jacinta, Our Lady must be coming; there's the lightning!" They all ran to the holm oak and we behind them. We knelt down on the rocks and stones. Lucia lifted up her hands as if she were praying and I heard her say: "You (Your Worship) asked me to come here; please tell me what you want."

Then we began to hear something like a tiny little voice, only we couldn't hear what it said. It was rather like the buzzing of a bee!

At this point, as if doubtful of our ability to understand her language, Maria da Capela asked anxiously:

"Does your Reverence understand about the bee?"

Sister Lucia has revealed to us what those fifty people were unable to understand:

"I want you to come here on the 13th of next month. Say the Rosary and after each mystery pray: *O my Jesus, forgive us and deliver us from the fire of hell: take all souls to Heaven, especially those who are most in need*.[2] I want you to learn to read, and afterwards I will say what else I want."

Lucia courageously asked for the cure of a sick person who had been recommended to her. Our Lady replied that if she were converted she would be cured within a year. Again the seer asked:

"Will you take us to Heaven?"

"Yes, I shall take Jacinta and Francisco before very long, but you will stay a little longer. Jesus wishes to use you to make me known and loved. He wishes to establish in the world devotion to my Immaculate Heart."[3]

"Must I stay here alone?"

"No, my child. Do not be sad because of this. I will never leave you. My Immaculate Heart will be your refuge and the way which will lead you to God."

These words were deeply impressed on Lucia's heart, and she was always to find that Heart a sure comfort in her sufferings, and strength in the terrible battle she would have to wage against the powers of Hell and the world, united in an effort to obstruct the grace and benefit which the Apparitions of Fatima have, under Divine Providence, brought to mankind.

> It was at the moment, when she said these last words (says Lucia), that Our Lady opened her hands and communicated to us once again the great light in which she was surrounded. In it we saw ourselves as if submerged in God. Jacinta and Francisco seemed to be in that part which was of Heaven and myself in that which was poured out upon earth. Our Lady's

[2] The souls in greatest danger of condemnation (Lucia).

[3] This is the first secret which Lucia revealed to her confessor. "On December 17th, 1927, I asked Our Lord how I could obey my confessor in the relation of certain graces if, among them, was the secret of Our Lady. Jesus in a clear voice, made me hear the following words: 'My daughter, write what your confessor commands you, write also all that the Blessed Virgin revealed in the Apparitions which refers to devotion to her Immaculate Heart. Continue to hide the rest of the secret.' "

right hand rested near a Heart, encircled by thorns which pierced it. We understood that it was the Immaculate Heart of Mary, calling for reparation for the outrages of humanity.

As in the first and subsequent Apparitions the Blessed Virgin spoke only with Lucia. Jacinta heard the words of both while Francisco heard nothing, and was afterwards informed by Lucia of what had been said. Why should this have been so we cannot tell. Our Lord distributes His grace when and how He will.[4] Maria da Capela continues:

> When Our Lady left the tree, it sounded rather like a rocket, a long way off, as it goes up. Lucia got up very quickly and, with her arm stretched out, cried: "Look, there she goes! There she goes!". We saw nothing except a little cloud a few inches from the tree which rose very slowly and went backwards, towards the east, until we could see it no more. Some people said: "I can still see it; it's still there . . ." until at last no one could see it any more.
>
> The children stayed, silently looking in that direction until at last Lucia said: "There, now we can't see her any more. She has gone back into Heaven, the doors are shut!" We then turned towards the miraculous tree and what was our admiration and surprise to see that the shoots at the top, which had been standing upright before, were now all bent towards the east, as if someone had stood upon them. Then we began to pull off twigs and leaves from the top of the tree but Lucia told us to take them from the bottom where Our Lady had not touched them. I then noticed a beautiful spray of rosemary growing near and took a piece of that, too, as a souvenir.
>
> Somebody suggested that we should say the Rosary again before going home, but others who had come a long way said that we could say the Litany now and the Rosary on the way back to Fatima. There was someone there who had a concertina but I don't remember hearing him play. After the Litany we all went back to Fatima with the children, praying as we went, and we arrived when the procession was just starting. People saw us arrive and asked us where we had come from. We replied, from the Cova da Iria, and that we were very glad to have come from there. Some of them were sorry at what they had missed but it was too late then.

In July, these fifty pilgrims increased to 2,000 or 3,000, a fact which can hardly cause us any surprise.

---

[4] A detail which we heard from the lips of Maria da Capela may explain a great deal. "On one occasion," she says, "I met Jacinta and Lucia. I asked Lucia why it was that Our Lady only spoke to her and not to Jacinta or Francisco. She said: 'Because Jacinta's tongue-tied. If she spoke, Our Lady would speak to her.' Jacinta looked at me and then at Lucia and smiled shyly!"

CHAPTER XI

DOUBTS AND THE DEVIL

IT was about four o'clock in the afternoon when the three children went home, followed by a multitude of curious people who at once began to torment them with futile remarks such as:

"Lucia, did the Lady appear on the top of the tree?"

"Jacinta, didn't the Lady say anything to you this time?"

"Well, how is it that you haven't gone to Heaven yet?"

For the children all this, and the implied irreverence towards the Lady was a real martyrdom.

At home Jacinta was silent and only replied in monosyllables to the questions which were not spared her even there. She repeated that it was necessary to say the Rosary every day, that the Lady would come back every month until October when she would say who she was and what she wanted. Of the secret part of the message not a word. She longed no doubt to throw her arms around her mother's neck and cry out that the Lady had promised to take her shortly to Heaven, but an imperious necessity which all three felt, imposed silence upon them.

On one subject, however, Jacinta felt free to speak, and that was of the loveliness of the vision, all of light and gold.

"Was the Lady as beautiful as so and so?" asked her family.

"Much, much more beautiful."

"Like that statue in church with the cloak covered in stars?" (St. Quiteria.)

"Much more beautiful!"

"Like Our Lady of the Rosary?"

"More beautiful still!"

And her mother and brothers and sisters passed all the images of the saints in church and at home in review, but the beauty of the Lady which Jacinta had seen in the Cova da Iria had no comparison here on earth.[1]

---

[1] On one occasion (related Fr. Manuel Ferreira, parish priest of Fatima, at the canonical inquiry into the Apparitions), it was August 21st, five ladies arrived in Fatima and asked me to accompany them on a visit to the children. Among them was a girl, about fifteen years old, dressed in white. When we arrived at Senhora Marto's house I called Jacinta who was alone in the house. The child was astonished

Jacinta bent her head and repeated that the Rosary must be said, that the Lady would come back, and that she had told them a secret which they must not tell to anyone. A secret! This was most intriguing. And from that moment Jacinta was to know no peace; everyone at home and outside, except her father, tried by means of persecution to force it from her. Senhor Marto describes it in his own words:

> All the womenfolk wanted to know what it was, but I never asked her anything about it. A secret is a secret and must be kept. I remember very well a time when some ladies came here with a lot of gold ornaments on them.
> "Do you like these?" asked one of them, showing Jacinta her bracelets and necklace.
> "Yes, I do."
> "Would you like them?"
> "Yes!"
> "Then tell us the secret!" and they pretended to be taking off the ornaments. But my little girl was very upset and cried out:
> "Don't, don't, I can't tell you anything! I couldn't tell you the secret even if you gave me the whole world!"
> Another day Senhora Maria das Neves came from Moita, with a little niece, and Jacinta on this occasion, too, was alone in the house.
> "Look, Jacinta, I'll give you this lovely gold necklace if you'll tell me the secret."
> "If you'll give me the medal hanging round your niece's neck, I'll tell you," replied Jacinta teasingly.
> "Well, I can't give you that because it's hers."
> "Then I'll give it to her," put in the niece.
> "Don't worry," said Jacinta with her little smile. "Nothing in the world could make me tell the secret!"

For all three children this insistent curiosity was a real torment, but it was not the greatest sacrifice, above all for Lucia. Trials even more severe were to come to purge the children's souls and prepare them for the extraordinary graces which had been destined for them.

The ways of Providence are like this. For his special and intimate friends Our Lord offers not a crown of roses but one of thorns; He does not lead them to Thabor but to

to see the visitors. After I had encouraged her a little I said to her: "Look, Jacinta, was the Lady you saw in the Cova da Iria one of these, or like one of these?" Jacinta looked at them in silence and said: "No, it wasn't one of these, the other one was more beautiful." Then I pointed out the girl in white and said: "Wasn't it this beautiful lady that you saw?" She replied: "This is a beautiful lady but the one I saw in the Cova da Iria was much more beautiful."

Calvary; does not offer them riches, honours, pleasures, but a cup of ignominy, a heavy cross.

According to the promise of the Blessed Virgin the two younger children were soon to be taken to Heaven, and it was necessary, therefore, that grace should work rapidly.

Lucia, for her part, had received the sublime mission of spreading in the world devotion to the Immaculate Heart of Mary and, consequently, the purification and embellishment of her soul in the crucible of suffering was no less urgent.

This and no other, is the explanation of the ceaseless conflict, the sometimes atrocious sufferings which the children had to bear in order to play their part.

The parish priest had advised Lucia's mother to allow her daughter to go to the Cova da Iria on the 13th of June, but told her to bring the child to the presbytery soon afterwards in order that he might question her. These recommendations were passed on to Senhor Marto, who relates what happened:

> I went as I had been asked, in good faith. "Reverend Father," I said, "my brother-in-law told me to come here with the children but I came to speak with you first to find out what we had better do." Then he said: "I'm sick and tired of this. First it's one thing and then another!" I kept quite calm and said: "Does your Reverence want the truth or not?" And he: "I've never heard such things in my life. And everyone else seems to know more than I do." He was obviously annoyed and said crossly: "If you want to bring them, bring them, and if you don't want to, don't. Do as you please." "Then I shall do what I think is right and that is, to come," I answered. We then went out on to the veranda and when I was leaving for home and was half-way down the steps, he said to me again: "This is your responsibility; bring them or not, as you please." At the bottom of the steps I turned round and said: "Your Reverence, I shall bring them because I think it is the right thing to do and not because I want to make trouble."

That same evening Lucia went to her cousins' house and told them:

"To-morrow we're to go and see the priest. I'm to go with mother and the others are doing their best to frighten me about it."

"We're going too," said Jacinta. "He told mother to bring us, but she hasn't said anything to us yet. Never mind, if they beat us we can suffer for Our Lord and for sinners."

On the next day (says Ti Marto), it was Maria Rosa who took the little girls and, I think, Francisco as well. When they came back she came to see me and said: "I've taken my Lucia and Jacinta to see Fr. Ferreira. He asked Jacinta questions but she wouldn't answer him a word." Then he said to her: "You don't seem to know anything; sit down there or run away if you like." Jacinta took out her Rosary and started to say it, while Fr. Ferreira began to question Lucia, who answered well. From time to time Jacinta got up and told Lucia to be sure and explain things properly. At that (continues Ti Marto) my sister-in-law was a bit surprised, and Fr. Ferreira said rather crossly to Jacinta: "When I was asking you questions you didn't know anything and wouldn't say a word, and now it's the other way about."

The interrogation clearly did not satisfy the good priest. Our Lady, he reasoned, could not have come from Heaven to earth just to tell people to say the Rosary every day, a custom more or less general in the parish. Also when things of this kind happen, Our Lord usually tells the souls to whom he makes his communications to reveal them to their confessors or parish priests. This girl, on the contrary, keeps things to herself when she can. It may be a trick of the devil; we shall see.

Perhaps his judgment would have been different if Lucia had been more open with him and had told him more of what the Blessed Virgin had told her. In any case it was within the disposition of Providence and gave the children further occasion for suffering and reparation for sinners.

"It might be a trick of the devil," Father Ferreira had said, and as parish priest his authority had commanded the utmost respect both from Lucia and all the other children of the village as well as their elders. In Lucia's mind the seed of doubt was sown. What if the good Father were right? Perhaps this was the sharpest thorn in the heart of the poor little girl (we must always keep in mind that she was but ten years old). It was incredible to her that the parish priest should be mistaken, and yet . . .

I began at that time to doubt and to wonder if the manifestations could be from the devil, trying to deceive me. I had always heard that the devil brought with him all kinds of disorder and war, and it was true that since these things happened there had been no more happiness or well-being at home. How much I suffered! I told my cousins of my doubts and Jacinta said: "No, no, it's not the devil! People say that the devil is very ugly and lives under the earth in hell, but that Lady was so beautiful and we saw her go up into Heaven."

Jacinta's words were like a ray of light in the dark night of Lucia's soul, fugitive none the less, for the sufferings which had been destined for her had not run half their course.

Gradually, the ardour which had made sacrifice and mortification sweet, lessened without her knowing how or why, and she felt a deadly apathy. She even reached the point where she wondered if it would not be better to say that she had lied and so finish with the whole thing.

Jacinta and Francisco, her consoling angels, said, however:

"Don't do that! Can't you see that it would be a lie and that lying is a sin!"

And then the sky cleared again, and again the storms returned. She was obsessed with the idea of being a plaything of the devil. Her fears were increased one night by a dream:

> I saw the devil laughing at having deceived me and trying to drag me into hell. Terrified at being in his clutches I began to scream so loudly, calling for Our Lady, that I awoke my mother, who was very upset and wanted to know what was the matter. I can't remember what I told her; I only remember that I was too terrified to sleep any more that night. This dream left a cloud of fear and apprehension in my soul.

A simple reflection of her state of mind. It was natural that her constant thoughts of the devil should turn into such a dream.

The only moments of peace for the children were enjoyed in the Cova da Iria by the oak tree. They were often met there by Senhora Carreira (Maria de Capela) who joined them in their prayers. Although weak from illness, she began to beautify the holy place as well as she could. In truth Maria da Capela was one of the first and most devoted believers in Our Lady of Fatima.

> On the same evening as the *festa* of St. Anthony (she tells us) when my daughters came back from Fatima they asked me: 'Well, mother, was it interesting in the Cova da Iria?' 'I was sorry you weren't there, too.' I replied. 'Did Our Lady really appear?' And then I told them all that had happened during the day. One of them said to me: 'We must go there on Sunday.' And so we did. We were praying by the oak tree when we saw two people from Lomba de Egua. They saw us, too, and said: 'Look, there are some more people.' We hid in the bushes to see what they did. They had some carnations and hung them on the branches of the tree and then

knelt and said the Rosary. We stayed where we were so as not to disturb them and only joined them when they had finished. From that time I always went to the Cova da Iria. At home I felt as if I had no strength, but when I got here I felt quite another person. I began to clean up a bit round the tree, and make a little clearing. I took away the gorse and prickles and cut paths with a pruning saw. I took away some of the stones and hung a silk ribbon on one of the branches of the tree. It was I who put the first flowers there.

CHAPTER XII

JULY THE THIRTEENTH

JACINTA and Francisco were filled with enthusiasm at the approach of the 13th of July. It was not so with Lucia, who was so depressed and uncertain that she almost decided not to go.

" The devil'll be there for sure," her mother said, echoing the words of Fr. Ferreira, who took no trouble to hide his opinions, which were entirely against any supernatural explanation of the events. Maria Rosa knew this very well. Once when she had been talking to him in the company of Senhor José Alves of Moita—one of the first believers in the Apparitions—he had said to her openly:

" This is the devil's work."

" No, Father," said the good man. " In the Cova da Iria people pray and surely the devil doesn't make people pray!"

" The devil goes to the Altar sometimes," put in the priest abruptly.

Humbly Senhor Alves agreed:

" You know more about it than I do, Father."

The constant repetition of these ideas nearly convinced Lucia of their truth. The poor child thought that all was over and on the eve of the 13th, when the people were already coming from all parts, she went to find Jacinta and Francisco and tell them her decision. No less firmly the two younger children gave her their answer:

" We shall go, anyway. The Lady told us to. *I* will speak to her," declared Jacinta. Then she broke down and cried.

" Why are you crying?" asked Lucia.

" Because you don't want to come."

" No, I'm not coming. Listen, if the Lady asks for me. tell her that I can't go because I'm afraid it is the devil!"

And, without another word, she went and hid herself from all the people who were trying to find and question her.

Her mother, who thought it was getting beyond a joke, reproved her:

" This is just the way to be a saint! When you ought to be with the sheep you get up to mischief and can't be found."

On the following day, however, when it was nearly time to leave for the Cova da Iria, an interior force which Lucia could not explain almost carried her on to the road. All the doubts and all the fears seemed to disappear as if by magic. As she passed her cousins' house she went in to see if they were still there. They were kneeling by their beds, both in tears.

" Aren't you going then?"

" Not without you. Come, Lucia, come. . . ."

" I'll come," was the immediate reply.

Happily as ever, the three made their way slowly through the crowds which were filling the roads and pressing round them to look at them closely or to question them or to give messages for Our Lady.

The children had not long left the house when Olimpia began to be nervous about their safety and she lost no time in running to Maria Rosa and putting her fears into words:

" We must go after them," she cried, " or we may never see our children again. Anything might happen, they might even be killed!"

" Now, keep calm," was the reply. " If Our Lady really appeared, then she will look after them; if not, well . . . I don't know. . . ."

Finally, after reflection, she resolved to go with Olimpia to the Cova da Iria. The two women threw their overskirts over their heads to conceal their identity and took a back road to the Cova. Each one carried a blessed candle and a box of matches:

> Because (says Olimpia), if we had seen anything evil we could have lit the candles. . . .

When they arrived at the Cova they hid themselves behind some rocks where they could observe what was happening. Their hearts beat violently in apprehension of what might happen.

Senhor Marto, on the contrary, was convinced of the sincerity of the children and, consequently, of the truth of the Apparitions. He, therefore, openly followed the little seers and approached as nearly as he could to the oak tree, round which a crowd of both curious and devout people had assembled from the early hours of the morning. Among them was Maria da Capela, with her husband and daughters and the cripple John, who sat on a stone and hoped that Our Lady would cure him of his deformity. Maria da Capela had, in fact, asked Lucia a few days earlier to ask Our Lady to cure her son, and the little girl had promised to do so. We will now quote Ti Marto, who has described the events of that day for us in his usual simple and graphic language:

> This time I left home determined to see what happened. How many times had I told Maria Rosa: "If people say that all this is an invention of the parents nobody knows better than you and I that it's not true. We have never encouraged the children, and even Fr. Ferreira says that it may be the devil all the time!" And with these ideas in my head I set off for the Cova. What a crowd of people there was! I couldn't see the children but there was a sort of clump of people in the road and I judged they must be there in front. I thought at first that I would stay behind but in the end I couldn't resist trying to get near to them. But how? That was the question! There was such a crush. At one moment, two men, one from Ramila and the other from here, made a barrier round the children so that they wouldn't be so crushed, and then seeing me there they pulled me by the arm and said: "Here's the father, let him through!" And so I got to my Jacinta. Lucia was kneeling a little way off saying the Rosary which the people were answering aloud. When it was finished she got up so quickly that it seemed as if she were pulled up. She looked to the east and then cried out: "Shut up your umbrellas (used for the sun) Our Lady is coming!" I looked as hard as I could but could see nothing at first. And then I saw what looked like a little greyish cloud resting on the oak tree, and the sun's heat lessened and there was a delicious fresh breeze. It hardly seemed like the height of summer. The people were so silent that you could have heard a pin drop. And then I began to hear a sound, a little buzzing rather like a mosquito in an empty bottle. I couldn't hear any words! I think talking on the telephone must sound like that though I've never done it! What is it?—I said to myself. Is it near or far away? All this was for me a great proof of the miracle.

In fact, the Blessed Virgin had descended for the third time to the oak tree and spoken to her three confidants. In the presence of the Vision an indescribable sense of happiness and peace filled the hearts of the children, especially Lucia, who could hardly believe what she saw.

With infinite love, as a mother with a sick child, the Lady
rested her eyes upon Lucia, reassuring her, encouraging her
against those now far-off temptations of the devil. Lucia
contemplated her as if in ecstasy, entirely absorbed by her
beauty. It was Jacinta who roused her from that contemplation by saying:

" Lucia, speak, Our Lady is talking to you."

Humbly, as if asking pardon for having doubted, Lucia
asked once more:

" What do you want of me?"

" I want you to come back here on the 13th of next
month. Continue to say the Rosary every day in honour
of Our Lady of the Rosary to obtain the peace of the
world and the end of the war, because only she can obtain
it. . . ."

The doubts of her mother, the taunts of the people, Fr.
Ferreira's devil; all these things passed through Lucia's
mind and she decided not to lose an opportunity.

" I would like to ask who you are and if you will do a
miracle so that everyone will believe that you appeared to
us."

" Come here every month and in October I will say who
I am and what I want. I will perform a miracle so that
everyone can believe."

This satisfied Lucia completely and she lost no time in
placing before the Blessed Virgin the requests with which
she had been entrusted. Our Lady replied gently that she
would cure some but not others. As to the cripple son of
Maria da Capela, she said that she would not cure him
nor relieve him of poverty, but that he must say the Rosary
every day with his family.[1]

One of those recommended was a sick person from
Atougia who asked to be taken soon to Heaven. Our Lady
gave the reply:

" Tell her not to be in a hurry. I know very well when
I shall come to fetch her."

There were requests for conversions; one from a Fatima
woman and her children; another from Pedrogão; others to
cure drunkenness, etc. Everyone must say the Rosary as
a general condition for the reception of grace.

In order to strengthen the failing fervour of Lucia, Our

---

[1] If Our Lady did not cure or enrich him she ensured him a means
of livelihood. He is to-day sacristan of the Chapel of the Apparitions.

Lady insisted again on the necessity for sacrifices and confided yet another secret.[2]

" Make sacrifices for sinners and say often, especially when you make a sacrifice: *O Jesus, this is for love of Thee, for the conversion of sinners and in reparation for sins against the Immaculate Heart of Mary."*

> As she said these words (continues Lucia) she opened her hands again as in the preceding months. The reflection which they gave out seemed to penetrate the earth and we saw a sea of fire and plunged in this fire devils and souls like transparent embers, black or bronzed, in human form, which floated in the fire and were carried by the flames which they themselves gave forth, together with clouds of smoke, falling on all sides— as the sparks fall in great fires—without weight or equilibrium, amidst cries of pain and despair which horrified us and made us tremble with fear.
>
> The devils could be distinguished by their horrible and terrifying forms of strange unknown animals but transparent like burning coal.
>
> At this moment (says Ti Marto) Lucia took a deep breath, went as pale as death, and we heard her cry out in terror to Our Lady, calling her by name.

The terrified children looked up at the Blessed Virgin as if asking for help and she sadly but kindly told them:

" You have seen hell where the souls of sinners go. To save them God wishes to establish in the world devotion to my Immaculate Heart. If you do what I tell you many souls will be saved and there will be peace. The war will end, but if men do not cease to offend God another worse one will begin.[3] When you see a night lit by a strange

[2] This is the secret which was to cause the children so much suffering. Only after the death of Francisco (1919) and of Jacinta (1920) did Lucia receive permission from Heaven to reveal the first and second parts. As to the third part, only in 1960 shall we know what the Blessed Virgin told the children of Aljustrel. It is in the possession of the Bishop of Leiria, written by Lucia and placed in a sealed envelope. " It may seem," she said later, " that I should have revealed these things sooner than I did and that their value would have been doubled. It might have been so if God had wished me to appear before the world as a prophetess, but such was not His Will. If it had been He would not have ordered me to keep silence (an order confirmed later by His representatives) but to speak. I think Our Lady only wished to make use of me to remind the world of the necessity of the avoidance of sin and of reparation for so many offences against God by means of prayer and penance." (*See* Appendix IV.)

[3] It is interesting to note that when in Lisbon, Jacinta repeated: " If men do not amend their lives, Our Lady will send the world a punishment worse than anything it has known before and it will come first to Spain." She spoke also of great events which would be realised about 1940. (Letters of Madre Godinho of 19th-30th November, 1937.)

unknown light, you will know that it is the sign that God gives you that he is going to punish the world for its crimes by means of war, hunger and the persecution of the Church and the Holy Father.[4] To prevent it I shall come to ask for the consecration of Russia to my Immaculate Heart and the reparatory Communion of the First Saturdays.

If my desires are fulfilled, Russia will be converted and there will be peace; if not, she will spread her errors throughout the world, causing wars and persecutions of the Church; the good will be martyred and the Holy Father will have much to suffer; various nations will be annihilated. *But in the end my Immaculate Heart will triumph.* The Holy Father will consecrate Russia to me and she will be converted and the world will enjoy a period of peace. In Portugal the Dogma of Faith will always be conserved. You must not tell this to anyone except Francisco."

In face of the terrible things which they had seen and heard, the children were bereft of speech, almost of their senses. After a few moments' silence Lucia asked:

" Do you want anything more?"

" No, to-day there is nothing more."

It was at that moment that a sort of thunderclap occurred, indicating that the Apparition was over. Says Ti Marto:

> We heard a large clap of thunder and the little arch which had been put up to hang the two lanterns on, trembled as if in an earthquake. Lucia, who was still kneeling, got up so quickly that her skirts ballooned round her and pointing to the sky she cried out: "There she goes, there she goes!" And then after a moment or two: "Now you can't see her any more."
> All this, too, was for me a great proof!

As usual, the Blessed Virgin rose and went from where she had come, disappearing into the blue immensity of the sky.

After the little cloud had disappeared from the tree and everyone had recovered somewhat from their emotion, they began to crowd round the children more than ever and torment them with questions:

" Lucia, what did the Lady say that made you so sad?"

Lucia recognised the sign of God in the extraordinary aurora borealis which illuminated the night sky on 24th-25th January, 1938. She was convinced that the world war was about to break out and did everything possible to hasten forward the recommendations of Our Lady. But she was to be convinced that the hour of mercy had not yet arrived.

" It's a secret."

" A nice one?"

" For some people it's good and for others bad."

" Can't you tell us?"

" No, I can't!"

The people crushed round them as if to suffocate them
and Ti Marto, suddenly seeing red, pushed a way through
the crowd with his elbows, snatched up his Jacinta, and
carried her in his arms to the road after having covered her
head with his hat to protect it from the blazing sun.

From their hiding place the two women clutched each
other in terror. The noise and shouting from the Cova
were positively alarming.

" Ah, Maria Rosa, they're killing our children!" sobbed
Olimpia.

A few moments later, however, she saw with relief that
Jacinta was safely in her father's arms, Francisco being
carried by someone else and Lucia in the herculean embrace
of Dr. Carlos Mendes (a lawyer from Torres Novas) which
caused her to exclaim:

" O Maria Rosa, what an enormous man!"[1]

Without waiting for anything more they set off at once
for home.

CHAPTER XIII

PENANCE

THE children returned to their normal work of pasturing
the sheep on the *serra*.

They went by little used paths, to hide from the people
who came to torment them with questions, and sought
solitude the better to meditate upon the mysteries which the
Blessed Virgin had revealed to them.

The hours passed in silence and the gay dancing of the
two girls and Francisco's little pipe were heard no more.

In the past year how entirely life had changed for these
three! Earlier, the Apparitions of the Angel and now the

---

[1] Dr. Carlos Mendes, however (now in charge of the sick at Fatima),
thinks that Olimpia is mistaken over this and that it was in September
that he picked up Lucia and carried her off to save her from being
crushed by the crowd.

Apparitions of Our Lady, especially the last, had begun to work a profound change in their souls.

Under the sweet and delicate influence of Our Lady, Lucia was no more the Lucia of other days and Jacinta and Francisco were no longer the gay and careless children, the babies of the Marto family. Concentrated in, almost submerged by the supernatural, they no longer lived the banal life of others but one infinitely superior.

They would sit on rocks or on the grass and recall to mind the tiniest details of what they had seen and heard, ever deepening their understanding of it and putting into practice the instructions which they had been given.

"What are you thinking of now?" Lucia asked Jacinta, noticing the sad look on her face.

"I'm thinking of hell and the poor sinners. How sorry I am for the souls who go to hell! And people burning there like coals. . . . O Lucia, why doesn't Our Lady show hell to sinners? If they saw it they certainly wouldn't sin any more! O Lucia, why didn't you ask Our Lady to show hell to those people?"

"I didn't think of it," answered Lucia sadly.

Then the little girl knelt on the ground and, joining her hands, repeated between her tears the words which Our Lady had taught them:

"*O my Jesus, forgive us and save us from the fire of hell. Take all souls to Heaven, especially those who are most in need.*"

The sheep wandered about quietly, searching for grass between the prickly weeds of the *serra*, while the children, prostrated on the ground, repeated incessantly:

"*O my Jesus, forgive us and save us from the fire of hell. . . .*"

As if waking from a dream, Jacinta interrupted the others with anguished words:

"Oh, Lucia, oh, Francisco, we must go on praying, praying, to save souls from hell. So many go there!"

And the three mingled their childish voices to ask pardon and raised their feeble little arms as if with a desperate effort they might avert the just arm of God which threatened sinners with hell.

It was not only Jacinta's heart that beat in pity; her intellect also demanded an answer to the terrible problem of hell:

"O Lucia, what sort of sins send people to hell . . .?"

"I don't know, perhaps not going to Mass, stealing, swearing, cursing. . . ."

"And just for that do they go to hell?"

"Yes, it's sin. . . ."

"O why can't they just go to Mass, it's not difficult? How sorry I am for sinners. If I could only show them hell!"

When their voices were weary and their arms fell to their sides they would go into the shade and meditate. This time Francisco asked a question:

"Why did Our Lady (referring to the June Apparition) have a heart in her hand and pour out that light which is God on the world? You, Lucia, were in the light which went down onto the world and Jacinta and I in the part which went up to Heaven?"

"Because," answered Lucia, "you and Jacinta are to go to Heaven soon, and I am to stay some time on earth."

"How long?"

"I don't know, many years."

"Did Our Lady tell you that?"

"No, but I saw it in the light which went into our hearts."

"Yes, I saw that too." put in Jacinta. "We're going to Heaven, how lovely!" But at once the thought of hell came back:

"I'm going to Heaven, but you're going to stay here. If Our Lady lets you, tell everyone what hell is like so that they won't sin and go there. Oh, so many people must go to hell!"

"Don't be afraid, you're going to Heaven."

"I know, but I want everyone else to go too. . . ."

The fresh morning hours were followed by a suffocating and windless heat. Thirst began to torment the children and there was no water anywhere.

"I'm glad." said Jacinta, "I'm thirsty, but I can offer it for sinners."

The sun burned pitilessly down. The hours passed, and at last Lucia began to fear for the two little ones and went to ask for some water at a nearby cottage. But when she offered it to Francisco he said:

"No, I don't want to drink; I want to offer it for sinners."

"Jacinta, you have some."

"No, Lucia, I want to offer it too."

> So I poured the water (writes Lucia simply) into a cavity in the rock for the sheep to drink, and went to give back the jug to the woman at the cottage.

Jacinta's sacrifice came near to heroism. With her aching head between her hands she seemed about to lose consciousness.

In the hottest part of the day the *serra* began to come alive with noise. The various kinds of crickets and frogs set up a discordant deafening cacophony. Jacinta felt she could bear no more and with enchanting simplicity turned to her cousin and said:

" Lucia, tell those things to be quiet. My head aches so!"

From his dry parched lips Fransico reproved her:

" Don't you want to suffer for sinners?"

" Yes, yes, I do. Don't tell them to stop, Lucia."

As we have already said, the well in Lucia's garden was the children's favourite place when they did not go out with the flocks or when they came home for the siesta hours in the height of summer.

In the shade of the fruit trees they continued to " think ". They had seen and heard so much that the time for meditation always seemed short, the flight of time too rapid for the assimilation of the mysteries with which they had been fed.

" Oh, Lucia, that Lady said that her Immaculate Heart would be your refuge and the way that would lead you to God. Don't you love that? I do. I love her Immaculate Heart."

Jacinta smiled as she said this, but two large tears coursed down Lucia's face.

" I would so love to go with you two to Heaven . . .!"

A few moments of silence and Jacinta's little treble was heard again:

" Lucia, do you remember, Our Lady's heart was being hurt by thorns."

" Yes, it was the Immaculate Heart of Mary wounded by the sins of men, asking for reparation."

" Poor, *poor* Our Lady. I am so sorry for her. She asked for Holy Communion to make reparation for the sins against her Immaculate Heart. But how can I do that when I'm not allowed to? I would so love to go to Holy Communion!"

"So would I!" cried Francisco. "But Father Ferreira won't let us!"

Sometimes, the better to immerse themselves in their thoughts, the three would separate. It was on one of these occasions that Jacinta, sitting alone on the well, had a vision which upset her greatly. Shortly afterwards she called Lucia, who had been with Francisco to search for some wild honey in a bank nearby, and unable to imagine that she would be favoured with anything hidden from her cousin, asked:

"Didn't you see the Holy Father?"

"No."

"I don't know how it was, but I saw the Holy Father, in a very big house, kneeling before a table with hands before his face, crying. He went to the door of the house and there were lots of people there throwing stones and cursing and saying horrible words. Poor Holy Father, we must pray for him, too!"

The Cabeço was another favourite place. It was a sure refuge from the questioners and there, too, Jacinta was favoured with a vision.

The children were prostrated on the ground saying the prayer of the angel, when suddenly Jacinta got up and cried out:

"Lucia, don't you see all those streets and roads and fields of people crying with hunger and with nothing to eat?[2] And the Holy Father in a church praying to the Immaculate Heart of Mary?"

Confiteor tibi Pater, quia abscondisti haec sapientibus et prudentibus et revelasti ea parvulis.

The events of Fatima were in accord with the ways of Divine Providence.

---

[2] Perhaps the exodus of the multitudes before the invading armies and under aerial bombardment. Perhaps the concentration camps?

CHAPTER XIV

TRIALS

THE two or three thousand witnesses of the third Apparition took care to spread far and wide the extraordinary news that Our Lady had appeared in the desolate *serra* of Aire to three children of the hamlet of Aljustrel. Thus, a large flow of pilgrims to the Cova da Iria was assured.

Near the miraculous oak tree, crowds of simple people came to kneel, to say the Rosary, and on their way home, to pass through Aljustrel and entrust the children with petitions which were to be presented to Our Lady if she should again appear.

However, it was not always faith which brought people to Ti Marto's and Maria Rosa's door, nor were they always simple folk.

Ladies came (says Ti Marto), goodness knows where from, well dressed and all. People went all over the place as they liked until one felt quite ashamed. Ugh! . . . weren't they curious. What they wanted was to get hold of the secret. They used to take Jacinta on their knees and worry her with questions. But she just answered as she wanted to! That secret . . . you couldn't get it out of her with a corkscrew! They tried offering presents and pleading with her but it was time wasted for them and for us, with our work and even our meals disturbed.

Fine gentlemen came too, just to make fun of simple folk who couldn't read or write. But sometimes it was we who had the laugh on them. Poor things, they had no faith, how could they believe in Our Lady!

When this kind came, it seemed as if the children knew beforehand and they were off to hide before you could so much as turn round.

One day I had to laugh. A car arrived with a large family, and the children . . . they were off in a flash. Lucia got under the bed and Francisco went up to the attic, while Jacinta who hadn't been so quick got caught.

When it was all over Lucia came out and asked her:

"What did you say when they asked for me?"

"I didn't say anything because I knew where you were and lying is a sin!" They both began to laugh and play, and Jacinta seemed pleased at the joke. *And* what questions they asked! It was a shame sometimes. Such as if Our Lady has sheep, and goats, and eats cheese, things which even ignorant people don't ask.

Ti Marto put his knotty hands to his head in a gesture of despair.

The clergy were not much less troublesome to the children.

> They questioned us (says Lucia), questioned us again, and then began all over again at the beginning. Whenever we saw a priest we took good care to escape and when we had to talk to one we offered to God one of our greatest sacrifices.

There were, however, exceptions, and the remembrance of certain among the clergy gives pleasure to Sister Lucia to this day.

> One of them said to me: "You must love Our Lord very much for all the graces and benefits which he is giving to you." These words, so graciously said, were imprinted deeply on my heart and from that time I began to say constantly to Our Lord: "My God I love You, and thank You for the graces You have given me."

She taught this prayer to her cousins, and Jacinta loved it so much that she would sometimes stop in the middle of her play and say:

"Have you remembered to tell Our Lord that you love Him for the graces He has given us?"

One day there came to Aljustrel the holy Father Cruz, who asked the children to take him to the place where Our Lady appeared. Mounted on a donkey with the little girls on either side, he went to the Cova da Iria, teaching them ejaculatory prayers, two of which Jacinta fixed in her memory and often repeated:

"O My Jesus, I love You," and "Sweet Heart of Mary, be my salvation." Both these were to comfort her greatly in her illness.

"I love to tell Jesus that I love Him! . . . When I tell it to Him a lot of times I seem to have a fire in my heart but it doesn't burn me. I love Our Lord and Our Lady so much and am never tired of telling them how much I love them!"

.The worst trials came from Lucia's family, who mocked and questioned until she hardly knew how to bear it. From her mother she had constant scoldings and punishments. The family was poor; a few head of sheep, a few plots of ground, among them part of the Cova da Iria, gave them their daily bread, maize and beans, also olives and acorns. Now, when the affair of the Apparitions began to be noised abroad it was good-bye to the produce of Cova da Iria! Pedestrians, donkeys, mules, trampled over it and spoiled what crops there were, preventing at the same time the sowing of any new ones. It was as if a cyclone had passed. Poor Lucia. . . !

> My mother was loud in lamentation and did not spare my feelings: "When you want something to eat, you had better ask Our Lady. . . ." And my sisters: "*You* can have what comes from the Cova da Iria."

It became a sort of martyrdom for the poor child even to reach for a piece of bread. The elder sisters, too, who contributed to the family income by sewing and weaving, suffered from lost time and had to watch the days pass without any earnings. The constant visitors and the flock which Lucia could no longer tend because of them, fell to their care, and finally they had to sell the sheep at a low price to anyone who would take them to pasture.

Blows rained on Lucia from all sides and this one in particular caused her acute suffering. Maria dos Anjos tells how it happened:

> One day a neighbour of ours, an elderly woman of about sixty, told our mother that she didn't wonder that the children were saying that they had seen Our Lady because she had seen a lady giving Lucia a ten cent coin. Without more ado mother called her and asked her if it were true. Lucia said that the lady had given a five cent coin, not ten cents. Mother didn't believe her and ended by beating her with the broom handle saying that those who told little lies told big ones, too. Soon after, Jacinta appeared and showed mother the ten cents which had been given to her and not to her cousin. But by that time even St. Anthony couldn't take away Lucia's bruises.

This incredulity was not peculiar to Maria Rosa and her family and there were other women who in no way lagged behind. They insulted the girl and if the occasion were propitious did not hesitate to give her a box on the ears or even a well-aimed kick.

Jacinta and Francisco had a much better time. There was always the vigilant Ti Marto nearby and he would not allow anyone to lift a hand to them. Oddly enough, in this matter Jacinta envied her cousin:

"I wish my parents were like yours! Then I could get beaten and have another sacrifice to offer Our Lord." Which is not to say that the good Olimpia did not occasionally dispense a few slaps. However, she was soon her old self again and explained:

"You got that for deceiving people. They all go to the Cova because of you."

"We don't tell them to go there," said Jacinta. "Those who want to go can go, and those who don't can stay at home. Those who don't believe will be punished and you, too, mother. . . ."

As for Ti Marto, like Jacob before the revelations of Joseph, and the incredulity of his brothers, he pondered everything in silence.

The 13th of August drew near, the day of the promised fourth Apparition in the Cova da Iria. By now the whole of Portugal knew the story and the Liberal press played no small part in spreading it about the country.

The facts were distorted and twisted, ridiculous details were invented; there was a new fabric of miracles invented by the priests—and why not the Jesuits?—who were luring the ignorant multitudes to the Cova da Iria in order to get their money, etc., etc. All this with satanic delight. As for the possibility of a supernatural intervention, the idea was beneath contempt!

Explanations were mobilised, epilepsy, cupidity, fraud; even the most moderate classified the affair as an obvious case of collective auto-suggestion. What better opportunity, in fact, had the Freemasons and supporters of the "New Order" to ridicule and belittle the Christian religion?

With such zealous publicity agents the name of Fatima became famous and the number of witnesses grew steadily and numbered thousands and tens of thousands at the last Apparitions.

CHAPTER XV

THE MAYOR

IN the background of the scene of the drama in which the chief personages were three unlettered children, lurked some-one in whom all the malice, all the perversity of the enemies of the Church, seemed to be incarnate.

He was the Administrator or Mayor of the county to which Fatima belonged, that of Vila Nova de Ourem.

Arthur Santos was a man of little culture and was a tinker by profession. He had, however, since his youth been interested in political questions and journalism, arriving at the editorship of the *Ouriense,* a small paper of purely local interest, in which he gave acid publicity to his antimonarchical and anti-religious prejudices. With the coming of the Republic the tinker of Ourem became the man of the moment. Only twenty-six years old at the time, he managed, with the aid of his Masonic friends, to be elected to the Lodge of Leiria, and later founded another Lodge, actually in Vila Nova de Ourem, to which county he became Administrator or Mayor, holding the post till 1918.

As President of the Municipal Chamber and Judge-Substitute of Comarca, Arthur Santos was the most prominent personality, the most feared and influential man in the county.

When the knowledge of events in Fatima came to his ears, he was overcome by a wave of zeal and impetuously decided that such things could not be allowed to continue. Such a crude recrudescence of the miraculous must be suffocated at birth. What sort of a figure would he cut before his colleagues if his own county were to become a focal point of a reactionary movement against the sacrosanct Republic?

There was no one in the county who did not fear this man and dread a summons to his presence. I beg my reader's pardon. There was one who, on being summarily ordered to appear before him with his children, calmly obeyed half of the order, and without the slightest sign of nervousness, appeared without them. He was Ti Marto. Here we will let the good old man take up the story:

My brother-in-law Antonio had received the same summons to appear with his daughter at the Town Hall of Ourem on 11th August at midday. They both came to my house in the morning while I was finishing my breakfast. Then Lucia asked me:

"Aren't Jacinta and Francisco coming?"

"What would two small children like them do there! I should think not . . . I'm going myself to answer for them!"

Then Lucia ran to Jacinta's room and we heard the latter say:

"If they kill you, tell them that Francisco and I are the same as you and that we want to be killed, too."

Then we all three left. On the way Lucia fell three times off her donkey and her father who was rushing along for fear of the Mayor, went ahead and when I arrived I found them already in the square. I said to him:

"Is everything all right then?"

He looked very heated and said: "The door was shut and no one there."

As it wasn't yet midday we waited a bit. Then we went

back to the Town Hall. Still shut. At last someone came
and told us that the Mayor didn't work there any more.
Finally we found him and he said to me at once:

" Where's the child?"

" What child?" I said.

He didn't seem to know that there were three children and,
as he had ordered me to bring one, I figured it out that he
didn't know what he wanted!

" Now, look, sir," I told him, " it's more than three leagues
from here to our village and the children couldn't walk all
that way, and they're not used to the donkey either." And I
wanted to add: " The idea of two children of that age being
called up!"—but I stopped myself in time. Then he got
annoyed—much I cared though! After that he began to
question Lucia and tried to get the secret out of her. But
as usual she wouldn't say a word about it. At one moment
he turned to Antonio and said:

" Do you believe in these things there in Fatima?"

" No, sir," said my brother-in-law, " we think it's all women's
stories."

Then I said:

" Here I am your worship and my children say the same
as I do."

" Do you believe it, then?"

" Yes, I believe what they say!"

They all laughed but it made no difference to me. There
were some men there who were going to put it all in the
papers and at last they let us go. But the Mayor kept on
threatening Lucia to the end and said that if she didn't tell
the secret he'd have her killed. As I was leaving I turned
round and said to the Mayor:

" If you send for us we shall have to come as many times
as you say but kindly remember that we have our lives to live."

This was the first interview that Lucia had with the lay
authorities. At home she ran at once to find her cousins,
who were sitting sadly on the edge of the well. They both
ran and embraced her and Jacinta sobbed out:

" Oh, Lucia, your sister told us that they had killed you!"
She had forgotten the Lady's promise that they would be
the first to go to Heaven. . . .

CHAPTER XVI

THE KIDNAPPING

THE Mayor maintained his ferocious attitude against Fatima. Orders from his Masonic superiors were both precise and rigid.

After the appearance of Lucia with her father and uncle in Vila Nova de Ourem, he set about giving the *coup de grâce* to Fatima. Ti Marto takes up the story:

On the morning of 13th August—it was a Monday—I had hardly set about my work on a plot of ground nearby when I was sent for to come home at once. When I got there I saw a great many people from outside but I was used to this and didn't take much notice. What did strike me as odd was that when I went into the kitchen to wash my hands I found my wife sitting there looking very upset. She didn't say anything but waved her hand towards the sitting-room. I said firmly: "Why such a hurry? I'm going there now." She seemed to be in a fuss but I washed my hands without hurrying myself, picked up a towel and took it with me into the sitting-room drying my hands as I went. The first thing I saw was the Mayor. Even on this occasion I wasn't very polite to him because I saw a priest there and went up to shake hands with him first. Then I said:

"I didn't expect to see you here, sir."

"No, I thought after all I would like to go to the miracle." My heart seemed to miss a beat, but he went on:

"Yes, we'll all go together and I'll take the children with me in the carriage. We'll see and believe like St. Thomas."

Now I could see he was nervous because he was looking all round him and he said at last:

"Aren't the children coming? It's late, we had better call them."

"There's no need to call them," said I. "They'll be ready all right when it's time to go." At that moment they came in, all three of them, looking just as usual and the Mayor asked them to go in the carriage with him. The children kept saying that it wasn't necessary. "It will be better that way," he insisted, "we can be there in a moment and no one will bother us on the way." I told him not to bother because the children could very well go alone. "Then we'll go to Fatima," he said, "I have something to ask Fr. Ferreira." And we went, Lucia's father, myself, and the three children. We had hardly arrived at the presbytery when the Mayor shouted: "Send the first!" "The first what?" I answered, worried, because I had a presentiment which in the end came true. He said arrogantly: "Lucia." "Go, Lucia," I told her. And she went in. It was all a trick to confuse us on the part of the

Mayor, and he did it just to impress us because, when it was
time to call my two, he said:

"It doesn't matter now, they can go, or rather we'll all go
because it's getting late."[1]

The children (continues Ti Marto) began to go down the
steps, and the carriage, without my noticing it had come up
quite close. It was all very well arranged and the Mayor
managed to get them in. Francisco went in front and the two
little girls behind. It was as cunning as you can imagine!
The horse went off at a trot towards the Cova da Iria and I
felt a certain relief but when it got on to the main road it
made a sudden turn and the horse was whipped up and went
off in a flash. It had been most cunningly arranged! Yes,
it was well managed, very well; and there was nothing to be
done.

"This isn't the way to the Cova," said Lucia, in the
carriage.

Then the Mayor tried to calm the children by telling
them that they were going first to Ourem to see the priest
there and that they would come back by motor car. On the
way, people began to recognise the Mayor's carriage and
its passengers, so he wrapped them up in a rug to hide them
from the curious eyes of the pilgrims who were by now
flocking along the road towards Fatima.

An hour, an hour and a half, and the tinker arrived in
triumph at his house with the three delinquents. There he
shut them in a room and told them that they would not
come out until they had revealed the secret.

"If they kill us," said Jacinta, "it won't matter because
we shall go straight to Heaven!"

Resigned, if not exactly in the best of spirits, they prepared to offer the sacrifice of their lives.

---

[1] Ti Marto is mistaken on this point. Lucia was in fact questioned
by the parish priest at the request of the Mayor, according to the
Canonical Inquiry.

"Who taught you to say the things which you are saying?"

"The Lady I saw in the Cova da Iria."

"Those who go about spreading such lies as you are doing will be
judged and will go to hell if they are not true. More and more people
are being deceived by you."

"If people who lie go to hell then I shall not go to hell, because I am
not lying and I saw only what I say and what the Lady told me. And
the people go there because they want to; we do not tell them to go."

"Is it true that the Lady told you a secret?"

"Yes, but I cannot tell it. If your Reverence wants to know it, I will
ask the Lady, and if she allows me to then I will tell it to you."

The Administrator said: "These are supernatural things. Let us go."

He got up and went out of the room, obliging the children to enter
the carriage in the presence of their fathers.

Events on this 13th of August, however, did not end so tragically as they promised to do. Instead of the executioner there appeared the kind-hearted wife of the Mayor, Senhora Adelina dos Santos, carrying an ample meal and a summons to play with her own children. Later she brought books and toys and tried in every way her motherly heart could think of to alleviate the distress of the three little *serra* children in the terrifying hours of imprisonment to which her husband had subjected them.

What meanwhile was happening in the Cova da Iria? Maria da Capela here takes up the story:

> As on the 13th June, I arrived very early at the Cova and sat down near the little tree where Our Lady appeared. I went in spite of the fact that many people had tried to frighten me. There were rumours that it was the devil who came and that he would wait until many people were gathered there and then open the earth and swallow them up. A woman from Santa Caterina told me this story and tried to prevent me from going. But I was not at all afraid. It couldn't be anything very bad, I thought, because there was so much praying. I asked Our Lady to guide me according to the Divine Will and there I went.
>
> If there were a lot of people in July, this month there were many, very many more. Some came on foot and hung their bundles on the trees, others came on horseback or on mules. There were many bicycles, too, and on the road there was a great noise of traffic.
>
> It must have been about 11 o'clock when Maria dos Anjos arrived, with some candles to light when Our Lady came.
>
> Round the tree, people were praying and singing hymns, but the children didn't come and they began to get impatient. Then someone came from Fatima and told us that the Mayor had kidnapped the children. Everyone began to talk at once and I don't know what would have happened if we hadn't heard the clap of thunder.
>
> It was much the same as the last time. Some said it came from the direction of the road, others from the tree; to me it seemed to come from a long way off. Anyway, people had rather a shock and some of them began to cry out that we would be killed. Everyone began to spread out away from the tree but, of course, no one was killed. After the thunderclap came the flash of lightning, and then we began to see a little cloud, very delicate, very white, which stopped for a few moments over the tree and then rose in the air and disappeared. As we looked around us we noticed the strange thing which we had seen before and were to see in the following months; our faces were reflecting all the colours of the rainbow, pink, red, blue. . . . The trees seemed to be made not of leaves but of flowers; they seemed to be laden with flowers, each leaf seemed to be a flower. The ground came out in colours and so did our

clothes. The lanterns fixed to the arch looked like gold. Certainly Our Lady had come although she had not found the children there!

As soon as the signs had disappeared all the people set off for Fatima shouting out against the Mayor, against the priest, against everyone who they thought had anything to do with the imprisonment of the children.

The noise was so great that it could be heard in Aljustrel! Ti Marto, who after the kidnapping of his children, had gone to the Cova, describes the disturbances on these usually peaceful *serras*:

"Let's go to Ourem and protest!" said some. "Let's go and beat them all up! Let's ;o and speak to the priest; it's his fault, too. Let's go and settle up with the Mayor!"[2] I thought to myself that they were right but at the same time the people were making such a clamour that I was quite alarmed. And then I began to shout, too: "Be quiet, everyone, there's no need to hurt anyone. Whoever has done wrong will be punished. All this is in the hands of God!" But they wouldn't take any notice and went on to Fatima while I went to my house where I found my poor wife in tears.

Indeed, Olimpia, who had followed her children to Fatima thinking that something had happened to them, learned finally that they had been taken to Ourem and ran back to Aljustrel to tell the sad news to her sister-in-law.

[2] That all this was not an empty threat is proved by the fact that the Rev. Ferreira, priest of Fatima, felt obliged to publish in the *Ordem*, of Lisbon, and the *Ouriense*, of Ourem, a defence of his attitude. He wrote a letter to the editor entitled:

To BELIEVERS AND NON-BELIEVERS:

Reluctantly as a Catholic priest, I beg to make known and to declare the following before all those who may know or hear rumours—infamous and damaging to my reputation as parish priest—that I was an accomplice in the imprisonment of three children in my parish who assert that they have seen Our Lady. I make this statement on the authority of the parents and for the satisfaction of the 5,000 to 6,000 persons who came many miles and with great sacrifice to see and speak with them. I deny this infamous and insidious calumny and declare before the whole world that I had nothing whatever to do, directly or indirectly, with this impious and sacrilegious action.

The Mayor did not confide his intentions to me. And if it was providential—which it was—that he acted secretly and without any resistance on the part of the children, it was no less than providential that the excitement to which this diabolical rumour gave rise was calmed, or the parish would certainly have had to mourn the death of its priest as an accomplice in the crime. That the devil did not succeed in this was due certainly to the Virgin Mother. The Mayor, after a protracted interrogation in their own houses, had the children brought to mine under the pretext of collecting more accurate information about the secret which they had refused to reveal to anyone. Then, at the time when he judged opportune, he ordered them into the carriage, and telling the parents that he was taking them to the Cova da Iria, in fact took

" What will become of us, Maria Rosa . . . they've taken our children?"

Lucia's mother, however, seemed not in the least perturbed over the affair; on the contrary she seemed rather pleased than otherwise:

" It'll teach them a lesson if they're lying, and if they're not then Our Lady will look after them!"

" You've only got one," sobbed Olimpia, " but we . . . we have our two . . . and such babies. . . ."

She wept inconsolably.

CHAPTER XVII

MARTYRDOM OF DESIRE

THE day broke sadly for the children imprisoned in the Mayor's house at Ourem. Jacinta missed her mother more than the others, though she tried to be brave and repeatedly asked the Blessed Virgin for courage to stand firm.

It was not long before the maddening questions began again, and the first comer was an old woman inquisitor who did everything possible to wheedle the famous secret out of them.

them to Vila Nova de Ourem. Why did he choose my house from which to act? In order to escape the consequences of his action? In order that the people should riot, as they did, and accuse me of complicity? Or for some other reason?

I do not know. I only know that I deny all responsibility in the matter and leave judgment to God. No one can prevent a work of God.

Thousands of eyewitnesses can attest that the presence of the children was not necessary for the Queen of Heaven to manifest her power. They themselves will attest to the extraordinary phenomena which occurred to confirm their faith. By now, it is not a trio of children but thousands of people of all ages, classes and conditions who have seen for themselves. If my absence from the Cova, as parish priest, gave offence to believers, my presence as a witness would have been no less objectionable to unbelievers. The Blessed Virgin has no need of the parish priest in order to manifest her goodness and the enemies of religion need not tarnish their benevolence by attributing the faith of the people to the presence or otherwise of the parish priest. Faith is a gift of God and not of the priests. This is the true motive of my absence and apparent indifference to such a sublime and marvellous event. This is why I have not replied to the thousand questions and letters which have been directed to me. The enemy is not asleep but like a roaring lion. The Apostles were not the first to announce the Resurrection. I abstain from any narration of the above-mentioned facts on account of the length of this letter and because the Press will most certainly have given its own accounts.

I am, yours faithfully,
FR. MANUEL MARQUES FERREIRA.

It was about ten o'clock when the three delinquents were taken before the Mayor. On the way they met a friendly priest still a stranger to them, Dr. Luis da Silva. They kissed his hand, and Lucia recounted simply all that had passed on the preceding day.

The Mayor questioned them closely, but neither threats nor promises could force from the children a word about the secret. Not even the shining coins or the beautiful gold chain which Mayor Santos laid before him on the table could break the extraordinary moral force of the little heroes.

They were taken back to the house for lunch where Senhor Santos's good wife saw to it that they lacked nothing. In the afternoon, more interrogations and fresh torment for the poor children.

It was at this point that they were imprisoned in the public gaol and told that they would be kept there until a cauldron of boiling oil had been made ready in which they would be thrown alive. They passed some two hours in this place in full expectation of a horrible death. Jacinta's tender little heart suffered the most. She could not keep back her tears and tried to hide them by looking out of the window which looked out on the market square. Lucia who was stronger, and, moreover, felt a maternal tenderness towards her younger cousins, went up to Jacinta and asked her:

" Why are you crying?"

" Because we shall be killed without seeing our parents. Neither yours nor ours have come to see us. They never bothered about us any more! If only I could see mother!"

Francisco, the little man, tried to encourage his sister:

" Don't cry. We can offer this sacrifice for sinners."

And the three joined their hands and said again: *O my Jesus, this is for love of You, for the conversion of sinners.* . . . Jacinta with fresh courage and careful not to forget a single intention recommended by the Blessed Virgin, added: *And also for the Holy Father and in reparation for sins against the Immaculate Heart of Mary.*

No one present, even the most hardened, could fail to be touched by this heart-rending scene. The other prisoners, crowding round, did their best to console them and to deter them from the resolution which had been the cause of their imprisonment.

"But you only have to tell the Mayor that secret. It doesn't matter about the Lady."

"No," said Jacinta, "we'd rather die than do that."

The little girl's face shone in such a manner that it cannot have failed to move those eyes, blind to the light of faith. Lucia and Francisco also looked radiant, and for a few moments it seemed as if they forgot that they were in prison and that they returned to the lightheartedness proper to their age.

This was, however, but a fugitive ray in the darkness, and soon Jacinta, who could not resign herself to dying without seeing her mother, fell to weeping again.

The prisoners returned to their self-imposed task of persuading the children to recant, but at last, unable to bear the sight of the children's distress they tried to distract them by songs and dances to the music of a concertina belonging to one of them.

It was not long before Jacinta dried her eyes and accepted the invitation to dance with a gaol-bird. The disproportion in size, however, was so great that at one moment the lady partner was whirled in the air like a feather, and her cavalier ended by dancing the fandango with her in his arms.

It was naturally not long before Jacinta remembered the Lady and her recommendations, while dancing could not be said to be the best preparation to martyrdom. So she pulled her medal out of her pocket and asked her partner to put her down so that she could hang it on the wall on a nail. She then knelt before it with the other two and began to say the Rosary. Automatically, the other prisoners knelt down, and as one of them kept his hat on his head, Francisco went up to him and said:

"When you pray you must take your hat off."

With an impatient gesture the man pulled it off and threw it on the floor. The little boy picked it up and put it gently on a bench.

Enchanting scene! Three children praying for the conversion of sinners of whom the first beneficiaries must have been their fellow-prisoners.

Suddenly there was a loud noise outside the door, and three little hearts beat loud and fast. It opened and a guard sternly ordered the children to follow him. They soon found themselves again in the presence of the Mayor, who began a new torment of questions. It was the secret which

Arthur Santos wanted at all costs to obtain, and in his methods he followed in the footsteps of the great persecutors of the primitive Church. In the presence of the children he gave orders for the preparation of a large cauldron of boiling olive oil in which these insolent, these stubborn and stiff-necked peasants were to be fried alive. Then he ordered them to be shut up in the next room. The first to be called was Jacinta, who cheerfully came forward for her supposed martyrdom, forgetting to say good-bye to her brother and cousin.

" The oil is boiling. Tell the secret . . . it's your last chance. . . ."

Jacinta trembled like a leaf but said nothing.

" Right," said the Mayor, " take her and throw her into the cauldron." A fierce-looking guard came in, seized Jacinta by the arm and took her into another room.

" Jesus . . . Our Lady . . . help me . . ." murmured the poor little girl.

But she stood fast. It seemed that a force not of this world upheld her in that moment.

During the interrogation, Francisco, to whom, more than to the others perhaps, the Blessed Virgin had communicated a nostalgia for Heaven, confided to Lucia :

" If they kill us as they say, we shall soon be in Heaven. That will be lovely! Nothing else matters!"

And shortly afterwards :

" I hope Jacinta won't be afraid. I think I had better say a Hail Mary for her."

And pulling his Rosary out of his pocket he began to pray. The guard looked at him suspiciously and asked :

" What are you saying?"

" I'm saying an Ave Maria for Jacinta so that she won't be afraid."

Minutes that seemed centuries passed in silence. The door opened again and the ferocious guard appeared. He put his hand on Francisco, saying :

" She's well fried. Now let's have this one. Come along now, out with the secret."

The little boy turned his clear eyes on this new Nero and said :

" I can't, sir. I can't tell it to anyone."

" Can't you, then . . . right . . . take him along and put him where his sister is !"

The guard's heavy hand came down on Francisco's

Pope Paul VI, with Bishop Venancio and Sister Lucia at 50th anniversary, May 13, 1967.

Olimpia and Ti Marto, parents of Jacinta and Francisco.

The three children (center) at the site of the apparitions, in the Cova. (photo taken later.)

Original chapel of the apparitions, built August 6, 1918, on the spot where they took place. It was destroyed by dynamite on March 6, 1922 by enemies, but soon restored.

Lucia's home, right foreground.

Hospital wher Jacinta was admitted, Feb. 2, 1920. Here she died 18 days later.

Pilgrims arriving at Fatima. Many walk hundreds of miles to reach the Shrine for the 13th, from May to October.

The Capelinha (Little Chapel) as it looks today on the interior.

Tomb of Francisco, in the Basilica at Fatima.

Jacinta's tomb, at the Fatima Basilica.

Statue of Our Lady of Fatima.

Rectory of St. Anthony's Church at Fatima, where the children were

The Sanctuary during the night vigil of the 12th to 13th October 1954

Pope Paul VI praying before the statue of Our Lady of Fatima, 13 May 1967

Pope John Paul II at the Capelinha, Fatima, May 13, 1982. It was the first anniversary of the attempted assassination on his life at St. Peter's in Rome.

Pope John Paul II places a Rosary around the hands of Our Lady's Statue, Fatima, May 13, 1982.

shoulder to take him to the death which for him was more a prize than a trial. But in the nearby room instead of the cauldron he found his sister safe and sound and happily smiling.

Lucia, now left alone, was convinced that the whole thing was no comedy with a happy ending but an authentic tragedy. She recommended her soul to the Blessed Virgin and asked her not to desert her in the coming agony.

The powers of darkness which had not prevailed against the weaker two were helpless before the stronger and more decided Lucia.

A few moments later the three were in each others arms, radiant after their victory. They knelt down to thank the Lady of the Cova da Iria for her timely protection. None of the three had vacillated, her approval was certain.

The Mayor, however, refused to admit defeat, and shot his last bolt. The ferocious guard was sent once more to tell them that they would all shortly be thrown together into a boiling cauldron. It was another trial and another victory. Fearless and strong in the grace of the Lady they waited once more for the hour when they would, as they thought, finally enter Heaven.

But the Blessed Virgin had not yet completed her work in this raw material of hers. More suffering was to purge the souls destined to be masterpieces of grace and the joy of Heaven and all the saints.

That night the three little confessors of the Faith laid their heads on their pillows and slept smilingly.

In the morning as the sun rose to the Feast of the Assumption, the Mayor at last admitted defeat, and after another feeble effort to drag the secret from them, put the children in his carriage and took them again to the presbytery of Fr. Marques Ferreira, parish priest of Fatima.

CHAPTER XVIII

REUNION

MASS of the Assumption had not yet finished. As soon as Fr. Ferreira had left the altar tongues began to wag, the topic of conversation being naturally the subject which occupied all minds on that day.

Someone asked Ti Marto about the children, to which he replied:

> I know absolutely nothing. They may even have been taken to Santarem. Nobody knows where they are. On the day when they were taken my stepson, Antonio, and some other lads went there and said they saw them playing on the veranda of the Mayor's house. That was the last I heard.
>
> The words were hardly out of my mouth (continues Ti Marto) when I heard someone say: "Look, Ti Marto, they're on the veranda of the presbytery!" I hardly knew how I got there, but I rushed up and hugged my Jacinta. I picked her up—I can even remember now that I sat her on my right arm. Women always put their children on the left arm so as to have the right arm free. I just couldn't speak. The tears poured down my face and made Jacinta's all wet. Then Francisco and Lucia ran up to me, crying: "Father, Uncle, give us your blessing!" At that moment there appeared a funny little official, a man who was in the service of the Mayor, and he shook and trembled in the most extraordinary way. I had never seen anything like it! He said: "Well, here are your children." Then I couldn't help myself and burst out: "This might have had a sorry ending and it's not your fault if it didn't. You wanted them to say they were lying and you couldn't make them. And even if you had made them I should have told the truth!"
>
> Then we heard a tremendous noise in the square. The people were waving and shouting, you never heard such a noise. Fr. Ferreira, who was in the church, went at once to the house, up the steps, and thinking it was I who was causing the riot, said: "Oh, Senhor Manuel, is it you making all this trouble?" But I knew how to answer him, too, and went inside. Then I turned to the people and with Jacinta still in my arms shouted: "Be quiet, all of you! Some of you are shouting against the Mayor, some against the priest and the *regedor* but it all comes from lack of faith and is allowed by God."

Golden words from old Ti Marto! Continuing, he says:

> Fr. Ferreira, who had heard it all, was satisfied, and said from the window: "Senhor Marto is quite right, quite right!"
> At this moment the Mayor arrived and showed himself to

the people, saying to me: " That's enough, Senhor Marto."
And I answered: " It's all right, it's all right, nothing has
happened." Then he went to Fr. Ferreira's office, called me in
and said to the priest:

" I prefer Abobora's (Lucia's father) conversation, but I must
see Marto, too." Then Fr. Ferreira said:

" Mr. Mayor, we cannot do without religion!" As Senhor
Santos was leaving he asked me to go and have a glass of wine
with him but I refused. But just then I saw a group of boys
below, armed with sticks, and I thought to myself that at this
stage it would be better to have no more trouble, so I said to
the Mayor:

" After all, sir, perhaps I'll accept your offer." He thanked
me kindly because he was beginning to realise the feeling
against him and that things were likely to warm up. At the
bottom of the stairs he said:

" You can be sure that I treated the children well."

" That's all right, sir, it's not I but the people who seem to
want to know that."

At that moment the children came down the steps and set
off for the Cova da Iria, where they said they were going to
pray. The people began to disperse slowly and I went with
the Mayor into the tavern, where he ordered wine and bread
and cheese to be brought. He started a silly conversation that
didn't interest me at all, but at a certain point he tried to make
me think that the children had told him the secret. And I
said, without moving a muscle:

" All right, all right. As they wouldn't tell it to their father
or mother it's natural that they should tell it to you."

When we came out the carriage was at the door; I said good-
bye but as I had to go to the post, which was some way along
the road to the town, he made me get in and go along with
him although it was so near. I got in and somebody shouted:
" There goes Ti Marto! He's talked too much and the tinker's
taking him to prison!"

The children's release, besides the natural joy it gave
their parents, also pleased large numbers of others who,
especially after the last Apparition of the 13th, had definitely come to believe in the reality of a supernatural intervention in the Cova da Iria. Of these, doubtless, the chief
was Maria da Capela, although the sky was not altogether
clear for her either. After the Apparitions she had invol-
untarily found herself in the position of receiver of alms
which the faithful left on a little table which she had
arranged with candles and flowers in front of the oak tree.
She herself relates the embarrassment which this caused her:

When the people in the Cova heard that the children had
been imprisoned on that 13th of August, and when they saw
those signs in the sky, you can't imagine how much money
poured on to that table. The people pushed so hard all round

it that I thought at one moment that it was going to upset.
They began to shout at me:

"Take the money, woman, take it and look after it; see that
you don't lose any. . . ." I had my lunch bag with me and
began to put the money in that. In the afternoon when there
weren't many people there, I saw Tia Olimpia's eldest son,
Antonio, passing by, and I said to him:

"Will you come here a moment?" He came but when he
saw what it was all about he wouldn't say anything and went
away. So I took the money home and counted it. It came to
13 'mil' and 40 'reis' if I remember rightly. The bag
was very heavy because in those days we had the other coinage.
So on the 14th I told my husband that it would be better to
go and take the money to Ti Marto. When we arrived we
found Senhora Rosa and Fr. Ferreira there, too. I can still see
him leaning against the wall. I was even rather rude because
I went straight up to Senhor Marto and gave him the money
instead of to the Rev. Father, as I should have done. But
Jacinta's father absolutely refused to accept it:

"Don't try me any more, woman, I'm tried enough already!"
Then I gave it to Lucia's mother but she said angrily: "God
forbid! I don't want it either. . . ."

I was getting upset by that time and turned to Fr. Ferreira
and offered it to him. He refused absolutely to take the money.
It might have had a curse on it. Then I saw red, too:

"I won't have it either," I declared. "I'll go out and put it
back where I found it!" Then Fr. Ferreira tried to calm me
and said:

"Don't do that, woman; keep it or give it to someone to
take care of until we see what comes of all this."

Some days later four men arrived and asked me for the
money to begin the building of a chapel. I told them that I
wouldn't give them a penny of it but afterwards I thought that
I shouldn't have done that without asking Fr. Ferreira. He
told me that he didn't want to have anything to do with it
but that, personally, he wouldn't give it to them as they had
no right to ask. He told me to do as I liked and said that
what I had done so far was all right. And so the muddle over
the money continued. Those whom I offered it to, wouldn't
take it, and those who wanted it didn't get it!

This went on until the 19th of August. It was a Sunday and
I went to Mass as usual. Afterwards I saw Lucia's father in
the square. Lucia was playing there, too. I thought I would
take the opportunity to try and straighten things out. People
had warned me to be careful of him because he was often
drunk and had been heard to say if he could catch me in the
Cova he'd soon put things right, etc. So I went up to him
and saw at once that he was sober. After greeting him I said:

"I think you are annoyed because I go on to your ground
at the Cova and put flowers, etc. I have come to ask your
permission to go there." And he answered:

"Put as many flowers as you like; what I don't want is
tabernacles on my land. Someone has already asked me and

I wouldn't give permission on account of the children getting into those crowds. If they're lying then they can look after themselves; and if they're not, well, then, it doesn't matter what happens, crowds or no crowds." I thought he was taking it well, all things considered, and I had confidence in Our Lady.

"Someone told me," he continued, "that you took a lot of money away from my land, but I don't want it."

"Nor do I," I said.

"What are you going to do with it, then?"

"I don't know. Perhaps I'd better have Masses said for the intentions of the people who gave it." At that moment the idea came into my head to ask Lucia to ask Our Lady what she wanted done with the money. She told me not to worry and that on the day of the next Apparition in September she would ask about it. That was a great weight off my mind.

The reply was not long in coming. Within a few days Lucia was able to tell Senhora Carreira the Lady's wishes on the matter. Two " andors " (processional biers) were to be bought, one of which was to be carried by Lucia and Jacinta and two more girls dressed in white, and the other by Francisco and three companions also dressed in white. The rest of the money was to be for the Festa of Our Lady of the Rosary. This did not altogether satisfy Senhora Carreira.

" Oh, Lucia," she lamented, " I wish the money could have been for a chapel, don't you?"

" Yes, I do, but Our Lady told me that. We must do as she says."

" Lucia, do ask her on September 13th if we can make a chapel, will you?"

CHAPTER XIX

VALINHOS

ON that Sunday, 19th August, the three children went to the Cova da Iria to say the Rosary after the parish Mass. They were joined by several other people, among them Lucia's sister Teresa, her husband, and a Senhor Alves of Moita, who took the children to have lunch with them after the prayers were finished. Only Lucia's mother was not pleased at this invitation fearing that her daughter would forget to take the flock to pasture in the cool of the evening. Lucia, however, was already a little woman and not one to neglect her duties, and at the proper hour she was again in Aljustrel together with Francisco and João, the eldest brother of the little seer. Jacinta had been called in by her mother as they passed the house and stayed at home to help her. The other three left for a small property, Valinhos, which belonged to one of Lucia's uncles. It lay near the village of Aljustrel.

At about four o'clock in the afternoon Lucia began to notice the atmospheric changes which usually heralded the Apparitions of the Lady in the Cova da Iria. There was a sudden freshening of the air, a dimming of the sunlight and the characteristic flash of lightning.[1]

"She must be coming," thought Lucia, "and Jacinta's not here!" Then she shouted to John:

"John, go and fetch Jacinta, Our Lady's coming!" But John, who wanted to see Our Lady, was not at all disposed to obey.

"Go, you must go," insisted Lucia. "I'll give you money if you'll go and fetch Jacinta. Look, here's something for you and you can have some more when you come back!"

The boy took the money, and in five minutes was at the door of the house.

"Mother, Lucia wants Jacinta to go to Valinhos."

"What's all this nonsense? Must the priest always have his sacristan?"

"Let her go, mother, it really is necessary."

"Necessary! What for I'd like to know!"

"Mother, Lucia gave me this money to fetch Jacinta." Olimpia was astonished.

"Now I'd just like to know exactly why Lucia wants Jacinta to go."

"Listen," said John impatiently, "Lucia saw the signs in the sky which mean that Our Lady is going to appear, and she wants Jacinta as quickly as possible."

---

[1] It was not only Lucia and Francisco who observed these phenomena. The above-mentioned sister, Teresa, who was returning home with her husband, relates the following:

"We were just coming into Fatima when we noticed that the air was fresher. The sun looked yellowish and took on various colours, as it had done on the 13th in the Cova. 'What is it?' I said to my husband, beginning to see the colours on his white shirt. 'I think we are all barking up the wrong tree! What do you mean?' he asked. 'Don't you see that it's just like it was on the 13th?' When we arrived at the church it had disappeared. Later we came to know that it was just at that moment that Our Lady appeared to the children at Valinhos."

" Well, go with God.   She's at her godmother's house."
This was what the boy was wanting to hear, and he was
off in a flash.   In a few moments he had told Jacinta what
had happened and his news made her more impatient than
he.   Hand in hand they ran to Valinhos where the Blessed
Virgin was waiting.

Olimpia, too, was overcome with curiosity and started to
walk in the direction of Valinhos.   She did not want to
lose what might be a unique opportunity.   But she delayed
a few moments in the godmother's house asking if the
children had left, and did not arrive in time.   John's pre-
cipitate haste did not avail him either.   All that he gained
from the affair was the money which Lucia had given him.
That night he confessed to his mother that for all his staring
he had seen absolutely nothing.   All he had heard was
something that sounded like a rocket when Lucia, after her
conversation with the Lady had said:

" Look, Jacinta, Our Lady's going away!"
As in the Cova da Iria only the three privileged children
saw the celestial visitor.   In the designs of Providence, they
and they alone were to be the instruments of the message.

The first flash of lightning was followed by another, and
it was at this moment that John and Jacinta arrived.   A
few moments later the Lady appeared on a small tree,
higher, however, than the holm oak of the Cova da Iria.
The Mother of God had rewarded her faithful little servi-
tors.

" What do you want?" asked Lucia again, this time with
filial confidence.

" Go again to the Cova da Iria on the 13th and continue
to say the Rosary every day."

Lucia again asked the Lady to perform a miracle that
all might believe in her.

"' I will," was the reply.   " In October, I will perform
a miracle so that everyone can believe in the Apparitions.
If they had not taken you to the town (Ourem) the miracle
would have been greater.   St. Joseph will come with the
Holy Child to bring peace to the world.   Our Lord will
also come to bless the people.   Our Lady of the Rosary
and Our Lady of Dolours will come too."

Lucia suddenly remembered the petition of Maria da
Capela and asked:

" What are we to do with the money and the offerings
which the people leave in the Cova da Iria?"

" Make two biers. You are to carry one with Jacinta
and two more girls dressed in white. Francisco is to take
the other with three more boys dressed in white. The
money for the biers is for the Festa of Our Lady of the
Rosary."[2]

Lucia, of course, did not forget the sick who had asked
her to remember them to the Lady, and she fervently asked
for their cure:

" I will cure some during the year," was the reply.

Sadly the Lady added: " Pray, pray very much and make
sacrifices for sinners, for many souls go to hell because no
one makes sacrifices for them."

After this the Blessed Virgin took leave of her little
friends and began to rise in the air in an eastward direction,
leaving in the children's souls a great longing for Heaven
and a true hunger for the sacrifice that could save so many
sinners.

When the people in the Cova da Iria pulled the leaves
and twigs off the oak tree the children reproved them, but
this time it was they themselves who cut the branch on
which the snowy mantle of the Lady had rested. Francisco
and Jacinta left John and Lucia to look after the sheep and
themselves returned in triumph to tell their parents the good
news and with the precious trophy in hand. At the door
of the Santos' house they found Maria Rosa, her daughter
Maria dos Anjos, and a group of neighbours. Maria dos
Anjos describes the scene:

> Jacinta, all excited, rushed up to my mother and said: " Oh,
> Aunt, we saw Our Lady again . . . at Valinhos!"
>
> " Ah, Jacinta, when will these lies end! Now you have to
> be seeing Our Lady all over the place, wherever you go!"
>
> " But we saw her!" And showing the branch: " Look,
> Aunt, Our Lady put one foot on this branch and the other
> on this one."
>
> " Let me see, let me see," said mother.
>
> When Jacinta gave it to her she sniffed and said:

---

[2] In Lucia's most recent manuscript (8th December, 1941) the seer
adds that the Blessed Virgin had said that the money for the " andors "
was to be destined for the Feast of Our Lady of the Rosary, and that
what was over was to be used for the construction of a chapel in the
Cova da Iria. We think that there is a confusion on Lucia's part, in
attributing this detail to the fourth Apparition when in reality it
occurred in the Apparition of September. The statement which she
made before the parish priest only two days after the Apparition of
Valinhos (21st August, 1917) concords with this, as do the declarations
of the Canonical Inquiry (8th July, 1924) and what we have heard from
the mouth of Maria da Capela.

"What smell is this? It's not scent and it's not the smell of roses . . . nothing that I know. But it's a good smell."

We all wanted to smell it and all found it very pleasant. Finally mother put it on the table and said:

"It had better stay here until we can find someone who knows what it is."

In the evening we couldn't find the branch and we never knew where she had taken it. But I think it was from that time that mother, and father, too, began to be kinder to Lucia and even defended her when we others teased her, telling us to leave her in peace because what she said might be true after all.

There was, however, no mystery about the disappearance of the scented branch. Hardly had Maria Rosa turned to her work when Jacinta stole in and took it to show to her parents. Ti Marto, as he tells us, only knew that night that the Blessed Virgin had appeared again:

That afternoon I had made a round of the land and at sundown I went home. I was nearly there when a man came up to me and said:

"Oh, Ti Manuel, the miracle's going well!"

"What do you mean? I don't know any more."

"Well, our Lady has appeared again, a little while ago, at Valinhos, to your two and Abobora's lad. I tell you, Ti Manuel, that your Jacinta has something special about her. She didn't go with the others and it was only when they called her that Our Lady appeared!"

Well, I said nothing at all to this but went into the yard to think it over. My wife wasn't there and I went into the kitchen and sat down. Then Jacinta came in looking as happy as anything, carrying a branch, about this size, in her hand.

"Listen, father, Our Lady appeared again to us at Valinhos."

And as she came in I smelt a most beautiful smell that I can't describe. I put my hand out to take the branch and asked her:

"What have you got there?"

"It's the branch that Our Lady stood on." I took it and smelt it, but the scent had gone.

CHAPTER XX

PENANCE

THE topic of the children's conversation hardly varied from day to day, and the word which Our Lady had spoken to them sank more and more deeply into their hearts.

" Pray, pray much, and make sacrifices for sinners. Many souls go to hell because there is no one to make sacrifices for them."

These words awoke in the children's hearts an insatiable hunger and thirst for suffering and sacrifice, such as we meet as a rule only in those few rare souls to whom it has been given to understand the ineffable mystery of the Cross.

The vision of hell on 13th July could not easily be erased from the simple imagination of the children, and the Blessed Virgin had added that many souls went to that horrible place because there were so few to make sacrifices for them.

Meditating almost incessantly on this, the children thought no effort or suffering too great if it could but shut the door of that fearful place and send the feet of sinners on the road to God. They passed hours at a time in the Loca do Cabeço, prostrate on the ground, repeating the prayer of the angel:

Oh, my God, I believe, I adore, I hope and I love You. I ask forgiveness for those who do not believe, nor adore, nor hope, nor love You.

And when the pain of lying in that position became intolerable, they would say the Rosary, never forgetting to interpolate the prayer that Our Lady had taught them:

O my Jesus, forgive us, and deliver us from the fire of hell. Take all souls to Heaven, especially those who are most in need.

In the practice of mortification they emulated the almost legendary feats of the Fathers of the desert. They wanted to convert many, if not all sinners, and laboured to invent new ways by which this might be accomplished by means of every conceivable suffering.

Nobody outside their own intimate circle knew of or even suspected the continual prayer, the hard, uninterrupted penance. If Sister Lucia had not in part lifted the veil we should never have known to what heroic lengths these children went.

"Why did you not speak of Our Lady's desire for sacrifice for the conversion of sinners?" Lucia was to be asked later.

"Because we were afraid they would ask us what sacrifices we did."

Humility's own reply. Lucia's manuscripts relate but few of these sacrifices and they nearly all refer to Jacinta, sufficient nevertheless to show us three little giants of Christian sanctity. We will take a few examples from Sister Lucia's account.

Thirst is one of the worst torments during the burning summer of the *serra*. It was one of their favourite mortifications. They passed nine days, and on one occasion a month without drinking, and this in the month of August!

One day, returning from the Cova da Iria where they had been to say the Rosary, they passed the Carreira pond, a dirty pool of water where the women wash clothes and the animals are brought to drink. Jacinta said to Lucia:

"My head aches so, and I'm so thirsty; I think I'll drink a little of this water."

"No, Jacinta, not from there. My mother doesn't want us to drink that water because it's dirty and might make us ill. Let's go and get some from Aunt Maria."

"No, I don't want to drink that good water. I'd like to drink this so that instead of offering Our Lady thirst I can offer this dirty water."

At other times fruit served as material for sacrifice. One day they were playing by the well when Olimpia brought some grapes to refresh them. As soon as her mother's back was turned Jacinta resolved not to eat them and to offer the sacrifice for sinners, and seeing some poor children in the road she ran and gave them the grapes.

On another occasion Olimpia brought them a beautiful basket of figs. The children were sitting on the ground and had begun to eat them when Jacinta suddenly remembered her sinners. She threw the fig which she already had in her hand back into the basket and ran away before she could have time to succumb to temptation.

No opportunity was allowed to pass that might serve their purpose. One day, while gathering some green grass that was growing between the stones, Jacinta felt the prick of a nettle. As if she had found a buried treasure she called to the others:

"Look, look, here's something we can make sacrifices

with!" Whatever it might cost them, the children never
lost an opportunity of consoling the heart of the Mother
of God. One day Lucia found a piece of cord on the *serra*.
Playing with it she knotted it round her arm and did not
fail to note that it hurt.

"Here's something that we can use for sacrifice," she
told the others. "We can knot it and put it round our
waists and offer the pain."

Even at night they did not take off those pieces of
knotted cord. Our Lady, in the September Apparitions, had
to tell them not to wear the cord at night.

What a contrast between these emulators of the saints
and the youth of to-day which only seeks comfort, pleasure
and amusement!

While the three children in perfect collaboration with
grace were seeking by every means in their power to please
Our Lady, the enemies of God could not rest until this
new flowering of grace in the "Terra de Santa Maria"
should be finally and completely annihilated.

CHAPTER XXI

The Thirteenth of September

The 13th of September was awaited by the children with
more impatience than usual, for the heroic sufferings of the
past month had deepened their desire to see the Lady who
had put them to the test.

The visits and questions of the curious did not diminish
but rather increased. The children were continually mocked
and even threatened as if they were criminals. The secret
was still the object of intense curiosity on the part of large
numbers of people, but all attempts to force the children to
speak were as useless as ever.

The continued disrespect for the Apparitions on the part
of the people of Aljustrel was a particular source of trial
for Lucia and the indifferent if not actually hostile attitude
of the parish priest and his colleagues in the surrounding
parishes was a torture for her sensitive heart.

And yet the number of believers increased in an extraordinary manner. In face of the prodigies of 13th of
August, witnessed by an enormous crowd of people from
all parts, and the superhuman constancy of the children

before the dreaded Mayor, it was difficult for people of good faith not to credit the good faith of the seers and, consequently, the truth of the Apparitions.

And so on the 13th of September there was a remarkable flow of pilgrims to the Cova. Many of them who set off on the evening before were not curious sightseers but souls desirous of witnessing as a reality what faith had taught them to be a fact.

As dawn broke on that 13th the roads round Fatima were blocked with people, most of them devoutly reciting the Rosary. An eye-witness gives her impressions:

> It was a pilgrimage really worthy of the name, a profoundly moving sight. I had never seen in all my life such a great demonstration of faith. At the place of the Apparitions all the men uncovered their heads and nearly everyone knelt and said the Rosary with evident devotion.

Among the crowd on this occasion were some priests and seminarists. One of the latter recalls:

> On the 13th of September the long vacation was drawing to a close and we seminarists did not want to return to the seminary without having been to Fatima about which we had heard so much in the country round about. So a group of four or five of us set out on foot to see what happened.
>
> We returned tired but very happy. There was quite a number of seminarists in Fatima on that day—some thirty perhaps—from various seminaries. This was not surprising for the same idea had brought them there. I only remember seeing two or three priests.[1]
>
> For a long time we went along, jumping from rock to rock and climbing walls and stiles, watching and commenting on all that we saw. One of the priests, however, called us and told us to be prudent because the whole thing might be of diabolical origin and, in any case, would probably end in a great fiasco. This was the mentality of most of them. In fact, we went back and watched from the high ground where the Basilica is now built, though very soon curiosity got the better of us and at the hour of the Apparitions we had come as near to the children as the crowds would allow.

Meriting particular attention among the priests was Mons. John Quaresma, Vicar-General of the Diocese of Leiria, and later a member of the Canonical Inquiry instituted by the Bishop. In a letter to Mons. Manuel do Carmo Gois, who also assisted at the September and October Apparitions, he minutely describes the events of that day.

---

[1] They were at least five: The parish priest of Sta. Caterina, Mons. Quaresma, Mons. Carmo Gois, Dr. Formigão, Fr. Manuel da Silva.

Fifteen years have passed since the extraordinary events of Fatima. Heavy clouds hung over Portugal and her people, while sadness and despair reigned in our country. In the midst of this darkness innumerable prayers were offered to God, asking for help and for mercy.

Men hoped for a ray of light in the storm which human passions had provoked. The Lord heard the prayer of His servants and in the sky of Fatima there appeared, like the rainbow after the flood, a Vision of Peace. The Vision spoke to three children and at once the terrible clouds began to disperse and souls breathed again as the burden of sadness was laid aside. Eyes, longing for the light, searched the skies where the morning star shone.

Now, may it not be that these simple children are mistaken? May they not have been victims of an illusion? Yet it is always possible that Our Lady may come to earth to bring us a message. Could there be some truth in what the children said? How explain these ever-growing multitudes that filled the Cova every thirteenth day of the month declaring that they witnessed extraordinary phenomena?

So on a beautiful September morning we left Leiria in a rickety carriage drawn by an old horse, for the spot where the much-discussed Apparitions were said to take place. Fr. Gois found the dominating point of the vast amphitheatre from which we could observe events without approaching too nearly the place where the children were awaiting the Apparition.

At midday there was complete silence. One only heard the murmur of prayers. Suddenly there were sounds of jubilation and voices praising the Blessed Virgin. Arms were raised pointing to something in the sky. " Look, don't you see?" . . . " Yes, yes, I do . . . !" Much satisfaction on the part of those who do. There had not been a cloud in the deep blue of the sky and I, too, raised my eyes and scrutinised it in case I should be able to distinguish what the others, more fortunate than I, had already claimed to have seen.

With great astonishment I saw, clearly and distinctly, a luminous globe, which moved from the east to the west, gliding slowly and majestically through space. My friend also looked and had the good fortune to enjoy the same unexpected and delightful vision. Suddenly the globe, with its extraordinary light, disappeared.

Near us was a little girl dressed like Lucia and more or less the same age. She continued to cry out happily: " I still see it! I still see it! Now it's coming down. . . .!"

After a few minutes, about the duration of the Apparitions, the child began to exclaim again, pointing to the sky: " Now it's going up again!"—and she followed the globe with her eyes until it disappeared in the direction of the sun. " What do you think of that globe?" I asked my companion, who seemed enthusiastic at what he had seen. " That it was Our Lady," he replied without hesitation.

It was my undoubted conviction also. The children had contemplated the very Mother of God, while to us it had been given to see the means of transport—if one may so express it—which brought her from Heaven to the inhospitable waste of the Serra de Aire. I must emphasise that all those around us appeared to have seen the same thing, for one heard manifestations of joy and praises of Our Lady. But some saw nothing. Near us was a simple devout creature crying bitterly because she had seen nothing.

We felt remarkably happy. My companion went from group to group in the Cova and afterwards on the road, gathering information. Those he questioned were of all sorts and kinds and of different social standing, but one and all affirmed the reality of the phenomena which we ourselves had witnessed.

With immense satisfaction we set off for home after this pilgrimage to Fatima, firmly resolved to return on the 13th of October for further confirmation of these facts.

The declaration of Mons. Quaresma is confirmed by thousands of eye-witnesses of this remarkable manifestation of Divine Power. Other phenomena took place which, like this one, were not seen by all. The sudden freshening of the atmosphere, the paling of the sun until the stars could be seen, a kind of rain of flower petals which disappeared before they reached the earth, these were some of the facts noted by hundreds and thousands of people.

But we must go back a short time.

From the early hours of the 13th the Santos and Marto houses were so seething with people that it was hardly possible to go from one room to another. Everyone wanted to see the children to recommend their petitions, their afflictions and their miseries. It was only with difficulty that the three seers managed to leave for the Cova da Iria. Lucia herself gives us an idea of what it was like:

When the time came I left with Jacinta and Francisco, surrounded by numbers of people who would hardly let us move along. The roads were crowded with people; everyone wanted to see us and speak to us and there was no human respect. The simple folk, as well as ladies and gentlemen, when they managed to break through the crowds, fell on their knees before us and implored us to place their necessities before Our Lady. Others who did not manage to get near shouted from far off. One of them said:

"For the love of God ask Our Lady to cure my cripple son."

"And mine who is deaf!"

"And mine who is blind!"

They asked for their husbands and sons to be brought back from the war, for the conversion of some sinner, for health for a consumptive, etc. All the ills of poor humanity seemed to be paraded before us and people climbed to the tops of

trees and walls to see us pass by.   Answering some and helping
others to rise out of the dust we went slowly along thanks to
some gentlemen who opened a way for us through the crowd.
To-day when I read in the New Testament of those touching
scenes of Our Lord in Palestine, I remember what He gave
me to see as a child on those poor roads from Aljustrel to
the Cova da Iria, and I thank God for the faith of our good
Portuguese people who if they fall thus before three poor
children to whom the grace to see Our Lady had been given
what would they do if they saw Our Lord Himself. . . ?

When the children finally arrived at the oak tree Lucia as
usual told the people to say the Rosary, at which she led
the prayers.   Everyone, rich and poor, fell to their knees and
answered aloud.

The children rose and turned towards the eastern horizon
before the Rosary was complete.   They had seen the
lightning flash and the Lady would not be long in fulfilling
her word. A few moments more and she shone, smiling,
above the oak tree.

" What do you want?" asked Lucia as usual.

" Continue to say the Rosary every day for the end of
the war."   And she repeated all that she had said in the
preceding month; that they were to come on the 13th of
October, when they would see St. Joseph and the Holy
Child, with Our Lord Himself and also the likeness of Our
Lady of Dolours and Our Lady of Mount Carmel.

" I have many petitions," said Lucia: " will you cure a
little deaf and dumb girl?"

" She will improve during the year."

" And the conversions and the cures?"

" Some will be cured, others not: Our Lord does not
trust them all."

The obstacle to miracle for some would be the lack of
proper dispositions, for others sickness would be better
than cure.

" The people would like to build a chapel here," continued
Lucia, remembering the recommendations of Maria da
Capela.

" Use half the money which you have received up to the
present for the ' andors ' and place on one of them the
Statue of Our Lady of the Rosary.   The other half may be
used to build a chapel."

" Many people say that I am deceiving people and that I
should be hanged or burned.   Will you do a miracle so that
they may believe?"

" Yes, in October I will perform a miracle," assured the Lady.

Then the Vision rose through the air which seemed charged with the supernatural and Lucia cried out to the people:

" If you want to see her look over there!" . . . and she pointed to the east where the Lady was disappearing. Avidly, all eyes followed the direction of her gesture and many noted the phenomena already referred to. The luminous sphere rose, carrying the Queen of Heaven home.

After a few minutes of stupefaction the people almost threw themselves upon the unfortunate children and besieged them with questions. It was with the greatest difficulty that their parents managed to get them back to their homes, which they found once more literally overflowing with people. The commotion continued until the veil of night enfolded the *serras* in silence.

CHAPTER XXII

INTERROGATION

AFTER this fifth Apparition people flocked to Aljustrel in greater numbers than ever to see the children and to talk with them. The majority of visitors was both foolish and curious and their questions had no other value than that of putting the patience of the children and their families to the test.

There was, however, a priest who had been following events with close interest and with the scrupulous care that they merited. He was a man of tact and prudence and soon gained the confidence of the little seers and their parents. He is Dr. Manuel Formigão, canon of the Patriarchal See of Lisbon, and Professor at the Seminary and Lyceum of Santarem.

On the 13th September, as we have said, this priest was present at the Apparitions. His first impressions, however, had not been particularly favourable. Taking up his position in the road some 200 metres away from the centre of events, he had observed, among the phenomena referred to, only the diminution of the light of the sun, which he attributed to the height of the *serra*.

His attitude, therefore, was one of reserve, also

benevolence, on account of the excellent personal impression which the children had made upon him.

To complete his first impressions and to gather further information for the work which he proposed to put in hand, he returned to Fatima on Thursday, 27th September. He wanted quietly and calmly to study and question the children in order to make up his mind as far as possible about the events which had occurred in the five months preceding.

The first conversation between himself and Francisco was as follows:

" What have you seen in the Cova da Iria during these months?"

" I have seen Our Lady."

" Where does she appear?"

" On the top of an oak tree."

" Does she appear suddenly or do you see her coming from anywhere?"

" I see her coming from the side where the sun rises and stop on the oak tree."

" Does she come slowly or quickly?"

" She always comes quickly."

" Do you hear what she says to Lucia?"

" No."

" Did you ever speak to the Lady? Has she ever spoken to you?"

" No, I have never asked her anything. She only speaks to Lucia."

" Who does she look at? At you and Jacinta or only at Lucia?"

" She looks at all three of us, but she looks longer at Lucia."

" Did she ever cry or smile?"

" Neither, she is always serious."

" How is she dressed?"

" She has a long dress and over it a mantle which covers her head and falls to the edge of her dress."

" What is the colour of the dress and the mantle?"

" It is white and the dress has gold lines."

" What is her attitude?"

" Like someone praying. She has her hands joined at the height of her breast."

" Does she carry anything in her hands?"

" Round the palm and the back of her right hand she carries a Rosary."

" And what does she wear on her ears?"

" You cannot see her ears because they are covered by the mantle."

" Is the Lady beautiful?"

" Yes, she is."

" More beautiful than that girl over there?"

" Yes."

" But there are ladies who are much more beautiful than that girl?"

" She was more beautiful than anyone I have ever seen."

After I had finished questioning Francisco (continues Dr. Formigão) I called Jacinta, who was playing in the road with some other children, and sitting her on a little stool at my side, I subjected her to a similar interrogation, and succeeded in obtaining complete and detailed replies as in the case of her brother:

" Have you seen Our Lady on the 13th of each month since May?"

" Yes."

" Where does she come from?"

" She comes from the sky from the side of the sun."

" How is she dressed?"

" She has a white dress, decorated with gold, and on her head a mantle, also white."

" What colour is her hair?"

" You cannot see her hair because it is covered by the mantle."

" Does she wear earrings?"

" I don't know because you cannot see her ears."

" How does she hold her hands?"

" Her hands are joined at the height of her breast, with the fingers pointing upwards."

" Are the beads in the right or the left hand?"

To this question the child replied at first that they were in the right hand, but just after, owing to a purposely captious insistence on my part she became perplexed and confused and was not able to indicate with certainty the hand in which the Vision held the Rosary.

" What was the chief thing that Our Lady told Lucia?"

" She said that we were to say the Rosary every day."

" And do you say it?"

" I say it every day with Francisco and Lucia."

Half an hour after this interrogation Lucia appeared. She came from a little property belonging to her family where she had been helping with the vintage.

Taller and better nourished than the other two with a clearer skin and a robuster, healthier appearance, she presented herself before me with an unselfconsciousness which contrasted in a marked manner with the shyness and timidity of Jacinta. Simply dressed like the latter, neither her attitude nor her expression denoted a sign of vanity, still less of confusion.

Seating herself on a chair at my side, in response to my gesture, she willingly consented to be questioned on the events in which she was the principal protagonist in spite of the fact that she was visibly fatigued and depressed by the incessant visits and the repeated and lengthy questionings to which she was subjected.

" Is it true that Our Lady has appeared in a place called the Cova da Iria?"

" Yes, it is true."

" How many times has she appeared to you?"

" Five times, once each month."

" On what day of the month?"

" Always on the 13th, except in the month of August, when I was taken to Ourem by the Mayor. In that month I only saw her a few days afterwards, on the 19th, at Valinhos."

" People say that Our Lady also appeared to you last year? Is there any truth in this?"

" She never appeared to me last year, never before May of this year; nor did I ever say so to anybody because it is not true."

" Where does she come from? From the east?"

" I don't know because I don't see her come from anywhere. She appears over the oak tree and when she goes away she goes into the sky in the direction where the sun rises."

" How long does she stay? A long or a short time?"

" A short time."

" Enough to be able to recite an Our Father and Hail Mary, or more?"

" A good deal more, but it is not always the same time; perhaps it would not be long enough to say a Rosary."

" The first time you saw her were you frightened?"

" I was, so much so that I wanted to run away with Jacinta and Francisco, but she told us not to be afraid because she would not hurt us."

" How is she dressed?"

" She has a white dress, which reaches to her feet, and her head is covered with a mantle, the same colour and the same length."

" Has the dress anything on it?"

" You can see, in the front, two gold cords which fall from the neck and are joined at the waist by a tassel, also gold."

" Is there any belt or ribbon?"

" No."

" Her earrings?"

" They are little rings."

" In which hand does she hold the Rosary?"

" In the right hand."

" Is it a Rosary of five or fifteen decades?"

" I didn't notice."

" Had it a cross?"

" Yes, a white cross and the beads, too, were white, so was the chain."

" Did you ever ask who she was?"

" I did, but she said she would only tell us on the 13th of October."

" Did you ask her where she came from?"

" I did, and she told me that she came from Heaven."

" When did you ask her this?"

" The second time, on the 13th of June."

" Did she smile sometimes, or was she sad?"

" She neither smiled, nor was she sad; she was always serious."

" Did she tell you and your cousins to say certain prayers?"

" She told us to say the Rosary in honour of Our Lady of the Rosary, to obtain the peace of the world."

" Did she say that many people were to be present in the Cova da Iria during the Apparitions of the 13th?"

" She said nothing about that."

" Is it true that she told you a secret that you were not to tell to anybody at all?"

" Yes."

" Does it only concern you or your cousins also?"

" It concerns all three of us."

" Could you not tell it even to your confessor?"

At this question Lucia was silent and appeared confused. I judged it better not to insist by repeating the question.

" In order to free yourself from the Mayor on the day he imprisoned you, did you tell him something as if it were the secret, thus deceiving him and boasting of it afterwards?"

" That is not true. Senhor Santos really did want me to reveal the secret, but I could not and did not do so, although he tried in every way to make me do what he wanted. I told the Mayor everything that the Lady had said to me except the secret. Perhaps it was because of this that he thought I had told him the secret too. I never wanted to deceive him."

" Did the Lady tell you to learn to read?"

" Yes, the second time she appeared."

" But if she told you that she would take you to Heaven in October next, what would be the good of learning to read?"

" That is not true. The Lady never said that she would take me to Heaven in October and I never told anyone that she had said such a thing."

" What did the Lady say was to be done with the money which the people left under the oak tree in the Cova da Iria?"

" She said that we were to get two ' andors ' and that I and Jacinta and two more girls were to carry one and Francisco with three more boys the other, to the parish church. Part of this money was to be for the Festa of Our Lady of the Rosary and the rest to help to build a new chapel."

" Where does the Lady want the chapel built? In the Cova da Iria?"

" I don't know; she didn't say."

" Are you glad that Our Lady appeared to you?"

" Yes."

" On the 13th of October will Our Lady come alone?"

" St Joseph and the Holy Child will come and a little time afterwards the world will have peace."

" Did Our Lady reveal anything more?"

" She said that on the 13th of October she would perform a miracle so that the people can believe that she appeared."

" Why do you often lower your eyes instead of keeping them on the Lady?"

" Because she sometimes blinds me."

" Did she teach you any prayer?"

" Yes, and she wants us to recite it after each mystery of the Rosary."

"Do you know this prayer by heart?"

"Yes."

"Say it."

"O my Jesus, forgive us and deliver us from the fire of hell. Take all souls to Heaven, especially those who are most in need."

CHAPTER XXIII

DR. FORMIGÃO AGAIN

WHAT impression did these interrogations make on the mind of Dr. Formigão?

A firm conviction of the absolute sincerity of the children, a conviction which nevertheless did not exclude a certain doubt as to the possibility of their being victims of a hallucination provoked by the spirit of darkness for unknown ends.

The tiny discrepancies in the replies of the seers did not create any serious difficulty, for they referred only to details of little or no importance, easily explained by the fatigue and mental perturbation caused by the incessant attacks from all sides since the news of the events began to circulate.

In order to test the case to his satisfaction Dr. Formigao resolved to go to Fatima for a further interrogation before the great day of the 13th on which the promised miracle was awaited.

From Santarem he took the train to Chão de Maças and from there to Vila Nova de Ourem and thence to Fatima by carriage. He arrived very late, too late to question the children, and passed the night in the home of the Gonçalves family in Montelo some two kilometres from Fatima. The eldest son of the house, Manuel Gonçalves, who is a man of intelligence and good sense and gifted with acute powers of observation, was able to furnish a number of useful facts about the families of the seers as well as his general impressions of the events of the last five months. This is the conversation exchanged between the two:

"Have the parents of these children a good name? Are they respectable, decent living people?"

"The parents of Jacinta and Francisco are very good people, profoundly religious and well thought of by everybody. Lucia's father is not a churchgoer but he is not at all a bad man.

On the 13th of June some of his more raffish friends succeeded in making him drunk in the hope of getting him to commit some folly or other in the place of the Apparitions, and although he had allowed his daughter to go to the place as usual he ordered the other people off, as proprietor of the ground where the oak tree grows. When the people saw that he was drunk they took no notice of his order but a man pushed him so that he fell to the ground. The mother is a pious hard-working woman."

"What do the inhabitants of Fatima think of the children's affirmations? Do they believe them? Do they think they are lying or perhaps victims of a hallucination?"

"At first the people did not want to go to the Cova. No one believed the children. On 13th June, the day of the second Apparition, there was a *festa* in the parish in honour of St. Anthony. In the Cova there were only about seventy people at the time of the Apparitions. The parents of Jacinta and Francisco had gone in the morning to Porto de Mós for the so-called 'Fair of the thirteenth' with the intention of buying oxen and returning at night. In their absence the house filled up with people who wanted to see the children and question them. At present a large proportion of the people thinks that the children are speaking the truth. For my own part I am convinced of this."

"On the days of the Apparitions are there extraordinary signs? Many people claim to have seen them?"

"The signs are very numerous. In August almost everyone who was present saw them. A cloud came down on the oak tree. In July the same thing was seen and there was no dust. The cloud seemed to sweep the air clean."

"Were there any other signs?"

"In the sky, near the sun, there were some white clouds which turned successively bright red (the colour of blood), pink and yellow. The people themselves turned this last colour. The light of the sun sensibly diminished in intensity and in July and August a noise was heard."

"Is it possible that anyone could have induced the children to play a hoax?"

"That would be impossible!"

"Have many people come from outside to talk to the children?"

"Innumerable people from all parts."

"Do they accept the money which is offered them?"

"They have accepted something from people who insist but they do not accept it willingly."

"Are the families poor? Do they live by their work? Do they own any property?"

"They are not poor and are indeed comfortably placed. If Lucia's family is not better off it is due to the fecklessness of the father."

"Are there people in Fatima who have been close to the children during the Apparitions?"

"In July, Jacinto Lopes da Amoreira and Manuel de Oliveira from this village of Montelo were near them."

"What does Lucia do during the Apparitions?"

"She says the Rosary. When she speaks to the Lady she speaks loudly. I myself heard her in June because I was near her. Some people say that they heard the sound of the reply."

"Is the place of the Apparitions much frequented on the other days?"

"Yes, many people go there especially on Sundays and mostly at night. People come from far and near, even more from outside the parish. They say the Rosary and sing hymns in honour of Our Lady."

After this conversation Dr. Formigao went to Aljustrel, where he found Lucia helping a mason who was repairing the roof.

As soon as she saw me (he says) she greeted me respectfully. Her mother appeared at that moment and willingly consented to my questioning her daughter again. First, however, I asked her a few questions among which the following may be of interest:

"I think that you have a book called *Short Mission*, which you sometimes read to your children. Is that so?"[1]

"Yes, I have read it to my children."

"Have you ever read about the Apparition of La Salette to Lucia or to other children?"

"Only to Lucia and the family."

"Did Lucia ever speak about the Apparition of La Salette, or show in any way that the story had made a great impression on her mind?"

"I don't remember her ever having mentioned it."[2]

The interrogation of Lucia was made before four reliable witnesses (notes Dr. Formigão):

"You told me some days ago that Our Lady wanted the money given by the people to be used for the Parish Church for two 'andors'. How are these 'andors' to be obtained and when are they to be taken to the church?"

"They must be bought with the money which is given, and carried on the Feast of Our Lady of the Rosary."

"Do you know for certain where Our Lady wants the chapel in her honour to be built?"

"I don't know for certain, but I think she wants the chapel in the Cova da Iria."

[1] Dr. Formigão had in mind the possible "suggestive" influence of this book.

[2] Impossible that any obsession or impression should not have been noticed by her mother.

"What did she say that she would do in order that people might believe?"

"She said that she would perform a miracle."

"When did she say this?"

"She said it several times, but once, during the first Apparition, I asked her."[3]

"Are you not afraid of what the people will do if nothing extraordinary happens on that day?"

"I am not at all afraid."

"Do you feel something inside you, some force which drags you to the Cova da Iria on the 13th of each month?"

"I feel I want to go there, and I should be sad if I didn't."

"Did you ever see the Lady make the sign of the cross, pray, or tell the beads?"

"No."

"Did she tell you to pray?"

"She told me to pray several times."

"Did she tell you to pray for the conversion of sinners?"

"No, she only told me to pray to Our Lady of the Rosary for the end of the war."

"Did you see the signs which other people said they saw such as a star, and roses falling from the Lady's dress, etc.?"

"I didn't see a star nor any other signs."

"Did you hear any noise or an earthquake?"

"No, I heard nothing."

"Can you read?"

"No."

"Are you learning?"

"No."

"Then you are not doing what Our Lady wants? . . ."[4]

"When you tell the people to kneel and pray is it the Lady who tells you to?"

"No, it is not the Lady. I tell them to."

"Do you always kneel when she appears?"

"Sometimes I kneel, sometimes I stand."

"When she speaks is her voice sweet and agreeable?"

"Yes."

"How old is the Lady?"

---

[3] One of the slips which Lucia occasionally makes and which are easily explained, as we have said, by the continual and ceaseless interrogations which everybody considered they had the right to make.

[4] Lucia did not wish to blame her mother who had said: "What does it matter to Our Lady if you can read or not!"

" She looks about fifteen years old."

" What colour is the Rosary chain?"

" White."

" And the crucifix?"

" White too."

" Does the veil cover the forehead of the Lady ? "

" It does not cover it; you can see her forehead."

" Is the light which surrounds her very beautiful?"

" More beautiful than the most brilliant light of the sun."

" Did the Lady ever greet you with her head or with her hands?"

" Never."

" Did she ever laugh?"

" Never."

" Does she usually look at the people?"

" I never saw her look at them."

" Do you hear the voices and the cries of the people while you are talking to the Lady?"

" No."

" Did the Lady ask you in May to come back every month until October to the Cova da Iria?"

" She said we were to come back from month to month on the 13th for six months."

" Do you remember your mother reading a book called *Short Mission*, where there is a story of an Apparition of Our Lady to a girl?"

" Yes."

" Did you think much about this story or speak about it to other children?"

" I never thought about this story and I never talked about it to anyone."

After hearing Lucia, Dr. Formigão went to Senhor Marto's house, and in his presence and of some of his daughters he questioned Jacinta:

" Did the Lady tell you to say the Rosary?"

" Yes."

" When?"

" When she appeared the first time."

" Did you hear the secret or was it only Lucia who heard?"

" I heard too."

" When?"

" At the second Apparition on St. Anthony's day."

" Is the secret that you will be rich?"

" No."

" That you will be good and happy?"

" Yes, it is for the good of all three of us."

" Is it that you will go to Heaven?"

" No."

" Can you tell the secret?"

" I can't."

" Why?"

" Because the Lady said we were not to tell it to anyone."

" If the people knew it, would they be sad?"

" Yes."

" How did the Lady have her hands?"

" She had them stretched out."

" Always?"

" Sometimes she turned the palms up to Heaven."

" In May did the Lady say she wanted you to go to the Cova da Iria again?"

" She said she wanted us to go there for six months running until October when she would say what she wanted."

" Has she light round her head?"

" Yes."

" Can you look easily at her face?"

" No, because it hurts my eyes."

" Do you always hear well what the Lady says?"

" Last time I couldn't hear everything because of the noise the people were making."

Then came Francisco's turn:

" How old are you?"

" Nine years old."

" Do you only see Our Lady or do you also hear what she says?"

" I only see her. I can't hear anything she says."

" Has she light round her head?"

" Yes."

" Can you look well at her face?"

" I can look but only a little because of the light."

" Has her dress some decoration?"

" It has some cords of gold."

" What colour is the crucifix?"

" White."

" And the chain of the Rosary?"

" White, too."

" Would the people be sad if they knew the secret?"

" Yes."

In face of these candid replies Dr. Formigao was further convinced of the sincerity of the children, and he awaited with redoubled impatience the day which would definitely decide whether or not the events of Fatima were super-natural. The children had affirmed that Our Lady had promised a sign from Heaven. She would certainly not fail in her word, if it were really she.

CHAPTER XXIV

APPREHENSION

IN *October I will perform a miracle so that everyone can believe.* This was the assurance of the Blessed Virgin to her confidant, and Lucia for her part repeated it to everyone who came to question her.

Everywhere in Portugal people talked about the miracle whose day, hour and place had been so accurately foretold. October the Thirteenth was to be the decisive day in the history of the Apparitions of Fatima.

The enemies of the Church mocked at this prophecy and at the simpletons who pinned their faith to it, rejoicing in the magnificent opportunity to bury once and for all the already moribund Christian religion in Portugal.

On 13th October Avelino de Almeida published a joking article in the *Seculo.* This article, however, served as an advertisement for Fatima not only in Lisbon but also in the provinces, for the *Seculo* was the paper with the largest cir-culation at that time.

In Fatima, and above all in Aljustrel where least credit was given to the Apparitions, consternation reigned. The children, the families, and above all Lucia, were seriously threatened if the miracle should not take place.

My family (Maria dos Anjos tells us) was much preoccupied. As the 13th drew nearer we kept on telling Lucia that it would be better if she did not keep up the affair any longer because ill would come of it to her and to us and we should all suffer because of the things she had invented. My father scolded her very, very much. When he had been drinking he was very bad but he did not actually beat her. It was my mother who did that most. It was said that they were going to put bombs down to frighten us and the children. Some people told us that if it were their children they would shut them up in a room until they came to their senses. We were all very much afraid. We wondered what would become of us.

all and said so behind Lucia's back. The neighbours said that the bombs would destroy our houses and our belongings. Someone came to my mother and advised her to take Lucia right away where nobody would know where she was. Everyone said something different and gave different advice until we didn't know what to do for the best. My mother said: "If it really is Our Lady who appears, she might have done a miracle already—made a spring come up or something. When it rains there is a tiny drop of water there but nothing more. . . . Oh, where will all this end!"

Only the children didn't seem to mind at all. One day—it was a few days before the 13th—I went to talk to them at the well and said: "Now aren't you three going to say that nothing happened after all in the Cova da Iria. People are saying that they will put bombs down to destroy our houses. Just tell me and I'll tell Fr. Ferreira and he can give it out in church. Shall I do that?"

Lucia wrinkled her forehead and said nothing and then Jacinta, between her tears and in her tiny little voice, said: "Say it if you like but we *saw* her. . . !"

There was such acute apprehension in Abobora's family that hardly had dawn broken on the 12th when Maria Rosa jumped out of bed and went to wake her daughter, saying:

"Lucia, we had better go to confession. Everyone says that we shall probably be killed to-morrow in the Cova da Iria. If the Lady doesn't do the miracle the people will attack us, so we had better go to confession and be properly prepared for death."

"If you want to go, mother, I'll come with you," said Lucia placidly, " but not for that reason. I am not afraid of being killed. I'm absolutely certain that the Lady will do all that she promised to-morrow."

No one spoke any more about confession.

In the Marto household things were more peaceful. Ti Marto was by now convinced of the truth of the Apparitions and nothing could shake his faith. He awaited events with the utmost calmness. Recalling that time he says:

A few days before 13th October, Fr. Poças, parish priest of Mós, and one of his parishioners came to see us to try and make the children deny what they had said.

By the time I arrived back home they had already questioned Francisco but without any result. They wanted to talk to the other two but they had gone to Boleiros with a donkey to get some lime. Although I told them that they would be back before long they went to find them with my John. It was not long before they all came back and I met them at the house of Lucia's sister, Maria dos Anjos. Then and there Fr. Poças attacked Lucia:

"Look here, child, you're just going to tell me that all this is stuff and nonsense and if you don't I will say so myself and tell everyone else, too. People believe me and, besides, they are going to the Cova to destroy everything and you won't escape either."

Lucia didn't say a word so I turned to Fr. Poças and said:

"Well, then, better telegraph the news everywhere."

"Yes, that's just what we ought to do and then nobody will come here on the 13th. It would be the best thing that could happen."

I was very angry, and Jacinta, who never liked to see anyone angry, suddenly disappeared. I turned to Fr. Poças and said:

"In any case, please leave the children alone. There's nothing to prevent your doing what you like about it."

Then the other man said furiously:

"This is nothing less than witchcraft. The same thing happened with a servant of mine some time ago and when she got the idea into her head nothing on earth could rid her of it!"

Without more ado we all went back to the house and found Jacinta on the doorstep playing with a child about her own age.

"Listen, Jacinta," said Fr. Poças again, "haven't you anything to say? You know Lucia has told us everything and now we know that it's all a lie."

"Lucia never said that!" replied Jacinta firmly.

And though he insisted she stood firm and repeated that Lucia had said nothing. I could see that they were all surprised at Jacinta's firmness; I even thought they believed in the Apparitions and at one moment the other man pulled a coin out of his pocket and tried to give it to Jacinta.

"You mustn't do that!" I told him.

"Surely I can give something to John then!"

"It's not necessary, but if you like you can give it to him."

When they were leaving Fr. Poças turned to me and said:

"Congratulations, you have played your part well!"

"Well or ill that's my way," I answered. "You haven't succeeded in making the children deny their story but even if you had I should still believe in them!"

CHAPTER XXV

THE THIRTEENTH OF OCTOBER

THERE was a marked contrast between the quite unjustified terror which reigned in Lucia's family, and among the greater part of the population of Aljustrel, and the tranquil faith with which pilgrims from all parts of Portugal took the road to the promised land.

It was indeed an extraordinary spectacle.

We have at hand various descriptions of this unique pilgrimage, and our only regret is that we cannot quote them
in full. We must content ourselves with a few passages.
We take the following from an article in the paper *O Dia* of
19th October, 1917, which we now know to have come from
the pen of Dona Madalena Patricio.

> The hamlets, villages and towns in the proximity appeared
> to be depopulated. For days beforehand groups of excursionists
> were to be seen on the way to Fatima. The fishermen from
> Vieira left nets, and wooden houses by the sea, and came
> swinging through the pinewoods. Artisans from Marinha,
> farmers from Monte Real . . . *serra* folk from much further
> afield, from every place where news of the miracle had pene-
> trated, the people left their houses and their fields and came to
> Fatima by horse, carriage, on foot, by every means of transport.
> The roads through the pines and the mountains echoed during
> these two days with the noise of traffic and the voices of the
> pilgrims.
>
> Autumn was reddening the vines, stripped after the vintage.
> The cold north-west wind announced the coming of winter . . .
> and all night and into the morning a sad drizzling rain fell.
> Damp and cold, it penetrated into the bones of those who,
> with their families and animals, were flocking along the roads
> which led to the miraculous mountain.
>
> The rain fell and fell. The cotton skirts of the women
> dripped and hung like lead around their ankles. Water poured
> from the new caps and hats which had been donned in honour
> of the day. Boots and bare feet splashed through the muddy
> puddles . . . and up on the mountain there was what appeared
> to be a large dark stain—thousands upon thousands of God's
> creatures waiting for a miracle, a blessing and an alleviation in
> the bitterness of life. . . .

From the other side, on the road from Chão de Maças
through Vila Nova de Ourem, the same scenes were
repeated. They were described by the special reporter of
the *Seculo*, Avelino de Almeida.

> On the road we can see the first groups of people making
> their way to the holy place, which is about twenty kilometres
> from here.
>
> Men and women are for the most part barefooted, the latter
> carrying their shoes in bags on their heads, while the men lean
> on thick sticks and are also prudently armed with umbrellas.
> Apparently indifferent to what is going on around them they do
> not seem to notice the countryside nor their fellow-travellers
> but murmur the Rosary as they go along immersed in thought.
>
> A woman recites the first part of the Ave Maria and imme-
> diately her companions continue the second part in chorus.
> They move rhythmically and rapidly in order to reach the
> place of the Apparitions before nightfall. Here, under the

stars they will sleep, keeping the first and best places near the little tree.

At the entrance to the town, women of the people, apparently influenced by the atheistic tone of the place, mockingly interchange impressions on the topic of the day, while the believers pursue their way indifferent to everything alien to the object of their journey. During the night the most varied types of vehicle have arrived in the square, bringing their loads of the devout and the curious.

At daybreak fresh groups hurry through the town and the habitual quiet is broken by singing of the most varied kind.

At sunrise the weather looks threatening. Black clouds gather exactly over Fatima but this does not deter the people who by now are flocking in from all sides, employing every means of transport. There are luxurious motor cars travelling at speed, ox-carts pulled in to the side of the road, victorias, closed carriages, carts in which seats are improvised and in which not another soul could be squeezed. Everyone is provided with food both for themselves and for the beasts . . . valiantly playing their part.

Here and there one sees a cart decorated with greenery, and although there is an air of discreet festivity people are sober and well-mannered. Donkeys bray at the side of the road and the innumerable cyclists make prodigious efforts not to collide with the carts.

By ten o'clock the sky was completely hidden behind the clouds and the rain began to fall in earnest. Swept by the strong wind and beating upon the faces of the people, it soaked the macadam and the pilgrims, often without protection against the weather, to the marrow of their bones. But no one complained or turned back, and if some took shelter under trees or walls the great majority continued on their journey with remarkable indifference to the rain.

The place where the Virgin is alleged to have appeared is fronted to a large extent by the road which leads to Leiria, along which the vehicles which bring the pilgrims are parked. But the great mass of the people congregate round the oak tree which, according to the children, is the Vision's pedestal. It can be imagined as the centre of a large circle round which the spectators gather to watch events.

Seen from the road the general effect is picturesque. The peasants, sheltering under their huge umbrellas, accompany the unloading of fodder with the singing of hymns and the recitation of the decades of the Rosary in a matter-of-fact way. People plod through the sticky clay in order to see the famous oak tree with its wooden arch and hanging lanterns, at closer quarters.

At one moment a terrified hare runs through the crowd and is hardly noticed except by half a dozen or so of small boys, who catch and kill it.

How many pilgrims came to Fatima on that memorable 13th October? In his account, Almeida Garrett, the well-known Professor of Coimbra University, computes the number at 100,000.[1]

The crowd did not consist of devout believers only. As on other occasions there was a good percentage of curious, incredulous and unbelieving people, who had come with the sole purpose of mocking the credulity of the simple faithful. Well sheltered in their comfortable motor cars they contemplated with supercilious amusement the scene before them.

Dr. Formigão, who was present at the miracle, relates an amusing detail:

> In a hired carriage a group of men who looked like small merchants were carrying on a heated conversation. One of them suddenly burst out in exasperated tones:
>
> "A good thing if they had cut off the heads of those children! Bringing us here in this weather just to get soaked!"
>
> "It's hardly their fault," replied another, "it's the parents who ought to be in prison!"
>
> "What fools we were," said a third. "Why didn't we stay in Ourem and have a decent meal there!"
>
> Even on the 12th (says Maria da Capela) there were so many people that we could hardly believe it. They made such a noise that you could hear it away in our village. They had to sleep out in the open because there wasn't a shelter of any kind here.
>
> Before sunrise they were praying and singing. I came here very early, too, and managed to get near the tree, which was now only a trunk, but I had decorated it with ribbons and flowers on the evening before. I felt sad because it was the last time that Our Lady was coming, but I was longing to see the miracle.
>
> Near the place of the Apparitions there was a priest who had spent the night there and was saying his Breviary. At midday the children arrived, dressed in white as if for First Communion, and the priest asked them what time Our Lady would appear.
>
> "At midday," said Lucia.
>
> The priest looked at his watch and said:
>
> "Look, it's midday now. Our Lady doesn't lie. Well! . . Well!"
>
> After a few minutes he said again:
>
> "It's past midday. You see, it's all a delusion! Run along, all of you!"
>
> But Lucia refused to go and the priest began to push the three children with his hands. Lucia, who was nearly crying, said to him:
>
> "If anyone wants to go they can go. I shall stay where I

---

[1] The *Diario de Noticias* reporter counted 240 carts, 135 bicycles, 100 cars. This only includes the number of vehicles which returned to Vila Nova de Ourem.

am. Our Lady said she would come. She came the other times and she will come this time, too."

At the same time she looked to the east and said to Jacinta: "Jacinta, kneel down; Our Lady is coming. I saw the lightning."

The priest didn't say another word and I never saw him again!

CHAPTER XXVI

THE LADY OF THE ROSARY

WE must again go back a little way. In Aljustrel, in the Santos' house, there was a great commotion. For the first time Maria Rosa was worried about her daughter, thinking it to be the last day of her life. With tears running down her cheeks she looked tenderly at Lucia who tried to comfort her mother while drying her tears.

"Don't be afraid, mother, dear. Nothing will happen to us I'm sure. Our Lady will do what she promised!" And she made ready to leave for her cousins' house. Then Maria Rosa in an access of maternal anxiety decided to go with her to the place of the Apparitions.

"If my child is going to die I want to die with her!"

Mother, father and daughter set off for the Marto cottage. They could only enter with the greatest difficulty.

The people filled the house so that you couldn't move (says Ti Marto). Outside it was pouring with rain so that one could hardly see through it and the ground was thick with mud.

My poor wife was very upset because the people got up on the chests and on to the beds, dirtying everything! And I said to her:

"Never mind, wife, it's so full now that nobody else can get in!"

When they came to leave I got ready to go with the children but at that moment a neighbour came up to me and whispered:

"Better not go, Ti Marto. You might be attacked. They won't hurt the children because they're so small, but with you it's another matter!"

"But I am going, because I have faith in it!" I told him. "I'm not at all afraid and am quite sure that everything will go off all right!"

With my poor Olimpia it was another matter. She was very much upset. Although she put her trust in Our Lady she didn't think things were going to be all right as I did, because the priests and so many other people had said the opposite. The children, too, were quite calm; neither Jacinta nor Francisco were in the least perturbed.

"If they harm us," Jacinta said to me, "we shall go to Heaven, but the poor people who do it will go to hell!"

A lady from Pambalinho brought dresses for the girls and she dressed them herself. Lucia's was blue and Jacinta's white, and she put white wreaths on their heads so that they looked like the little angels in processions.

We left the house in such rain as you never saw! The road was thick with mud but this did not prevent the women and even ladies from kneeling in front of the children. "Leave them alone, good people!" I cried. For they seemed to think that they had the power of saints. After a lot of trouble and interruptions we at last arrived at the Cova da Iria. The crowd was so thick that you couldn't pass through. It was then that a chauffeur picked up my Jacinta and pushed and shoved his way to the lantern arch, shouting out: "Make way for the children who saw Our Lady!" I went behind him and Jacinta, who was frightened to see me among so many people, began to cry out:

"Don't push my father, don't hurt him!"

The chauffeur at last put her down by the tree but there, too, the crush was so great that she began to cry. Then Lucia and Francisco made their way into the middle of it. My Olimpia was somewhere else, I don't know where, but Maria Rosa was quite close. At that moment I saw a man bearing down on me with a stick and thought there was going to be trouble, but the people made ranks in front and behind and when the moment came everything was quiet and orderly.

"The moment", as we may guess, was the hour of noon. A few seconds later Lucia cried out:

"Be quiet, be quiet, Our Lady is coming!"

And, in fact, the Mother of God came for the last time to the little tree now gay with the flowers and ribbons which the devoted hands of Maria Carreira had placed there. The face of the seer was transformed by the supernatural. Her features looked more delicate, her colour heightened and her expression was grave and sweet. She entered at once into communication with the Vision and did not hear her mother's warning voice behind her:

"Look carefully, Lucia, make no mistake!"

A misty cloud like incense enveloped the little group as the spontaneous question came:

"What do you want of me?"

"I want a chapel to be built here in my honour. I am the Lady of the Rosary. Continue to say the Rosary every day. The war will soon end and the soldiers will return to their homes."

"I have many petitions, will you grant them?"

"Some, yes; others, no. People must amend their lives

and ask pardon for their sins. They must not offend Our Lord any more for He is already too much offended."

" Do you want anything more?"

" Nothing more."

And the Lady of the Rosary took her last leave of her three little friends. She opened her hands which were reflecting the solar rays, and while she rose her light was thrown back to the sun so that she was more brilliant than the sun itself. Lucia, fixing her eyes on the radiant vision, cried out to the people:

" There she goes, there she goes! *Look at the sun!*"

CHAPTER XXVII

The Miracle of the Sun

" Look at the sun," Lucia had cried to the people. What was happening in the miraculous skies of Fatima during those incredible moments? The answer is a miracle, a stupendous miracle, such as no one had dared to imagine. The children saw a series of tremendous visions: first St. Joseph with the Holy Child and Our Lady—the Holy Family. St. Joseph, robed in white, seemed to lean from the clouds, half hidden, holding the Child which was fully visible and dressed in red, upon his arm. Our Lady on the right of the sun wore a blue mantle which covered her head and fell loosely round her. St. Joseph traced the sign of the Cross three times over the vast kneeling crowd and then the vision faded to give place to another of Jesus Christ, vested in red and His Mother under her symbolism of Our Lady of Dolours.[1] The Redeemer also gave His blessing to the people. As this vision faded it was succeeded by yet another seen by Lucia alone, of Our Lady of Mount Carmel with something falling from her hand.

What, meanwhile, had the people seen? We will let Ti Marto speak first:

> We looked easily at the sun, which did not blind us. It seemed to flicker on and off, first one way and then another. It shot rays in different directions and painted everything in different colours—the trees, the people, the air and the ground. What was the most extraordinary was that the sun did not hurt our eyes at all. Everything was still and quiet; everyone was

[1] Without the sword piercing the Hear'

looking upwards. At a certain moment the sun seemed to
stop and then began to move and to dance until it seemed that
it was being detached from the sky and was falling on us. It
was a terrible moment!

Maria da Capela saw much the same thing:

> It turned everything different colours, yellow, blue, white,
> and it shook and trembled; it seemed like a wheel of fire which
> was going to fall on the people. They cried out: "We shall
> all be killed, we shall all be killed!" Others called to Our
> Lady to save them and recited acts of contrition. One woman
> began to confess her sins aloud, saying that she had done
> this and that. . . . At last the sun stopped moving and we all
> breathed a sigh of relief. We were still alive and the miracle
> which the children had foretold had taken place.[2]

Yes, the miracle had taken place and it was seen not only
by the simple and humble but by the whole multitude (some
70,000 people), believers and non-believers, many of whom
have given testimony of this extraordinary occurrence.

Owing to the impossibility of quoting the various accounts
of the scene in full we will choose two passages from the
principal Lisbon papers, *O Dia* and *O Seculo*. The former
of 17th October, 1917, says:

> At one o'clock in the afternoon, midday by the sun, the
> rain stopped. The sky, pearly grey in colour, illuminated the
> vast arid landscape with a strange light. The sun had a trans-
> parent gauzy veil so that the eyes could easily be fixed upon it.
> The grey mother-of-pearl tone turned into a sheet of silver
> which broke up as the clouds were torn apart and the silver sun,
> enveloped in the same gauzy grey light, was seen to whirl and
> turn in the circle of broken clouds. A cry went up from every
> mouth and people fell on their knees on the muddy ground. . . .
> The light turned a beautiful blue as if it had come through
> the stained-glass windows of a cathedral and spread itself over
> the people who knelt with outstretched hands. The blue faded
> slowly and then the light seemed to pass through yellow glass.
> Yellow stains fell against white handkerchiefs, against the dark
> skirts of the women. They were repeated on the trees, on the
> stones and on the *serra*. People wept and prayed with un-
> covered heads in the presence of a miracle they had awaited.
> The seconds seemed like hours, so vivid were they.

In the *Seculo*, Avelino de Almeida recorded his impressions:

---

[2] In more or less the same words as Ti Marto and Maria Carreira, the
" Miracle of the Sun " has been described to us by many other people.
Up to the present we have not met a single person among the many we
have questioned who has not confirmed the phenomenon.

From the road, where the vehicles were parked and where hundreds of people who had not dared to brave the mud were congregated, one could see the immense multitude turn towards the sun, which appeared free from clouds and in its zenith. It looked like a plaque of dull silver and it was possible to look at it without the least discomfort. It might have been an eclipse which was taking place. But at that moment a great shout went up and one could hear the spectators nearest at hand shouting: "A miracle! A miracle!"

Before the astonished eyes of the crowd, whose aspect was Biblical as they stood bareheaded, eagerly searching the sky, the sun trembled, made sudden incredible movements outside all cosmic laws—the sun "danced" according to the typical expression of the people.

Standing at the step of the Torres Novas omnibus was an old man, whose appearance in face and figure reminded one of Paul Déroulède. With his face turned to the sun he recited the Credo in a loud voice. I asked who he was and was told Senhor João da Cunha Vasconcelos. I saw him afterwards going up to those around him who still had their hats on and vehemently imploring them to uncover before such an extraordinary demonstration of the existence of God.

Identical scenes were repeated elsewhere and in one place a woman cried out: "How terrible! There are even men who do not uncover before such a stupendous miracle!"

People then began to ask each other what they had seen. The great majority admitted to having seen the trembling and the dancing of the sun; others affirmed that they saw the face of the Blessed Virgin; others, again, swore that the sun whirled on itself like a giant catherine wheel and that it lowered itself to the earth as if to burn it in its rays. Some said they saw it change colours successively. . . .

We also quote the relevant part of a letter which the well-known professor of Coimbra, Dr. Almeida Garrett, wrote to Dr. Formigão who asked him for an account of what he saw on that memorable 13th October:

While I was looking at the place of the Apparitions in a serene, if cold, expectation of something happening and with diminishing curiosity because a long time had passed without anything to excite my attention, I heard a shout from thousands of voices and saw the multitude which straggled out at my feet, here and there concentrated in small groups round the trees, suddenly turn its back and shoulders away from the point towards which up to now it had directed its attention, and turn to look at the sky on the opposite side.

It must have been nearly two o'clock by the legal time and about midday by the sun. The sun, a few moments before, had broken through the thick layer of clouds which hid it and shone clearly and intensely. I veered to the magnet which seemed to be drawing all eyes and saw it as a disc with a clean-cut rim, luminous and shining, but which did not hurt

the eyes. I do not agree with the comparison which I have
heard made in Fatima—that of a dull silver disc. It was a
clearer, richer, brighter colour, having something of the lustre
of a pearl. It did not in the least resemble the moon on a clear
night because one saw it and felt it to be a living body. It
was not spheric like the moon nor did it have the same colour,
tone, or shading. It looked like a glazed wheel made of mother-
of-pearl. It could not be confused, either, with the sun seen
through fog (for there was no fog at the time), because it was
not opaque, diffused or veiled. In Fatima it gave light and
heat and appeared clear-cut with a well-defined rim.

The sky was mottled with light cirrus clouds with the blue
coming through here and there but sometimes the sun stood
out in patches of clear sky. The clouds passed from west to
east and did not obscure the light of the sun, giving the impression of passing behind it, though sometimes these flecks of
white took on tones of pink or diaphanous blue as they passed
before the sun.

It was a remarkable fact that one could fix one's eyes on
this brazier of heat and light without any pain in the eyes or
blinding of the retina. The phenomenon, except for two interruptions when the sun seemed to send out rays of refulgent
heat which obliged us to look away, must have lasted about
ten minutes.

The sun's disc did not remain immobile. This was not the
sparkling of a heavenly body for it spun round on itself in a
mad whirl. Then, suddenly, one heard a clamour, a cry of
anguish breaking from all the people. The sun, whirling
wildly, seemed to loosen itself from the firmament and advance
threateningly upon the earth as if to crush us with its huge
and fiery weight. The sensation during those moments was
terrible.

During the solar phenomenon, which I have just described in
detail, there were changes of colour in the atmosphere. Looking at the sun, I noticed that everything around was becoming
darkened. I looked first at the nearest objects and then extended my glance further afield as far as the horizon. I saw
everything an amethyst colour. Objects around me, the sky
and the atmosphere, were of the same colour. An oak tree
nearby threw a shadow of this colour on the ground.

Fearing that I was suffering from an affection of the retina,
an improbable explanation because in that case one could not
see things purple coloured, I turned away and shut my eyes,
keeping my hands before them to intercept the light. With my
back still turned, I opened my eyes and saw that the landscape
was the same purple colour as before.

The impression was not that of an eclipse, and while looking at the sun I noticed that the atmosphere had cleared. Soon
after I heard a peasant who was near me shout out in tones of
astonishment: "Look, that lady is all yellow!"

And in fact everything, both near and far, had changed,
taking on the colour of old yellow damask. People looked as
if they were suffering from jaundice and I recall a sensation

of amusement at seeing them look so ugly and unattractive. My own hand was the same colour. All the phenomena which I have described were observed by me in a calm and serene state of mind and without any emotional disturbance. It is for others to interpret and explain them.

We have quoted this testimony at length because we think it best interprets the impressions of the generality of people to whom we have spoken about the solar prodigy. We add, however, a few more accounts of this indisputably miraculous event. Dr. Domingos Pinto Coelho said in the paper *Ordem*:

> The sun, at one moment surrounded with scarlet flame, at another aureoled in yellow and deep purple, seemed to be in an exceedingly fast and whirling movement, at times appearing to be loosened from the sky and to be approaching the earth, strongly radiating heat.

On the night of that same 13th, Fr. Manuel Pereira da Silva wrote to his colleague, Canon Pereira de Almeida, the following description:

> The sun appeared with its circumference well-defined. It came down as if to the height of the clouds and began to whirl giddily upon itself like a captive ball of fire. With some interruptions, this lasted about eight minutes. The atmosphere darkened and the features of each person became yellow. Everyone knelt even in the mud. . . .

In a carriage near Dr. Formigão, a middle-aged, well-dressed woman turned to a lad who looked like a university student, and asked him with some emotion: " My son, do you still doubt the existence of God?" " No, mother," he answered with his eyes swimming in tears, " now it is impossible!"

We also transcribe the following passage from a letter written by Dona Maria do Carmo da Cruz Menezes:

> Suddenly the rain stopped and the sun broke through, casting its rays on the earth. It seemed to be falling upon that vast crowd of people and it spun like a firewheel, taking on all the colours of the rainbow. We ourselves took on those colours, with our clothes and even the earth itself. One heard cries and saw many people in tears. Deeply impressed, I said to myself: " My God, how great is your power!"

While writing this book in the very place of the Apparitions it occurred to us one day (at the conclusion of a retreat for professional men) to ask Senhor Alfredo da Silva Santos, who was present at the solar prodigy, his impressions of that event.

On the day before (he told us), I was in the Café Martinho, in Lisbon, when my cousin, João Lindim, from Torres Novas, entered and said to me:

" Everyone is going to Fatima to-morrow. There seems to be something extraordinary in the air and we are all full of curiosity to know what it is all about."

" I will go with you," I told him.

We made our arrangements and went in three motor cars on the early morning of the 13th. There was a thick mist and the car which went in front mistook the way so that we were all lost for a time and only arrived at the Cova da Iria at midday by the sun. It was absolutely full of people, but for my part I felt devoid of any religious feeling. Although I was some distance away, I still seem to see Lucia and Jacinta. When Lucia called out: " Look at the sun! " the whole multitude repeated: " Attention, to the sun! " It was a day of incessant drizzle but a few moments before the miracle it left off raining. I can hardly find words to describe what followed. The sun began to move and at a certain moment appeared to be detached from the sky and about to hurtle upon us like a wheel of flame. My wife—we had been married only a short time— fainted, and I was too upset to attend to her, and my brother-in-law, João Vassallo, supported her on his arm. I fell on my knees oblivious of everything and when I got up I don't know what I said. I think I began to cry out like the others. An old man with a white beard began to attack the atheists aloud and challenged them to say whether or no something supernatural had occurred.

" Could it have been a case of collective suggestion? " we asked Dr. Santos.

" I think," said he smiling, " that the only collective thing on that day was the rain which wet us to the bone! "

It is interesting to note that the phenomenon was seen not only in the Cova da Iria but was noticed by people kilometres away. This fact destroys any possible hypothesis of a collective hallucination as the Bishop of Leira observes in his pastoral letter on Fatima.

The poet Afonso Lopes Vieira saw the prodigy from his residence some forty kilometres distant from Fatima.

On that day, 13th October, 1917, without remembering the predictions of the children, I was enchanted by a remarkable spectacle in the sky of a kind I had never seen before. I saw it from this veranda.

Another extremely interesting description is that left by the late Fr. Inacio Lourenço, which we have personally verified from the mouths of various people of his parish,

Alburitel, and especially from the school teacher, Dona Delfina Pereira Lopes, to whom he refers:

> I was only nine years old at this time (runs Fr. Lourenço's account) and I went to the local village school (18 kilometres from Fatima). At about midday we were surprised by the shouts and cries of some men and women who were passing in the street in front of the school, The teacher, a good, pious woman, though nervous and impressionable, was the first to run into the road, with the children after her.
>
> Outside, the people were shouting and weeping and pointing to the sun, ignoring the agitated questions of the schoolmistress. It was the great Miracle, which one could see quite distinctly from the top of the hill where my village was situated—the Miracle of the sun, accompanied by all its extraordinary phenomena.
>
> I feel incapable of describing what I saw and felt. I looked fixedly at the sun, which seemed pale and did not hurt the eyes. Looking like a ball of snow revolving on itself, it suddenly seemed to come down in a zigzag, menacing the earth. Terrified, I ran and hid myself among the people, who were weeping and expecting the end of the world at any moment.
>
> Near us was an unbeliever who had spent the morning mocking at the simpletons who had gone off to Fatima just to see an ordinary girl. He now seemed to be paralysed, his eyes fixed on the sun. Afterwards he trembled from head to foot, and lifting up his arms fell on his knees in the mud, crying out to Our Lady.
>
> Meanwhile the people continued to cry out and to weep, asking God to pardon their sins. We all ran to the two chapels in the village, which were soon filled to overflowing. During those long moments of the solar prodigy objects around us turned all the colours of the rainbow. We saw ourselves blue, yellow, red, etc. All these strange phenomena increased the fears of the people. After about ten minutes the sun, now dull and pallid, returned to its place. When the people realised that the danger was over there was an explosion of joy and everyone joined in thanksgiving and praise to Our Lady. . . .

After the solar phenomenon another prodigy, inexplicable by natural means, took place. The people, who had been soaked by the rain, found themselves suddenly and completely dry. The Blessed Virgin had multiplied her miracles in order absolutely to confirm the veracity of the children.

No one can escape from these hard facts inexplicable by the ordinary laws of nature—no one that is, who takes the trouble to examine them scientifically, without philosophic prejudice or a dogmatic *parti pris*. Yet in this poor world there will always be proud and sceptical men who deny and interpret everything according to their own feeble reasoning powers, blurred by passion.

We cannot end this chapter in a more fitting manner than by quoting the words of D. José Alves Correia da Silva, Bishop of Leiria, in his pastoral letter on the Apparitions:

> The solar phenomenon of 13th October, described in newspapers of the time, was of a most marvellous nature and caused the deepest impression on those who had the good fortune to witness it.
>
> The children had foretold the day and the hour at which it would occur. The news spread rapidly throughout Portugal and in spite of bad weather thousands and thousands of people congregated at the spot. At the hour of the last Apparition they witnessed all the manifestations of the sun which paid homage to the Queen of Heaven and earth, more brilliant than the heavenly body itself at its zenith of light.
>
> This phenomenon, which was not registered in any astronomical observatory, *and could not, therefore, have been of natural origin,* was witnessed by people of every category and class, by believers as well as unbelievers, journalists of the principal daily papers and even by people kilometres away, a fact which destroys any theory of collective hallucination.*

CHAPTER XXVIII

THIRD INTERROGATION

ON the same day at seven in the evening, Dr. Formigao undertook a new interrogation of the children, for it was of the first importance not to delay this and to ensure that they were not left alone together before being questioned.

It is unfortunate but natural that the fatigue of the seers after a day of so much emotion and agitation should have in some measure prevented the complete success of the only serious interrogation of the day. In fact the children had not had a single moment of peace since daybreak and the strain was intensified after the miracle.

By the assertion of his authority as a priest, Dr. Formigão managed at last to rid the children of the redoubtable crowd of curious and importunate people which had gathered in the house, and tranquilly and deliberately began his interrogation. The three must also have felt a great relief at finding themselves again with their kind priestly friend. The first to be questioned was Lucia:

"Did Our Lady appear again to-day in the Cova da Iria?"

* Appendix V.

" Yes."

" Was she dressed as on the other occasions?"

" She was dressed in the same way."

" Did St. Joseph and the Holy Child appear?"

" Yes."

" Did anyone else appear?"

" Our Lord appeared and blessed the people and Our Lady of the two cards."

" What do you mean by Our Lady of the two cards?"

" Our Lady appeared dressed like Our Lady of Dolours but without the sword in her heart, and Our Lady dressed I don't quite know how, but I think it was Our Lady of Mount Carmel."

" They all came at the same time, did they not?"

> With my presentiment of the truth of the Apparitions I confess that it was with trepidation that I asked this question, purposely giving it an affirmative form (Dr. Formigão told us). Although it would not have been, strictly speaking, impossible for the children to have had a simultaneous vision of the three Images of the Blessed Virgin, it would clearly have created a serious difficulty.

" No.   First I saw Our Lady of the Rosary, then St. Joseph and the Holy Child.   After that I saw Our Lord, then Our Lady of Dolours and at the end what I think was Our Lady of Mount Carmel."

" Was the Holy Child standing or being carried by St. Joseph?"

" He was being carried by St. Joseph."

" Was He already a big child?"

" No, He was little."

" How old would He have been?"

" About a year."

" Why did you say that the Lady at one moment seemed to be dressed like Our Lady of Mount Carmel?"

" Because she had two things hanging from her hand."

" Did they appear on the oak tree?"

" No, they appeared near the sun, after the Lady had dis· appeared from the oak tree."

" Was Our Lord standing?"

" I only saw Him from the waist."

" How long did the Apparition on the oak tree last? Long enough to say the Rosary?"

" I don't think it was as long as that."

" Did the figures you saw in the sun last long?"

" No, only a short time."

" Did the Lady say who she was?"

" She said that she was the Lady of the Rosary."

" Did you ask what she wanted?"

" Yes."

" What did she say?"

" She said that we were to amend our lives and not offend Our Lord any more because He was too much offended already, and that we were to say the Rosary and ask pardon for our sins."

" Did she say anything else?"

" She said that a chapel was to be built in the Cova da Iria."

" Where was the money to come from?"

" I think it would be what was left there."

" Did she say anything about our soldiers who were killed in the war."

" No, she said nothing about them."

" Did she tell you to tell the people to look at the sun?"

" No."

" Did she say that the people were to do penance?"

" Yes."

" Did she use the word penance?"

" No. She said we were to say the Rosary and amend our lives and ask pardon of Our Lord, but she did not use the word penance."

" When did the sign in the sun begin? Was it after the Lady disappeared?"

" Yes."

" Did you see the Lady come?"

" Yes."

" Where did she come from?"

" From the east."

" And the other times?"

" I didn't look the other times."

" Did you see her go?"

" Yes."

" In which direction?"

" To the east."

" How did she disappear?"

" Little by little."

" What disappeared first?"

" Her head. Then her body, and the last thing I saw was her feet."

" When she went did she go with her back towards or away from the people?"

" With her back towards the people."

" Did she take long to go?"

" Only a short time."

" Was she surrounded by any light?"

" I saw her in the middle of brilliant light. This time, too, she was blinding. Sometimes I had to rub my eyes."

" Will Our Lady appear again?"

" I don't think so; she said nothing about it."

" Will you return to the Cova da Iria on the 13th?"

" No."

" Will Our Lady do any miracles? Cure any sick people?"

" I don't know."

" Didn't you ask her anything?"

" I told her to-day that I had various petitions to give and she said she would grant some and not others."

" Did she say when she would grant them?"

" No."

" Under what title is the chapel of the Cova da Iria to be?"

" She said to-day that she was the Lady of the Rosary."

" Did she say that many people were to go there from all parts?"

" She didn't say that anybody was to go."

" Did you see the signs in the sun?"

" I saw it going round."

" Did you see signs on the oak tree?"

" No."

" When was the Lady the most beautiful, this time or on other occasions?"

" She was the same."

" How long was her dress?"

" It fell below the middle of her legs."

" What colour was Our Lady's dress when she was near the sun?"

" The mantle was blue and the dress white."

" And Our Lord and St. Joseph and the Holy Child?"

" St. Joseph's was red and I think Our Lord and the Child wore red too."

" When did you ask Our Lady to make the people believe in her Apparitions?"

" I asked her several times. I think the first time I asked was in June."

" When did she tell you the secret?"

" I think it was the second time."

After this it was Jacinta's turn:

" Apart from Our Lady, who did you see to-day when you were in the Cova da Iria?"

" I saw St. Joseph and the Holy Child."

" Where did you see them?"

" I saw them near the sun."

" What did the Lady say?"

" She said that we were to say the Rosary every day and that the war would end to-day."

" To whom did she say this?"

" To Lucia and to me. Francisco didn't hear."

" Did you hear her say when our soldiers would come back?"

" No."

" What else did she say?"

" She said that a chapel was to be built in the Cova da Iria."

" Where did the Lady come from?"

" From the east."

" And where did she go when she disappeared?"

" She went to the east."

" Did she go away backwards facing the people?"

" No, she turned her back to the people."

" Did she say that she would come back to the Cova da Iria?"

" She said before that it was the last time she would come, and to-day, too, she said it was the last time."

" Did the Lady say anything else ? "

" She said to-day that we were to say the Rosary every day to Our Lady of the Rosary."

" Where did she say that people were to say the Rosary?"

" She did not say where."

" Did she say that they were to go to the church?"

" She never said that."

" Where do you like to say the Rosary best; here, at home, or in the Cova da Iria?"

" In the Cova da Iria."

" Why do you like to say it there?"

" I don't know."

" With what money did the Lady say the chapel was to be built?"

" She said a chapel was to be built, but I don't know about the money."

" Did you look at the sun?"

" Yes."

" Did you see the signs?"

" Yes."

" Did the Lady tell you to look at the sun?"

" No."

" Then how did you see the signs?"

" I turned my eyes to the side."

" Was the Holy Child on the right or the left of St. Joseph?"

" On the right."

" Was he standing or being carried?"

" He was standing."

" Did you see St. Joseph's right arm?"

" No."

" How tall was the Child? Did his head come up to St. Joseph's chest?"

" He didn't reach St. Joseph's waist."

" How old do you think the Child was?"

" The age of Deolinda Neves." (A child of about two years.)

Finally it was Francisco's turn:

" Did you see Our Lady this time?"

" Yes."

" What Lady was she?"

" She was the Lady of the Rosary."

" How was she dressed?"

" She was dressed in white with a Rosary in her hand."

" Did you see St. Joseph and the Holy Child?"

" Yes."

" Where did you see them?"

" By the sun."

" Was the child being carried by St. Joseph or was he standing? Was he big or little?"

" He was little."

" Was he the size of Deolinda Neves?"

" Yes, he was just her size."

" Did the Lady hold her hands?"

" She had them joined."

" Did you only see her on the oak tree or by the sun as well?"

" I saw her near the sun too."

" Which was the brighter, the sun or the face of the Lady?"

" The Lady's face was brighter; she was white."

" Did you hear what the Lady said?"

" I heard nothing that she said."

" Who told you the secret; was it the Lady?"

" No, it was Lucia."

" Will you tell it?"

" No."

" You are afraid of being beaten by Lucia if you tell it, aren't you?"

" No."

" Then why don't you tell it?   Is it a sin?"

" Perhaps it is a sin to tell the secret."

" Is the secret for the good of your soul, and Jacinta's and Lucia's soul?"

" Yes."

" Is it for the good of Fr. Ferreira's soul?"

" I don't know."

" Would the people be sad if they knew?"

" Yes."

" From which side did the Lady come?"

" From the east."

" And did she disappear in the same direction?"

" Yes, she went to the east."

" Did she go backwards?"

" She turned her back to us."

" Did she go slowly or quickly?"

" Slowly."

" Did she walk as we do?"

" She didn't walk. She just went without moving her feet."

" What part of the Lady disappeared first?"

" The head."

" Did you see her easily this time?"

" I saw her better than last month."

" When was she most beautiful, now or the other times?"

" As beautiful now as last month."

CHAPTER XXIX

EXHAUSTION

ON the 13th of October both Lucia and Jacinta affirmed that they heard from the lips of the Blessed Virgin the words: " The war will end to-day."

Such a statement on the part of the seers could create very serious objections to the veracity of the Apparitions and it was for this reason apparently that Dr. Formigão decided to go back to Aljustrel and subject the children to vet another severe inquest. He arrived on the 19th of October at 3 o'clock and stopped on the road where it passes the site of the Apparitions.

> In the Cova da Iria (runs Dr. Formigão's narrative) there were a few pious women saying the Rosary near the oak tree. The latter, reduced to a mere trunk a few inches high, was surrounded with branches of wild plants and flowers. The devotion of the pilgrims who wished to have a souvenir of the Virgin's pedestal had almost entirely annihilated it though everything else was in the same state as on the eve of the last Apparition. I then went to the house of the Marto family where I found the three seers undergoing an interrogation from the Rev. Laçerda, parish priest of Milagres, director of the weekly paper, *The Leiria Messenger,* and also chaplain to the Portuguese Expeditionary Force. Home on leave for a short time he wished to see the children of Aljustrel before going back to France. He was accompanied by another priest from Leiria and the parish priest of Fatima.

At this point Dr. Formigão made a bitter discovery. The children were in such a state of physical and moral exhaustion that they were quite unable to respond seriously to the questions which he had prepared.

> Lucia especially, (wrote Dr. Formigão), on account of the severe ordeal by interrogation which she had undergone, was utterly worn out and excessive fatigue prevented her replying with the care and attention which we desired. Her answers were at times almost mechanical and she was frequently unable to recall certain circumstances of the Apparitions which was not the case before 13th October. If the children are not spared the fatigue of these frequent and long inquiries, there is a serious risk to their health.[1]

[1] Fr. Laçerda regretfully recognised the same fact:
" Jacinta's mother did not receive me with open arms. At my request for permission to question her daughter she hesitated and only after I had told her that I wanted to tell the soldiers in France about the

It would, in fact, have been a prudent safeguard to have taken the seers away from Aljustrel to some place where they were not known because their parents had not enough firmness and authority to prevent even the least important visitor from plaguing them with questions at will.

Shocked as he was, Dr. Formigao nevertheless subjected the children to another detailed interrogation which in the interests of historical criticism we reproduce in full.

The following questions were put to Lucia:

" On the 13th of this month Our Lady said that the war would finish on that same day? What were the words she used?"

" She said: ' The war will end to-day. You can expect the soldiers very shortly '."

(Dr. Formigão here asked Lucia to specify which of two current Portuguese words for " soldiers " Our Lady had used and her form of address).

" But listen, Lucia, the war is still going on. The papers give news of battles after the 13th. How can you explain that if Our Lady said the war would end that day?"

"" I don't know; I only know that I heard her say that the war would end on that day."

" Some people declare that they heard you say that Our Lady had said that the war would end shortly. Is that true?"

" I said exactly what Our Lady had said."

" On the 27th of last month I came to your house to speak with you. Do you remember?"

" I remember seeing you here."

" Well, on that day you told me that Our Lady had said that on the 13th of October she would come with St. Joseph and the Holy Child and that *afterwards* the war would end, not necessarily on the 13th."

" I can't remember now exactly how she put it. She might have said that or perhaps I did not understand her properly."

" On the 13th did you tell the people to look at the sun?"

" I don't remember doing that."

Apparitions of Our Lady did she consent. Senhora Olimpia had every justification for her attitude. So many people had appeared in Aljustrel on the pretence of seeing the children that they no longer knew how to reply. Some people had been there to try and surprise the children into contradictions. The children's father took up the same attitude and reproached us, as priests, for doubting the children's word."

" Did you tell them to shut their umbrellas?"

" In the other months I did; I don't remember about this last time."

" Did you know when the sign in the sun was going to begin?"

" No."

" Did you look at it?"

" Yes, it looked like the moon."

" Why did you look at the sun?"

" I looked because the people said so."

" Did Our Lady say that she would pray to her Divine Son on behalf of the soldiers who had been killed in the war?"

" No, Father."

" Did she say that the people would be punished if they did not amend their lives?"

" I can't remember if she said that; I don't think so."

" On the 13th you did not have any doubts about what the Lady had said. Why have you these doubts now?"

" I remembered better on that day, it was nearer the time."

" What was it that you saw about a year ago? Your mother said that you and some other children had seen a form wrapped up and hidden in a cloth. Why did you tell me last month that it was nothing?"

Lucia could not reply clearly to this.

" Did you run away that time?"

" I think I did."

" On the 11th of this month you did not want to tell me that Our Lord would appear and give his blessing to the people. Was it because you thought I would laugh at you like other people had done and say it was impossible? Or was it because there were many other people there at the time and you did not want to say it in front of them? You know that Jacinta has told me everything?"

No coherent reply.

" When did Our Lady tell you that there would be these Apparitions on the 13th of October?"

" It was the day that she appeared at Valinhos or on another 13th. I can't remember well."

" Did you see Our Lord?"

" I saw the figure of a man; I think it was Our Lord."

" Where was this figure?"

" It was near the sun."

" Did you see it bless the people?"

" I didn't see it, but Our Lady said that Our Lord would come to give his blessing to the people."

" If the people knew the secret that Our Lady told you, would they be sad?"

" I think they would be about the same."

Francisco's interrogation:

" Did you see Our Lord bless the people on the 13th of this month?"

" No, I saw Our Lady."

" Did you see Our Lady of Dolours and Our Lady of Mount Carmel?"

" No. Our Lady was the one I saw down below (on the tree). She was dressed the same."

" Did you look at the sun?"

" Yes."

" Did you see St. Joseph and the Child Jesus?"

" Yes."

" Were they near to or far from the sun?"

" They were near."

" Which side of the sun was St. Joseph?"

" On the left side."

" And on which side was Our Lady?"

" On the right side."

" Where was the Child Jesus?"

" He was near St. Joseph."

" On which side?"

" I didn't notice which side."

" Was the Child big or small?"

" Small."

" When Our Lady was over the oak tree did you hear what she said to Lucia?"

" No."

" Did you hear the sound of her voice?"

" No."

" Did it seem as if she were not speaking?"

" Yes."

" Did you see her lips move?"

" No."

" Did you see her laugh?"

" No."

" Did you see the signs in the sun? What were they?"

" I looked and saw the sun going round; it looked like a wheel of fire."

" When did the signs begin, before or after Our Lady disappeared from the oak tree?"

" When Our Lady disappeared."

" Did you hear Lucia tell the people to look at the sun?"

" I did. She gave a shout when she told the people to look at the sun."

" Was it the Lady who told her to tell the people to look at the sun?"

" Yes, the Lady pointed towards the sun."

" When did she do this?"

" When she disappeared."

" Did the signs begin at once?"

" Yes."

" What colours did you see in the sun?"

" I saw very pretty colours: blue, yellow and others."

Jacinta was questioned while she and Dr. Formigão were walking from Aljustrel to Fatima.

" On the 13th of this month did you see Our Lord near the sun and Our Lady of Dolours and Mount Carmel?"

" No."

" But on the 11th of this month you said they would appear?"

" Yes, I did. Lucia saw the other Lady; I didn't."

" Did you see St. Joseph?"

" Yes. Lucia said that St. Joseph gave a blessing." (Jacinta said " *Peace*.")

" Did you look at the sun?"

" Yes."

" And what did you see?"

" I saw it red and green and other colours, and I saw it going round."

" Did you hear Lucia tell the people to look at the sun?"

" Yes. She told them in a very loud voice. The sun was already going round."

" Did the Lady tell her to tell the people?"

" The Lady said nothing about it."

" What did the Lady say this last time?"

" She said: ' I have come here to tell you that people must not offend Our Lord any more because he is very much offended and that if the people amend their lives the war will end and if not the world will end.' Lucia heard better than I did what the Lady said."

" Did she say that the war would end on that day or shortly?"

" Our Lady said that the war would end when she arrived in Heaven."

" But the war has not ended."

" But it will end, it will."

" When will it end?"

" I think it will end on Sunday."

*   *   *   *

The somewhat unsatisfactory interrogations of the 19th of October were thus concluded, and as can be seen the question of the end of the war is one of several contradictory or ambiguous statements. Did Our Lady really say that the war would end that day or did the children misunderstand her words, or, which is more likely, did the continuous questioning which was often prolonged into the night cause such excessive fatigue to the nervous systems of the children that they were unable to co-ordinate their ideas with precision and exactitude?[2]

At the official enquiry of 8th of July, 1924, which took place in the tranquil surroundings of the convent of Vilar, Lucia expressed herself as follows:

> I think that Our Lady added this: " People must be converted. The war will end to-day and the soldiers can be expected soon." My cousin Jacinta, however, told me afterwards at home that Our Lady had said this: " People must be converted. The war will end within a year." I was so preoccupied with all the petitions which people wanted me to lay before Our Lady that I could not give all my attention to her words.

Apart from this, we must also bear in mind that the actual date of the end of the war would not make the same impression on the mind of a child of ten years as on that of an adult. Again, among the many references to the declarations of the children on the 13th of October we find no allusion to the expression " the war will end to-day " but " shortly," as, for example, in the " Seculo " and in the other reports which we have at hand.

It is psychologically impossible that if anyone had heard such an expression used by the children after the miracle which had, in fact, swept away all doubt as to the veracity of the Apparitions, that such news would not have run like

---

[2] Dr. Formigao affirms that on the night of 18th-19th October Lucia did not sleep at home but stayed at the Marto house in order not to be submitted to insidious and useless questions until a very late hour.

wild fire up and down the country and caused an outburst of jubilation.

The first time that Lucia and Jacinta declared that the war would end that day was in the presence of Dr. Formigão at 7 o'clock in the evening, when they were already exhausted in body and mind and in no condition to reply with exactitude to the questions put to them.

Can we then discover among the different affirmations of the children the nearest approach to the exact truth? We think that it lies in the declaration of Jacinta on the 13th of October when she and Dr. Formigão were quietly walking along the road from Aljustrel to Fatima. When asked what Our Lady had said on the last occasion she replied: " I have come here to say that men must not offend Our Lord any more because He is already very much offended, and that if they amend their lives the war will end and if not the world will end."

This is the solution arrived at by Dr. Fischer, who has made a close and conscientious study of the facts, and it is one which we feel best resolves the difficulties which such contradictions raise.

Dr. Formigão returned once more to Aljustrel to question the children on the 2nd of November of that same year. Although not of capital importance, we reproduce it in order that the convincing candour of the three children may be thrown into relief. This quality was so marked in them that perhaps it is the best proof of the genuineness of the Apparitions. The latest interrogation also drew forth a few details previously lacking and are therefore of interest for this reason alone.

To Jacinta:

" Which side of the sun did the Child Jesus stand when you saw Him on the 13th of October?"

" He stood in the middle, at the right side of St. Joseph; Our Lady was on the right side of the sun."

" Was the Lady you saw near the sun different from the one you saw on the oak tree?"

" The Lady I saw near the sun had a white dress and a blue mantle. The one I saw on the oak tree had a white dress and mantle."

" What colour were the feet of the Lady who appeared on the oak tree?"

" They were white; I think she wore stockings."

" What colour was St. Joseph's dress and the Child's?"

" St. Joseph's was red and I think the Child's was red, too."

" When did the Lady reveal the secret?"

" I think it was in July."

" What did the Lady say the first time she appeared in May?"

" Lucia asked what she wanted and she said we were to go there every month until the last month, when she would say what she wanted."

" Did Lucia ask anything else?"

" She asked if she would go to Heaven and the Lady said yes. Then she asked if I would go to Heaven too and she said yes. Then she asked if Francisco would go and she said yes, but that he would have to say many Rosaries."

" Did the Lady say anything else?"

" I don't remember anything else."

" What did the Lady say the second time, in June?"

" Lucia said: 'What do you want?' and the Lady replied: 'I want you to learn to read '."

" Did Lucia ask anything else?"

" She asked about the sick people and sinners. The Lady said that she would make some better and convert them, but not others."

" Did the Lady say anything else?"

" On that day she didn't say anything else."

" What did the Lady say in August?"

" In August we didn't go to the Cova da Iria. You mean what did the Lady say at Valinhos? Lucia asked her if she was to bring Manuel and the Lady said she could bring everybody."

" What else?"

" She said that if they had not taken us to Ourem, St. Joseph with the Holy Child would come to give peace to the world. And Our Lady of the Rosary with two angels, one on each side."

" What else?"

" She said we were to make two 'andors' and to take them to the *festa* of the Rosary, I and Lucia with two girls dressed in white; and that Francisco and two other boys were to take the other."

" Anything else?"

" I can't remember."

" What did the Lady say in October?"

" Lucia said: 'What do you want?' and she replied: ' Do

not offend Our Lord any more because he is very much offended.' She said that He would pardon our sins if we wanted to go to Heaven. She said also that we must say the Rosary and that we could expect our soldiers back very soon and the war would end that day. She said that we were to build a chapel and I don't know if she said ' to the Lady of the Rosary ' or just that she herself was the Lady of the Rosary."

Lucia's interrogation:

" Did the Lady wear stockings? Are you sure of this?"

" I think they were stockings, but they might not have been."

" You said once that the Lady wore white stockings. Were they stockings or were they feet?"

" If they were stockings, then they were white, but I am not sure if they were stockings or her feet."

" Was the dress always the same length?"

" The last time it seemed longer."

" You have never told the secret nor even said that the people would be sad if they knew. Francisco and Jacinta said they would be sad. If you cannot say this how can they say it?"

" I don't know if they ought to say that the people would be sad. Our Lady said that we were not to tell anybody anything, so I cannot say anything."

Francisco's interrogation:

" Which side did the Child Jesus stand when you saw Him near the sun?"

" He stood nearer the sun, on its left side, but on the right of St. Joseph."

" Was the Lady you saw near the sun different from the one over the oak tree?"

" The Lady I saw near the sun looked the same as the one I saw below."

" Did you see Our Lord bless the people?"

" I didn't see Our Lord."

CHAPTER XXX

BLASPHEMY

AT first sight it would seem that the events of 13th October, unanimously considered miraculous, would have silenced the enemies of the supernatural in general, and of Fatima in particular, once and for all. One would have expected a prudent reserve on their part, at least during the primitive period when the enthusiasm of the people for Fatima was at its peak. Such, however. was not the case. In an access of fury they planned a coup some ten days later which, by holding Catholic devotion and faith up to ridicule, was to throw new discredit on religious institutions. This time it was the Masonic Lodge of Santarem which took the initiative.

With the tree, and the devotional objects which the faithful placed at its feet, they planned to hold an exhibition in the capital of the district and afterwards organise a procession along the principal roads of the neighbourhood.

This plan, well conceived, was carried out to perfection.

During the night of October 23rd-24th—as the *Diario de Noticias* informs—some individuals from Santarem (whose names are given) joined by others from Vila Nova de Ourem went to the Cova da Iria.

> With an axe (runs the newspaper report) they cut the tree[1] under which the three shepherd children stood during the famous phenomenon of the 13th of this month, so largely referred to in the Press. They took away the tree together with a table on which a modest altar had been arranged and on which a religious image (of Our Lady) had been placed. They also took a wooden arch, two tin lanterns and two crosses, one made of wood and the other of bamboo cane wrapped in tissue paper.

---

[1] " On this occasion," says Maria da Capela, " they took the lanterns, the table and the arch for their parody in Santarem. They thought they had taken the tree but they made a mistake and took another."

Lucia also refers to the event: " Meanwhile the Government did not leave things where they stood. In the place of the Apparitions people had put an arch and lanterns which were kept alight. One night some men came in a motor car to tear down the arch and to cut the tree where the Apparitions had taken place. In the morning the news spread rapidly and I ran to see if it was true. Imagine my joy when I saw that those wretched men had made a mistake and instead of taking the real tree (which was by then nothing but a small trunk) they had cut one of the saplings nearby. I asked Our Lady to forgive them and I prayed for their conversion."

These stolen objects were placed on exhibition (with an entrance fee) in a house near the Seminary of Santarem. The result, however, was far from satisfactory in spite of the fact that the profits were to be devoted to a local charity. The money was handed over to the Director of the Misericordia who very creditably refused to accept the proceeds of such a disgraceful proceeding. On the same night the procession was held.

> It was headed by two drums (relates the " Seculo "), while behind came the famous tree on which Our Lady had appeared. Next, the wooden arch with the lanterns alight, the table and other objects which the faithful had placed on the improvised altar. To the sound of blasphemous litanies the procession passed through the principal streets of the city, returning to the Sá da Bandeira Square where it dispersed.

Many of the demonstrators reunited, however, in a nearby street, and it was at that moment that a woman poured a bucket of water out of a window which found its target and also a policeman. It was only after some time that a picket of police dispersed the gathering.

> The affair was a disgrace (concludes the journalist). How is it possible that the authorities tolerate such a thing while at the same time they refuse permission for the processions of the Church to which nearly the whole population belongs and whose ceremonies in no way offend the convictions of others?

The general reaction was one of revulsion and disgust not only on the part of Catholics but also of any who retained some sentiments of decency and respect. From all sides protests poured in, and we transcribe one of the most notable, from Dr. Almeida Ribeiro to the Minister of the Interior:

> As believers, and sons of a nation which has been made great by the faith of its warriors and the heroism of its saints; as citizens of a city which has been in the forefront of civilisation and culture we strongly and earnestly protest against the scandalous procession tolerated by the public authorities, which, on the night of the 24th of this month passed through the streets of Santarem.
>
> In this procession, which was worthy only of savages, the objects stolen from a place where people gather with the most pacific of intentions, were shamelessly exhibited. It took place in the presence of the whole population which, however, was disgusted at this degrading action on the part of a few people who can only be called pustules of society. The Cross of Our Redeemer . . . and the image of the Virgin who has presided

over our destinies in all periods of our history, were held up
to sacrilege and profanation.

The Litany of Our Lady, whose name is the strength and
comfort of our soldiers on the field of battle, was drunkenly
intoned by the organisers of this satanic orgy.

There has not been in living memory such a repugnant attack
on the faith of our people, directed against the traditions and
dignity of a nation which prides itself on its respect for the
beliefs of others.

It is impossible for us not to raise our voices against such
flagrant provocation, and to repudiate this horrible parody with
the greatest energy. Impossible not to make public our bitterness of heart in face of such an attack on the faith of our
fathers and our own; an attack also on the honour of this
city on the part of a few miserable youths.

If we did not publish our disclaimer we should be considered
at home and abroad as the most cowardly and unworthy of
Portuguese.

We, therefore, proclaim blessed the Cross of Christ which
in other days rode the seas with our caravels when they went
forth to conquer new worlds for the Faith and for civilisation.

We also proclaim blessed the great Protectress of Portugal
who, through the troubles and trials of our history has watched
with maternal solicitude over our destiny. May God forgive
these impious men, destitute of all decent feeling, who
blaspheme her adorable name and may He withhold the
punishment which would justly fall on a nation which consented to such crimes.

Santarem, 28th October, 1917.

Signed: " A Group of Catholics."

In their almost satanic anxiety to demolish Fatima as
rapidly as possible, and to finish once and for all with so-
called " Jesuitical inventions ", these unfortunates contributed in no small manner to the unexpected and almost
sensational increase of faith in the miracle and to the re-
birth of religion in the *Terra de Santa Maria.*

CHAPTER XXXI

FIASCO

ANOTHER personage at this point takes the stage: Senhor
José Vale, editor of the paper *O Mundo.* In politics an
anarchist and in religion an atheist, he was a frequenter of
taverns, and when in his cups wielded a doughty pen.

Now this man conceived a magnificent idea for putting
an end to the fantasies of Fatima. He distributed in Torres

Novas, Vila Nova de Ourem and neighbouring districts, a series of pamphlets filled with invective against the supposed Apparitions, and the priests and the Jesuits who were the customary authors of all ill. Finally, all liberal-minded people were invited to assemble on the following Sunday outside the church of Fatima at the close of the parish Mass, in order to unmask the comedy of Fatima and its players.

This news naturally spread like wildfire through the whole district, and was a source of serious preoccupation to the parish priest who, in order to avoid disorders, resolved to celebrate Mass on that Sunday in the Chapel of Our Lady of Ortiga. Fearing also that the seers might be the object of malicious action he sought to arrange for their departure from Aljustrel. Things could not have turned out more propitiously, for it happened at that time that a young nobleman named Dom Pedro Caupers was staying at an ancient *quinta* some six kilometres from Fatima, and it was decided without further delay to send the children there with some members of their families. We will let Ti Marto tell the story in his own graphic style:

An hour before sunrise we set off for the Quinta, fleeing from persecution like St. Joseph and the Holy Family. We hurried along but when we arrived the door of the chapel was already chock-full of people. Lucia and Jacinta had their shawls over their arms and Francisco carried his cap in his hand. We asked if Mass had begun and were told that it was already the Offertory. At this moment a servant of the house arrived and took us into the chapel by way of the house which led into a choir where the whole family were assembled. We heard Mass right by the altar. When Mass was over Dom Pedro came up and said to Lucia: " Say the Rosary where you are." She looked as if she would refuse but in the end she began to pray. When she had told all the beads Dom Pedro said to her: " Lucia, when you say the Rosary you always say an Ave Maria too much in each decade. . . !" I said to him: " You see, Dom Pedro, the extra Ave Maria belongs to the Pater Noster and this makes eleven Aves to each mystery. I always do that when I pray alone; the Pater Noster isn't complete without an Ave after it—so I was always taught."

When we had had something to eat the servants showed us over the house, room by room. Such huge rooms, my word! Lucia amused us all very much because each time she went into one she said astonished: " Oh, what a barrack!" And the servants kept on saying: " Lucia, do you want to see another barrack?" And the " barracks " went on until we had seen the whole house!

Then Dom Pedro sent for three lambs and took the children's photographs with the lambs on their shoulders. After that we had something more to eat and then Dom Pedro said to me: " Oh, Senhor Marto, will you stay here with Francisco because I have to go to Vargos and I have only room in the car for the two little ones." So they went to the *quinta* on the way to Torres Novas while Francisco and I went for a long walk round the property. The others were away a long time but they came back that day. We went home late and it was night when we arrived.

What had been happening meanwhile in Fatima?

Certain that everything would turn out in the best possible way, José Vale, the Mayor of Ourem, and other friends, as well as some guards, kept their appointment at the appointed hour. What, however, was their astonishment at finding, not the vast applauding multitude of their imagination, but only Francisco da Silva, *regedor* of the parish and an influential democrat of the district. The fiasco could not be more complete! What then was to be done? An ignominious withdrawal?

It was decided at last to go to the Cova da Iria on a forced pilgrimage, and here at least there was no lack of an audience.

A man from Lomba da Egua had even prepared a magnificent reception. Assembling a variety of donkeys he tied them to the trees and on the arrival of the " protest meeting " from Fatima, placed under the nose of each a bowl of a certain liquid which caused him to bray with exceeding loudness to the great embarrassment of the visitors. Another pleasant surprise awaited them on their arrival at the oak tree, now little more than root. Fodder, the customary food of beasts, had been placed there for their reception!

We did it to annoy them (says Maria da Capela) and they knew it. When I arrived at 11.30 with two of my neighbours we hid near the place where the Chapel of Penance was later built. Higher up three men climbed on an oak tree. Then someone began to preach against religion and every time he said something particularly bad we answered: " Blessed be Jesus and Mary." A lad from Quinta da Cardiga who was perched up in a tree on the other side also said in a loud voice: " Blessed be Jesus and Mary," and made a salute with his hat. They were so furious that they sent two guards down to us but we ran away through the trees and they lost sight of us.

Then the lads and men who had been to Mass at the Ortiga chapel arrived and, seeing what was happening in the Cova da Iria, began to shout out to the speakers and the guards:

"Fools! beasts! etc., etc." And they shouted back: "Country bumpkins, fools, too!" The guards tried again to catch them but not one did they get! We all ran away wherever we could jeering and laughing at them as hard as we could. After a bit they went off in the direction of Fatima village and we never saw or heard anything of them again!

CHAPTER XXXII

RESURGENCE

THE sacrilegious theft and the parody in Santarem did not, however, in any way react against Fatima. Nor did the numerous pamphlets* which were widely distributed, an example of which we give in an appendix and which show clearly how matters stood.

Once more the Portuguese found the principle of their salvation in the Blessed Virgin, through her latest Apparition on their *serras*. "Europe's garden by the sea" has throughout her history, through all her troubles and vicissitudes, enjoyed the special love and protection of the Mother of God who has now placed her tabernacle in the very heart of this privileged nation.

Her sons answered the call and from that memorable 13th day of October began to flow in ever-increasing numbers towards the Serras of Aire. There, where the Mother of God pours out her most precious graces, began that gradual transformation of family and social life which will before long restore the Portuguese nation to its ancient splendour.

As usual the simple people of the countryside were the first to answer the Blessed Virgin's call. *Evangelizare pauperibus misit me*, Our Lord has said, and the poor were the first beneficiaries of His Mother's largesse. Then came the others until the whole of Portugal went on pilgrimage to the Cova da Iria.

> After the day on which the sun danced (says Maria da Capela) there was an endless procession of people here, especially on Sunday afternoons and on the 13th of each month. There were people from hereabouts and people from other parts. The men came with their sticks and a bundle on their shoulders, and the women carried their children and there were even old people with very little strength. They all knelt near the tree where Our Lady had appeared and no one seemed weary or tired. Here nothing was sold, not a cup of water or wine—nothing! Oh, what good times those were for penance! We often wept with emotion.

* Appendix II.

It was in fact with tears running down her cheeks that Senhora Carreira told us about those first pilgrimages of which she holds such happy memories:

> Here there were many tears and prayers for Our Lady, and when there were plenty of people we sang our favourite hymns. What wonderful times those were! People did so much penance and all with a smile. I think if I had died in those times Our Lady would have taken me straight to Heaven. Now it's over and I can't help longing for those days. . . !

> Everyone went home happy. They had come to ask Our Lady for miracles and she always heard their prayers. In those days I can't remember anyone saying that Our Lady had refused a miracle. All who came, came with faith or found it here. One day a man who had come a long way was soaked with the rain. I went to him and asked him if he felt any ill effects. " No," he answered, " I am quite all right and have never passed such a happy night as this. I have come eleven leagues and yet I don't feel at all tired. I am so happy in this place." Apart from the rain it was very cold, being winter, and the man had passed the whole night in the open air because in those days there was no shelter here.

> Once there arrived a group of gentlemen and ladies, with Padre dos Reis do Montelo, who is now parish priest of St. Sebastian in Lisbon. I found out afterwards that they had been to a christening and to a dinner and had come here out of curiosity but without believing anything. They began to pray round the box where the alms are collected and which had lighted candles on it. Fr. Reis took off his hat and began to answer our Rosary. When it was finished I heard someone —I think it was he—say: " Even if Rome never approves this I shall always believe that something extraordinary happened here."[1]

Twenty-five years later the Vicar of Christ was heard in that same place speaking to the world in the Portuguese tongue and consecrating the human race to the Immaculate Heart of Mary in accordance with the desire expressed by the Mother of God.

---

[1] Dona Maria de Aguiar writes to us as follows:

" On 8th December, 1917, a great solemnity took place in the Quinta de Nossa Senhora da Piedade (near V.N. de Ourem), which belongs to Dona Rita de Faria. There was sung Mass in honour of the Immaculate Conception and the preacher was Fr. Oliveira Reis, the present parish priest of St. Sebastian in Lisbon, but at that time Vicar of Vara near Torres Novas. After the *festa*, Fr. Reis, a Madam Amado and myself were taken to Fatima in a coupé drawn by a pair of powerful mules belonging to Dona Maria Pena from a neighbouring *quinta*.

It was a cold winter afternoon and a fine rain was falling when we arrived at the Cova da Iria and came upon a spectacle which moved us profoundly. Near a mast which marked the place where Our Lady appeared, and the box for alms, some men and women were kneeling

How little did those humble folk dream, as they prayed so devotedly by the broken trunk of a tree, that Rome itself would recognise in such a solemn manner the vision of their shepherd children!

CHAPTER XXXIII

THE CHAPEL

THE chapel which Our Lady had asked for had not yet been started and this fact worried Lucia and her cousins, as well as the Carreiras.

There had been no lack of alms; the people left food and coins of every value as well as objects in gold and silver, but other obstacles stood in the way of the realisation of the project. In the first place there was the vigilant opposition of the civil authorities of Vila Nova de Ourem, and secondly the indifference if not hostility of the parish priest. A year and a half passed, therefore, before the realisation of Our Lady's wishes.

As we know, Maria Carreira was the custodian of the almsbox, and every day she collected the money in her little bag and sold the articles of food and other objects which the clients of Our Lady left there in fulfilment of their promises. After a time there was a considerable sum of money but no sign of a chapel and naturally evil tongues began to murmur as is always the way in our poor world. It was said that the Carreiras of Moita had known how to use their opportunity.

> My daughters (says Maria da Capela) went out to work by the day in the fields and those who worked with them used to taunt them if they had new dresses or shoes. The people began to murmur and so I went to the priest and asked him to take charge of the money because I was tired of the criticism.

in fervent prayer. One of them was praying in a loud voice, imploring the protection of Our Lady for our unhappy country. So irresistible was it that we fell on our knees and joined the prayer. It seemed inspired. . . .

It must have been on this occasion that Maria da Capela heard the vicar of Torres Novas affirm that, even if Rome never approved Fatima, he on the contrary would continue to believe in it.

On the way back to the Quinta do Caneiro we heard that there had been a revolution in Lisbon and that communications were interrupted and train lines cut. It was on this afternoon of such fervent prayers to Our Lady that the victory of Sidonio Pais occurred."

Then Fr. Ferreira took me to his office and showed me a letter from the Cardinal Patriarch which said that the money was to be kept carefully by some reliable person (but not the children's parents) until further notice. This time I went home in a happier state of mind.

But the persecutions went on and this upset me a great deal. One day I heard a sermon by the parish priest of Santa Catherina on All Souls' Day. He said from the pulpit that people who looked after the money for *festas* were always criticised and that there were always evil tongues ready to wag. But we must suffer such persecutions patiently for His sake as He suffered for us. And from that time I determined to bear my trouble.

It was not long, however, before another worry loomed up. A man from the Mayor—the one we called the Tinker—came to the house with a notice for my husband to appear at the tribunal. We and the neighbours thought that it would be about the money:

" Be careful, Ti Manuel," they said to my husband. " Think out what you're going to say!"

" I needn't do that!" said he.

Although we didn't know for certain we were nearly sure that it would be about the money and when he arrived at the town hall the people in the office asked him:

" What do you want?"

" The Mayor sent for me and I have come to find out what he wants."

" Where do you come from?"

" From Moita, near Fatima."

" Ah, yes," put in the Mayor, who was sitting there, too, " Then you are Senhor Carreira?" My husband replied that he was.

" Then you live near the Cova da Iria?"

" Yes, sir."

" Do you go there often?"

" I have been there."

" What do you do there?"

" I do what the others do."

" Do you see Our Lady, too?"

" No, sir, I haven't seen her up to now."

" Then what do you do there?"

" I go with the other people."

" What do they say?"

" I don't know. Some say one thing, some another."

" There must be plenty of money left there?"

" I don't know, sir."

" Don't you see it, then? Don't you know anything about it?"

" I know nothing about it, sir."

" Who keeps this money?"

" I don't know, sir."

" You seem to be a very ignorant man!"

" That I am, sir!"

Behind the Mayor was Senhor Julio Lopes, from the tribunal,

and he nodded to my husband approving the way he was talking and telling him to go on. My Manuel kept on pretending
he knew nothing and returned home very pleased at having got
the better of the Mayor. But our troubles didn't end here.

One day—it was a Sunday—my eldest son came back from
Mass and said to me:

" Mother, listen; I have just been talking to João Nogueira
and he told me that the *regedor* intended to come here to see
father again about that money. I don't know if he was joking,
but I don't think so because he spoke seriously. You had
better think out what you're going to say when he comes."

" I shall tell him it was stolen," I said promptly.

" Then you should have said something about it before or
he will know you're lying."

" Then I shall go and make a complaint now," I said.

At this moment José Alves' wife came along and I pretended
to be very upset. When she asked me what was the matter I
said:

" They've stolen Our Lady's money. . . ."

" *Stolen* it? But didn't you keep it safely somewhere?"

" No, I kept it in a tin under a stone in the garden." The
woman seemed surprised but she believed me:

" Well, it serves you right for being such a fool."

" Yes," I said, with my hands in front of my face.

Shortly afterwards Antonio Joaquim's wife came along and
I played the same game with her, pretending to be upset and
telling her the story of the tin under the stone.

" You were asking for it, weren't you!" she said. (The next
door family were known not to be very reliable.) And she
went away.

This happened in the morning and by nightfall everyone in
Moita knew that Our Lady's money had been stolen. I felt my
ears burning! Some days later Senhor Alves' wife came back
and said:

" You were lying, weren't you! The money wasn't stolen.
I could see you were only pretending to be upset."

Then I told her everything. Sometimes one has to lie!

Some time passed and when I saw that there was no more
danger from the authorities in Ourem I went to the priest and
asked for his permission to begin building the chapel. I told
him that we intended to put the statue of Our Lady in it and
the gifts which the people brought which were often spoiled
by the rain as things were at present. Fr. Ferreira answered
as if he didn't care one way or the other and finally said that
he didn't want to have anything to do with it.

" If we build it with the money we have shall we be doing
anything wrong?"

" I don't think so," he replied.

He spoke like this because he didn't want it to be said later
that he had ordered the chapel to be built. He had orders
from the Cardinal Patriarch not to take any part in the affair.
For myself, I had heard enough and I went home happy. I
told everything to my Manuel and he went and spoke to Lucia's
father because he was the owner of the land.

Senhora Abobora gave his permission and said we could make it any size we liked. All the same he was very upset and with good reason. The people spoiled everything so that nothing would grow there. They spoilt the trees cutting branches—big branches, not twigs—right and left until there was nothing left growing near the tree of the Apparitions. When he saw people going by with branches in their hands he knew that they had come from his property. When the little tree disappeared they began to attack the big ones and if my Manuel had not protected them with thorn bushes the big trees in the Cova would not be there now.

The chapel took more than a month to build and everyone wanted to have a finger in the pie. Some wanted it one way, some another. Each one had his own idea, the more so because no priest would have anything to do with it. It became so difficult that I went and spoke to the mason, who was a man from Santa Catherina, a very good religious man and clever at his work.

"Don't worry about it, woman," he said to me. "If this is God's work there's bound to be trouble at the beginning."

It was a dear little chapel when it was finished but it was not much more than a depository because it had nothing inside. No priest would come and bless it and it was only much later that this was done by Dr. Marques dos Santos.[1] It had a little covered balcony in front, very tiny—with six people it was full. It was later enlarged to the size it is to-day.

The arrival of the image was delayed yet another eight or ten months. It was on 13th May, 1920 (hidden in a cart among farm tools) that the famous statue came to occupy its niche in the chapel of the Apparitions. At Fatima there was a delay, and it remained there some time, being blessed in the interval by the parish priest. When the box was opened people rushed forward to kiss the statue which seemed so perfectly to reproduce the serious and beautiful vision described by the children. A girl of thirteen leaned over it with tears running down her cheeks. It was Lucia. The statue before her revived poignant memories both of the events which it symbolised and of her companions in them, now happily in possession of the Reality.

---

[1] At present Vicar-General of the Diocese of Leiria.

CHAPTER XXXIV

INCREASE OF GRACE

WITH the story of Fatima hastening to its close, let us for a moment retrace our steps to that cold November afternoon in 1917 when Dr. Formigão carried out his interrogation of the children under such disheartening conditions.

We can easily realise that the former peace and quiet of these simple families of Aljustrel had departed never to return. The children were questioned for the thousandth time and more by people of all classes and conditions, about the Apparitions, about the secret, about all that could satisfy, if not the pious feelings, at least the curiosity of those who at all costs wished to see and speak with the mortal eyes and lips that had communicated with the Mother of God.

All who did so returned with excellent impressions. It was sufficient to see the children once in order to believe in them implicitly. Candid smiles and the guileless souls which shone from eyes which had confessedly beheld the sublimest work of God's hands, their gestures and their words, all proclaimed the impossibility of falsehood, its utter incompatibility with such beings. The toughest sceptics melted before their candour. Their replies were always the same. Francisco continued to affirm that he had only seen, never heard the Lady and that her light had blinded his eyes. Lucia alone had held conversation with her. Jacinta knew rather more, but ingenuously confessed that at times she had difficulty in hearing the Lady's words; that many things had escaped her memory and that she must ask her cousin if people wanted to know the details of what happened. It was, therefore, to Lucia that the majority of people went to satisfy their curiosity, and she was obliged to repeat the same things and the same words over and over again.

It was only when someone attempted to unveil the secret that the two girls retired into absolute silence, even to the point of rudeness. With ordinary people this did not trouble them, but in the case of priests their delicate consciences were perturbed as to the lawfulness or otherwise of refusing the requests of ministers of Christ.

It was at this moment that Divine Providence guided into

their path a priest who gained their absolute confidence. He was Father Faustino Ferreira, vicar of Olival.

From his first encounter with them, this wise and prudent priest recognised that he was in the presence of privileged beings, and with admirable tact sought to guide their souls —already so sensitive to the supernatural—into yet higher paths of grace. He let no occasion pass by, and every time that he passed through Fatima he called at Aljustrel and by other strategems managed to see as much as possible of the children.

Father Faustino in the first place put their consciences at rest with regard to the secret and their reluctant refusal to reveal it to priests. But where his influence was most fruitful was in the admirable manner in which he taught them to try to please Our Lord in everything, and above all to make a constant offering of all small sacrifices.

" If you specially want to eat something," he told them, " eat something else instead and offer the sacrifice to God. If you want to play, offer that too; and if you are obliged to answer questions, then that is God's will and you can offer Him yet another sacrifice."

This language was, of course, perfectly understood by the children, and Father Faustino Ferreira was in fact Lucia's first Spiritual Director whom she keeps in most holy and grateful remembrance. This good priest, now in Heaven, must contemplate his work with great satisfaction and smile perhaps at the excessive prudence of his sometime colleagues!

However, the true Spiritual Director of the children was doubtless the Blessed Virgin in person. She herself supervised the master work which she had taken in hand and carried it to a successful conclusion. From her powerful hands came three angels clothed in flesh—angels and authentic heroes. The raw material was of an admirable plasticity and of the artist, what can we say? In her school the three little village children were in a short time to take giant steps on the road to perfection. In them were to be verified to the letter those words of St. Grignion de Montfort: " In the school of the Blessed Virgin the soul progresses further in a week than in a year elsewhere." The teaching of the Mother of God is unique. In two years she raised Jacinta and her brother Francisco to consummate heights of Christian sanctity. The portrait of her cousin, traced by the sure hand of Lucia, reveals much.

Jacinta was always serious, modest and kind, and seemed to carry the presence of God into all her actions in a manner more proper to people of advanced age and virtue. After the Apparitions I never saw her drawn by any childish enthusiasm for frills and fancies. If children were not attracted to her as they were to me it was perhaps because she did not know so many songs and stories or perhaps because she was so serious for her age. If in her presence a child, or even a grown-up, did or said anything unseemly, she would say: " Don't do that because it offends God and He is so much offended."

Identical impressions were made on Dr. Formigão, Dr. Carlos Mendes,* Baron Alvaiázere, in fact on everyone who had the happiness of knowing her. Unfortunately for reasons of space we are unable to quote at length from their written testimonies.

As for Francisco we will limit ourselves to the salient features of his personality.

One day two ladies came to see him and began to question him about the career which he had in view.

" Do you want to be a carpenter?"

" No, madam."

" A soldier?"

" No, madam."

" Surely you would like to be a doctor?"

" No, not that either."

" Then I know what you would like to be . . . a priest! Then you could say Mass and preach. . . ."

" No, madam, I don't want to be a priest either."

" Well, then, what *do* you want to be?"

" I don't want to be anything. I want to die and go to Heaven. . . ."

Ti Marto, who was present on this occasion, called it a " real proof ".

Another episode illustrating the same trait in his character occurred one day when the children were pasturing their sheep about the time of the Apparitions. In order to prevent the flocks from eating certain young crops the children divided, the girls going one side and Francisco, who showed a preference for solitude, choosing the fringe of the wood.

Lucia who was always careful of the younger ones, told Jacinta at a certain moment to go and see if her brother was all right as he had been such a long time alone. Jacinta called several times, but there was no reply from Francisco and finally, worried as to his whereabouts. she hurried back

* Appendix I.

to her cousin and told her that she thought her brother was lost. Lucia immediately went in search of the little boy and found him prostrate on the ground behind a stone wall. Approaching him, she touched his shoulder, then shook him and said in a loud voice:

"What are you doing?"

As if dragging himself from a long sleep the boy replied: :

"I began to say the prayer of the angel and then . . . I started thinking."

"Didn't you hear Jacinta call?"

"No, I didn't hear anything."

The desire of Heaven and the contemplation of Divine things had had their effect on the soul of Francisco.

One afternoon the three inseparables took their sheep to the slopes on the other side of Fatima. When they had arrived at the prearranged feeding ground Francisco withdrew to a solitary place. Time passed and the little boy did not return. At the meal time Jacinta discovered him praying in secret behind a rock.

"Come," she called, "come and have your lunch."

"No, I don't want to. You have yours and call me when you say the Rosary."

Respecting the desires of this small ascetic they rather sadly ate their meal without him and later went to call him for the Rosary. Then Lucia asked:

"What were you doing all that time?"

"I was thinking of God Who is so sad because of all the sins. If only I could comfort Him!"

One thought dominated the boy's mind: "Jesus is sad and I want to console Him with prayer and penance."

"I loved seeing the angel," he said, "and I loved seeing Our Lady even better, but what I liked best of all was seeing Our Lord in that light which Our Lady put into our hearts. I love God so much, but He is so sad because of all the sins. We mustn't commit even the tiniest sin!"

His desire for Heaven was not so much for his own consolation as for that of his God:

"Soon Jesus will come and take me to Heaven with Him and then I shall always be able to comfort Him. . . ."

We could relate many similar incidents in the paths of grace which the children travelled hand in hand with their heavenly teacher.

We already know what a profound impression the vision

of hell had made on their souls: " We must make many sacrifices and pray very much for sinners," said the youngest repeatedly, " so that they do not go into that prison of fire. . . ."

It is hardly surprising therefore, in face of such extraordinary fervour, that the Blessed Virgin should manifest herself again to the children.

From the official testimony of the parish priest, completed in August, 1918, and handed to the ecclesiastical authorities on 28th April, 1919, we know that Our Lady appeared to Jacinta at least three times during the short space of time between October, 1917, and August, 1918. The visions took place in various places, one of them in the presence of Senhora Olimpia who confirmed it in the presence of the parish priest and also to us.

During this same period, more precisely between May and June, 1918, Jacinta must have made her First Communion.   It is a point on which the Martos are explicit, and it seems to us that their affirmations are worthy of confidence.   The late Father Ferreira, parish priest of Fatima, was of the same opinion.   In the preceding year, at the peak period of the Apparitions, Jacinta and Francisco made their first confessions.   With regard to this we quote Ti Marto:

> About that time, it must have been after the second Apparition, I took the two of them to the church to make their confessions.   I went with them to the sacristy and said to Fr. Ferreira:
> " Father, here are my two children; they want to go to confession.   Your Reverence can ask them any question you like.   (I confess that I put a little malice into those words!)
> Then the priest replied:
> " These things (the Apparitions) do not belong to confession, my friend!"
> " That's true," I said, " and if they don't belong I needn't bring them here again."
> But the children made their confession, though Fr. Ferreira thought they should wait another year for Holy Communion.
> The next year, in May, they went back to be examined in the Catechism.
> Jacinta answered well but Francisco got muddled somewhere in the Creed—I can't remember where—and so in the end Jacinta was allowed to make her Communion while Francisco could not.   He went home in tears, but there was nothing to be done!

We can only imagine with what fervour Jacinta must

have received Our Lord for the first time, prepared as she was for that reception by His own Mother. Would not her heart have been, as was St. Gertrude's, another paradise?

CHAPTER XXXV

THE FLOWERING OF GRACE

WE already know the heroic mortification which the children imposed upon themselves after the first Apparition —sacrifices which, in their consuming desire to save sinners, they were not to relax until their deaths.

Any sacrifice seemed to them but a little thing. Penances which seem to us excessive if not imprudent, such as the wearing of a tight-knotted cord round the waist, were to them insignificant and of little account. Our Lady herself in the September Apparition modified this ardour in suffering and told them explicitly to take off the cord before sleep.

The heroic virtue of the three children, although hidden, attracted the simple people like a magnet and these confided their necessities to them and implored their intercession. It is not surprising that even in this life their prayers were heard and miracles performed through their sacrifices.

In Fatima, the school is not far from the church and the children, on entering and leaving their classes, would use the occasion for a visit to the Blessed Sacrament, sometimes passing long hours before the Tabernacle. Jacinta and Francisco especially, with their foreknowledge of imminent death, considered themselves exempt from lessons and went more often to the church to talk with " hidden Jesus ". But even there the people did not leave them in peace and swarmed around with their requests and petitions which the children were begged to place before the Virgin Mother.

" They seem to guess where we are." complained Jacinta, " and they won't let us talk to Jesus!"

It was not only in church that this happened.

We were met one day (says Lucia) by a poor woman, who knelt down weeping before Jacinta, imploring her to obtain from Our Lady the cure of a terrible disease from which she suffered. Jacinta, seeing the woman kneeling before her in such a manner, was much troubled and tried to lift her up by the hands. Unable to do this, she knelt down, too, and prayed three Hail Marys with her. Afterwards she told her to get up, saying that Our Lady would cure her, and she never ceased to pray daily for the woman until the latter returned to thank Our Lady for her cure.

On another occasion a soldier appeared, crying like a child. He had received orders to leave for the front, leaving a sick wife and three small children behind. He implored the cure of his wife or the cancellation of the order. Jacinta told him to say the Rosary, and added that Our Lady was so good that she would certainly grant him the favour he required. She never forgot her soldier, and at the end of the Rosary always added a Hail Mary for him. Some months later he appeared again with his wife and children to thank Our Lady for two graces conceded. On account of a fever which developed on the eve of departure he had been exempted from military service, and his wife declared that she herself had been cured by a miracle of Our Lady.

Lucia in her memoirs refers to another extraordinary happening, not unknown in the annals of sanctity. She says:

> One of my aunts (Victoria), who lived in Fatima, had a son who was a real prodigal. I don't know why but he had some time before abandoned his father's house and nobody knew what had become of him. In great affliction of mind my aunt came one day to Aljustrel to ask me to pray to Our Lady for this son and, unable to find me, she put her request to Jacinta, who promised to comply. After some days, he came home and asked his parents' forgiveness, and later went to Aljustrel to recount his misfortunes. Having spent all that he had stolen—according to his own story—he had been arrested and imprisoned in Torres Novas. He eventually managed to escape and hid himself among some unknown hills and pinewoods. Thinking that he was completely lost, he was seized with a sudden terror of the wind and darkness and as a last resort fell on his knees and prayed. He declared that after a few moments Jacinto appeared and, taking him by the hand, led him on to the road which leads from Alquidão to Reguengo, making signs to him to continue on that way. At daybreak he found himself on the road to Boleiros, and recognising exactly where he was he went straight to his parents' house overcome with emotion.
> Now he had declared that Jacinta had come to him and that he recognised her perfectly. I asked Jacinta whether she had in fact been there with him. She answered no, and that she did not even know those hills and pinewoods where he had been lost.
> "I only prayed," she said, "and asked Our Lady very much

about him, because I was so sorry for our aunt Victoria."
This was her answer. How, then, can the fact be explained?
God alone can answer.

Having seen some of the graces obtained by Jacinta's
intercession when she was still alive, we may pass on to
those granted to Francisco who exerted much the same
power of prayer.

One day when she was setting out for school Lucia met
her sister Teresa who had been recently married and who
said that a woman from a neighbouring hamlet had come
to ask for prayers for her son who was in prison accused
of a grave crime.

Lucia, on the way to school, told the story to her cousins.
When they arrived at Fatima, Francisco, who was seen to be
much perturbed, said to the two girls:

" Listen, you go to school and I will go and stay with
hidden Jesus and ask Him for this grace."[1]

After school Lucia went to find him and asked whether
he had asked Our Lady about the lad.

" Yes," was his reply, " you can tell your sister that he
will be freed." And so it turned out. In a few days the
prisoner returned home and on the 13th went to the Cova
da Iria to thank Our Lady.

We cannot close this chapter without referring to an

[1] In this connection there is an interesting parallel between Francisco
and another child who received from the Blessed Virgin the same
assurance that he would shortly be taken to Heaven, Guido de Fontgalland. Both, in the certainty that they would shortly die, gave scant
attention to studies. In his Paris College, the young Count Guido was
always distracted in class, spending his time in scribbling prayers and
ejaculations in an alphabet of his own invention. In Fatima, the
unlettered Francisco hid himself in church instead of going to school.
While the Countess de Fontgalland, however, insisted on the studies of
her son, the Marto parents and the teacher took little notice of the
preferences of Francisco.

The following notes written by a former schoolfellow of Francisco,
(now Director of the Seminary of Leiria) throw an interesting light on
their schooldays.

" I had the good fortune to attend the same school as Francisco
Marto, from February to June of 1917. Francisco distinguished himself from the others by reason of his humility and kindness, virtues
which, however, caused him much suffering, thrown as he was among
companions under the influence of a teacher without Christian formation.
He was very backward at his lessons and was still in the lowest form,
a misfortune which drew upon him the strictures of his teacher and
schoolfellows. It is obvious, however, that he was occupied with the
sublime thoughts which the angel had brought to birth in his mind
and that he cared little or nothing for the ordinary instruction of the
school. Francisco would humbly bow his head, and, we may be sure,

extraordinary grace obtained by Lucia in favour of her mother who fell seriously ill at this time. Mario dos Anjos gives us the details:

Our mother was so ill that we thought she would die. She had long attacks of breathlessness and the doctor said she suffered from her heart. It was a great sorrow to us because we had just lost our father. It was then that I said to Lucia, who was sitting on a bench by the hearth:

" Listen, Lucia, father is dead and if mother dies we shall be orphans; if you really saw Our Lady, ask her to make mother better."

Lucia didn't reply but she got up and went to her room and put on a thick woollen skirt because it was winter and raining hard, and went off in the direction of the Cova da Iria. When she came back she was carrying a handful of earth and told my sister, Gloria, to make an infusion with it for mother. She had also made a promise to Our Lady to return there with her sisters and go on the knees from the street to the chapel for nine days running and during the same time to feed nine poor children.

Gloria prepared the infusion and gave it to mother.

" What sort of tea is this?" she asked.

" It's made of flowers," we said, and she drank it all.

Then the attacks gradually began to get less and she no longer suffered from breathlessness but breathed easily and well. And her heart also improved and within a very short time she was able to get up.

with his soul united to God, received the censures of his master and companions.

At the break which we had at midday he would eat his lunch and stay quietly with a few other boys until the teacher gave the sign for them to go into school again. I remember playing with him and enjoying it because Francisco was always pleasant and friendly with everyone.

In the evening he went his way and I mine which was in the opposite direction and for this reason I do not know how he passed the rest of the day. From February to May, the life of Francisco in the school at Fatima was more or less as I have described and such was the attitude of his teachers and fellows towards him. In the last half of May the news of the Apparitions spread through the village and the attitude of the school towards him began to alter somewhat. The teacher, a good professor but a bad educator, took advantage of Francisco's scant interest in his lessons to dub him a fraud and a liar. He never ceased to point out his defects, I don't know whether with the intention of shaming him into greater efforts, or to induce us to take his part against the little seer.

We, mere children as we were, naturally followed the teacher's lead and often joined with him in humiliating poor Francisco. The worst of it was that our words were sometimes translated into actions, and he sometimes had to spend the recreation period pinned against the wall unable to free himself from the ill treatment meted out to him by certain stronger boys among us. This all took place during the last half of May and the whole of June. After the long vacation I entered the seminary and lost touch with the seers. . . ."

> She was able to work again after this and did not seem like
> an old woman. We began at once to go to the Cova to fufil
> the promise. For nine days, after supper—because in the day-
> time we had to work and also we didn't want to be seen—we
> went on our knees from where the main gate is now to the
> little chapel. Mother also came with us but she walked behind.

Amid doubts and difficulties these graces came like
showers of rain to refresh the parched earth and like rays
of light in the darkness. Heaven which had closed after the
last Apparition nevertheless opened from time to time as
the Lady of the Cova da Iria watched over her little friends
and gave them palpable evidence of her watchfulness.

CHAPTER XXXVI

THRESHOLD OF HEAVEN

EIGHTEEN months had passed since the last Apparition, and
it was time for Francisco to go to Heaven. He must have
said the required number of Rosaries.

About the middle of October the little boy fell ill,
together with Jacinta, his other brothers and sisters, and his
mother. The only person to remain well was Ti Marto who,
as he tells us, was the nurse of the " hospital ".[1]

> When my wife went down, it was all I could do to look after
> them all and go about my work and the errands as well! One
> of the girls had to have a caustic plaster, another something
> else, and so forth. But the hand of God was here and He
> helped me. I never had to beg from anyone. We always had
> money enough.

Lying in their beds, Jacinta and Francisco began to
realise clearly that their illness would end in Heaven. However, they improved to some extent and were even able to
get up but had a further relapse. A fortnight passed in this

---

[1] The publications on Fatima (Dr. Formigão and Dr. Fischer,
Fonseca, etc.) give the beginning of Francisco's illness as occurring at
the end of December, on the 23rd, precisely. This date must mark the
beginning of a relapse and not the illness itself. The following detail
will affirm our assertion. Throughout Portugal it is the custom on All
Saints' Day for children to go from house to house begging for sweets,
apples, etc. Now Senhor Marto remembers perfectly that children came
on that day as usual and that when they knocked on the door his son,
João, called out: " It's no use coming here, we are all ill!"—and that
he had to repeat this each time children called.

way, and according to Olimpia the illness (the malignant influenza of that year) was so severe that Francisco, especially, could not move hand or foot.

It was at this time that Our Lady appeared to them assuring them once again that she would shortly come to take Francisco to Heaven and that Jacinta would follow before long.

"Lucia," cried Jacinta happily, "Our Lady came to tell us that she would fetch Francisco very soon. And she asked me if I would like to convert still more sinners. I told her yes, and Our Lady wants me to go to two hospitals but not to get cured. I am to suffer more for the love of God and to convert sinners and to make up for the sins against the Immaculate Heart of Mary. She said that you wouldn't go there but that mother would take me and then I should have to stay alone."

From that moment the little girl and boy redoubled their love and desire for Heaven and tranquilly and happily awaited their death. For them death meant Heaven and Jesus and happiness.

Olimpia describes Francisco's illness for us:

> The little boy took any medicine we gave him and was not difficult about anything. I never knew what he liked and what he didn't. If I gave him a little milk he took it, and if it was an egg he took that too. Bitter medicines he swallowed without making a face. Poor little boy! He was so good that we thought he would get better but he always said that all the medicines were useless because Our Lady was coming to take him to Heaven.
>
> In January he got better again for the second time and he even got up for a bit, which made us very hopeful. But he never believed he was better and always repeated the same thing, that Our Lady would soon come to fetch him.
>
> I remember once (said Ti Marto on the occasion of this conversation) that he went out and fetched a small basket of olives and then sat on a bench and began to cut them. "Francisco," I said, "how nice to see you work; do you feel better?" But he said nothing and looked thoughtful. He seemed to know that in spite of everything he was going to die.
>
> "Yes, he knew!" put in Olimpia.

During this short space of time, when the little boy felt better and was able to get up and take a few short walks, it was always to the Cova da Iria that he went, with its memories of the dazzling Lady of the Apparitions. He would kneel by the root of the oak tree and there, where that blinding light had forced him to turn his eyes away, he would contemplate in memory the beauty and the tenderness of his vision of the Mother of God, so soon to be his for ever.

"You'll get better," said his father encouragingly, "and be a big strong man yet!"

"It won't be long before Our Lady comes," was his invariable and serene reply.

Ti Marto sadly recognised that some knowledge from Heaven was illuminating Francisco's mind, and as the truth began to dawn on him tears ran down his honest old face. It was all useless; Francisco would die as the child himself assured his godmother who wanted to make a "promise" in simple country style, of Francisco's own weight in wheat if he should be cured.

And, in fact, a few days later, he returned to bed never to rise from it again. His condition became steadily worse until his parents at last realised that they would lose him. Every encouraging word of theirs brought forth the same reply:

"It's no use, Our Lady wants me in Heaven with her."

And yet he was so cheerful, so happy and smiling that the illusion remained until the end. The high fever was gradually and implacably undermining his enfeebled organism until only a thread held him to earth.

Lucia, who had escaped pneumonia, and when the work of her house which was also transformed into a hospital permitted, constantly visited the Marto family to help where she could, and above all to see her cousins and use to the full the last precious days together. She divided her time equally between the two of them, while the confidences poured forth.

"Have you made a lot of sacrifices to-day?" was always the first question put by Jacinta. "I have, because when mother went out I wanted to go and see Francisco and I didn't go!"

The elder girl then confided her own, and these perhaps we shall never know. She told of her industry and invention in the interests of sinners and of the ejaculations which had accumulated on the day before. They were those which Father Cruz had taught them and which they had known so well how to use.

"I do so love Our Lord and Our Lady," said Jacinta to Lucia one day. "I think I never get tired of telling them

I love them and then I tell them, I have a fire here in my chest, but it doesn't burn me."

The two would revive in memory the happy hours of the Apparitions and the places which Our Lady had made holy by her presence.

" If only I could go to Cabeço," sighed Jacinta, " and say the Rosary in our favourite place! But I can't do that now. When you go, say the Rosary for me. I am sure I shall never go there again."

The same scenes were repeated in Francisco's room where Lucia often went at Jacinta's request, the latter avid for more sacrifice by the privation of her cousin's company.

" Do you suffer very much, Francisco?" Lucia asked him.

" Yes, I do, but I do it for Our Lord and Our Lady. I would like to suffer more, but I can't."

Then, assuring himself that the door was safely closed, he searched for the penitential cord among the bed-clothes and gave it to Lucia:

" Take it before mother sees. Now, I can't manage the cord."

Later Jacinta also gave her cord into the safe hands of her cousin, telling her to keep it:

" I'm afraid mother will find it. If I get better I shall want it again."

This cord was the only thing in the world to which the children were attached and in the eyes of Jacinta and Francisco the sole object of value. What precious relics they would have been for us if Lucia had not burned them before leaving for the convent school of Vilar!

" Listen, Lucia," continued Francisco, " I haven't much time left. Jacinta must pray very hard for sinners and for the Holy Father and for you. You must stay, because Our Lady wants it and we must do all that she says. . . ."

> While Jacinta (comments Lucia, thus throwing invaluable light on the individual sanctity of the two children) seemed only to think of converting sinners and saving souls from hell, Francisco's chief thought was to console Our Lord and Our Lady, who had seemed so sad.

" I'm very ill, Lucia," he repeated. " I shall go to Heaven very soon."

" Don't forget to pray for us and for sinners and the Holy Father."

" I won't forget, but Jacinta must remember, too, because I'm afraid I shall forget when I see Our Lord and shall want to comfort Him first."

CHAPTER XXXVII

FRANCISCO'S CALL

LUCIA'S visits were much appreciated by the Marto family.

> We were always glad to see her (Olimpia says), because it made me sad to see Jacinta passing hours on end with her hands over her face without moving. If I asked her what she was thinking about she would answer: "Nothing!" But with her cousin she had no secrets. When Lucia came to the house happiness came with her. She was like a ray of sunshine. The two used to talk and talk for hours but we could never catch a word they said. As soon as anyone came they would lower their heads and say nothing. We couldn't understand all the mystery!

When Lucia was making ready to go Olimpia would try and get her to talk:

"What was Jacinta telling you?"

But Lucia would smile and hurry off. There seemed to be no means of extracting these secrets from her.

When the sick children were alone they spent much time in prayer. Rosary succeeded Rosary, seven or eight a day, Olimpia assures us, and also innumerable ejaculatory prayers. But in his last days Francisco could not pray and this caused him intense sorrow. Sometimes night would come and he would not have managed to get through even one Rosary. His mother divined the bitterness of his heart and tried to console him:

"Mother, I can't pray; my head goes round so. . . ."

" If you can't pray with your lips, then pray with your heart; Our Lady will understand just the same. . . !"

Suddenly his condition worsened; a thick expectoration in the throat; rising fever; inability to take any food and a feebleness and exhaustion so marked that now there could be little doubt that Francisco's days were numbered.

"Father, I want to receive Holy Communion before I die."

" I'll go and see about it," said Ti Marto, his heart torn with anxiety not only because he feared for his son's life but in case the priest should once again refuse him his " hidden Jesus." Anxiously he made his way to the presbytery.

At that moment Fr. Ferreira was away and had appointed as his substitute Rev. Fr. Moreira, of Atouguia, who at once agreed to take the Blessed Sacrament to Francisco.

" On the way," recalls Ti Marto, " we said the Rosary and I remember very well that I had forgotten my beads and so I counted the Ave Marias on my fingers."

Meanwhile Francisco had asked his sister Teresa to go secretly and call Lucia, who lost no time in hurrying to the Marto cottage. She describes the scene in the following words :

> Francisco asked his mother and the rest of the family to leave the room because he wanted to tell me a secret. When they had gone he said:
>
> " I'm going to confession now and then I shall die. I want you to tell me if you have seen me commit any sin and to ask Jacinta if she saw any, too."
>
> " You were disobedient sometimes to your mother when she told you to stay at home, and you ran away to be with me or to hide."
>
> " Yes, I did do that. Now go and ask Jacinta if she remembers anything."
>
> I went and, after a moment's thought, she said :
>
> " Listen, tell him that before Our Lady appeared he stole a ' tostão ' (about a penny) from José Marto, of Casa Velha, and that when the Aljustrel boys threw stones at the ones from Boleiros, he threw them, too."
>
> When I gave this message Francisco replied :
>
> " I have confessed those already but I'll confess them again. Perhaps it is because of those sins that Our Lord is so sad. But even if I don't die, I'll never commit them again. I'm *very* sorry for them."
>
> And joining his hands, he said the prayer : *Oh, my Jesus, forgive us and deliver us from the fires of hell, etc.*
>
> " Lucia, you pray to Our Lord, too, and ask Him to forgive me my sins."
>
> " Yes, I will, you can be sure. If Our Lord hadn't forgiven them Our Lady wouldn't have told Jacinta the other day that she was coming soon to take you to heaven. Now I am going to Mass and I will pray to hidden Jesus for you."

That same day Fr. Moreira came to confess the little boy.

> I was very much afraid that he would refuse Francisco Holy Communion (confesses Ti Marto) because in his weak state he might easily have muddled the Catechism. But after all he came through all right and Fr. Moreira was satisfied.

" To-morrow I will bring Our Lord," he promised.

Francisco was blissfully happy. The desire of his heart was to be granted and he would have his hidden Jesus. He awaited the moment with the utmost impatience and made his mother promise that she would give him nothing after midnight so that he could be fasting " like everyone else."

At last the day dawned, the 3rd of April, a radiant spring morning. The fields were gay and fragrant with flowers, the birds sang and new life burst into being on the *serra*.

When Francisco heard the tinkling of the little bell which announced the Royal Coming, he tried to sit up in bed, but his strength failed him and he fell weakly back on his pillows.

" You can receive Our Lord lying down," said his godmother, who had come on purpose to assist at this First and Last Communion. Then the priest, bearing Jesus hidden under the Sacramental Species, entered the humble little bedroom. He placed the pyx on the table covered with the best lacy towel, and wishing peace to that house and all who lived in it, he placed the Body of Our Lord upon the tongue of the dying child, by now more angel than boy.

By the bedside his sister and cousin wept unconsoled, for very soon their beloved little companion would be with them no more. But Francisco closed his eyes in ecstatic happiness. In that moment he died to this world and when a day later his soul left his body it was already plunged in the reality of Heaven.

His first words when he opened his eyes again were:

" When will you bring me hidden Jesus again ? "

This was the only desire which could keep Francisco on earth, but, in fact, his hours were numbered. The high fever prostrated him, and his already enfeebled organism could not resist the mounting infection which spread rapidly through his body. On that vigil of his translation to Heaven Lucia did not leave his bedside for an instant and, as he could not pray, he asked her and Jacinta to say the Rosary for him.

In a moment of fleeting improvement he confided to Lucia:

" I shall miss you very much in Heaven! If only Our Lord would let you come soon!"

And Lucia playfully replied:

" Miss me . . . of course, you won't! Just think of being near Our Lord and Our Lady!"

" Yes, perhaps I had forgotten. . . ."

Night, the last night, fell at length. Francisco's condition
had become alarming. He was thirsty but could not
swallow the spoonfuls of water which he was given from
time to time. When asked how he felt, he replied:

" All right; I have no pain."

To his companions who did not leave him for a moment,
he whispered:

" I shall be going to Heaven very soon and I must ask
Our Lord and Our Lady to fetch you, too."

" Give my love to Our Lord and Our Lady," said Jacinta,
" and tell them that I'll suffer as much as they want, to convert sinners and to make up to the Immaculate Heart of
Mary."

Lucia was silent. She knew the long exile that she must
endure on earth before joining them in their home.

Later, when the *serra* was wrapped in darkness, Francisco
called his mother, who came to him with her heart heavy
beyond words. The pain, as she looked at him, was acute.

" Mother, look at that lovely light by the door!"

And a little later:

" Now I can't see it any more."

The night passed and in the morning (Friday, 4th of April)
it became clear that the end was at hand. Francisco's last
words were for his godmother. He asked her blessing and
her pardon for anything he had said or done to hurt her. At
10 o'clock, when the strong sunlight was pouring into his
wide, open windows, Francisco's face lit up in a singular
manner. A smile passed over his lips as he drew his last
breath. Sweetly and calmly, without agony or suffering, his
soul passed, it cannot be doubted, to Heaven.

On the following day a humble little procession brought
his body to Fatima. At the head, a Cross; then some men
in green capes preceding the surpliced priest. Four boys in
white bore the body, while Lucia followed weeping behind.
Jacinta, whose illness prevented her from leaving the house,
passed the time at home in prayer.

In the tiny cemetery Francisco was buried with no other
memorial but a simple Cross, differing in no way from the
others, set up by Lucia's hand. She let no day pass without
kneeling there to converse with her beloved little friend.
Later in the convent school at Tuy these words fell from
her lips in a moment of longing:

" What a wonderful priest he would have made!"

Our Lady, for inscrutable reasons, did not wish it so, for she had reserved another priesthood for the shepherd boy of Fatima.

CHAPTER XXXVIII

The Hospital

AFTER the last Apparition in the Cova da Iria Heaven did not close completely for the three children. The official Apparitions had ended, but not the familiar communications of Our Lady with her friends.

We have already referred to her Apparitions to Jacinta and Francisco when the two were ill in bed. With Jacinta, however, Our Lady did not content herself with a few passing words, but was to communicate with her at some length.

Jacinta was the youngest and perhaps the one to whom Our Lady destined the most abundant outpouring of grace. Correspondence to the graces and gifts of God is one of the most profound of mysteries; on the other hand, extraordinary grace does not always correspond to the degree of perfection possessed by a particular soul. We must make it clear, therefore, that in referring to the predilection of the Mother of God for the youngest child we in no way suggest that Lucia and Francisco were less generous or less ready to correspond with the supernatural.

From Lucia's various references to her cousin, and from the sources of knowledge which we possess of the principal protagonist of Fatima, only one conclusion can be drawn; that all three, with equal fervour, and with all the strength at their disposal—often it might seem, above the physical capacity of children of whom the eldest was ten—sought to translate into fact, the fact of blood, their correspondence to divine grace.

We think it necessary to make these observations before speaking of Jacinta's illness and holy death in the Estafânia hospital in Lisbon, in order to avoid any possibility of seeming to place Lucia and Francisco on a secondary plane. For us, we repeat, all three merit the same admiration, the same praise.

The death of her cousin made a profound impression on Lucia and perhaps even more on Jacinta. Seated on her bed, the little girl passed hours together in a profound melancholy. When she was asked why she was so sad she would answer:

" I am thinking of Francisco and of how I would like to see him!"

But it was not only the thought of Francisco that saddened the little girl. She was obsessed with thoughts of the war, of hell, and of the other sad things told her by Our Lady.

" I am thinking of the war which will come," she once told Lucia. " So many people will die and go to hell. So many houses will be destroyed and priests killed. Listen, I am going to Heaven soon, but when you see that light that Our Lady told us of, you must go there too."

" Don't you see that one can't just go to Heaven when one wants to," said Lucia sensibly.

" Yes, that's true, but don't be afraid. I will pray very much for you in Heaven and for the Holy Father and that the war may not come to Portugal, and for all the priests."

As when Francisco was alive, Lucia never let a day pass without going to the Marto house. She wrote later that every free moment and every opportunity was used to spend time with Jacinta.

The little girl suffered greatly in her illness. Except for a few days in which she felt slightly better, she had not left her bed since the last days of October in the preceding year. Such is the way of Our Lady with her special friends. After bronchial-pneumonia a kind of purulent abscess formed in the pleura, which caused her acute pain. But Jacinta bore her martyrdom with heroic resignation and a joy which was truly astonishing. To her mother, naturally worried by her condition, she said:

" Don't worry, mother, I am going to Heaven and I shall pray for you very much. Don't cry, because I'm all right."

But afterwards she gave her instructions to Lucia:

" Don't tell anyone how much I suffer, especially mother. I don't want her to worry."

Jacinta, reduced in a few months from the most exuberant health and spirits to a thin little skeleton on the edge of the grave, still thought not of herself but of others.

The doctor, seeing the gravity of the case and the unsuitability of her surroundings, advised the parents to send her to the hospital of Vila Nova de Ourem. Jacinta knew that hospital treatment could not restore her to health but would,

on the contrary, only increase her suffering. But in this
way she would convert many sinners and console the Heart
of Mary. Things could not be better!

" You will go to two hospitals," Our Lady had told her,
" not to be cured but to suffer more for the love of God and
for the conversion of sinners and to make reparations for
the sins against my Immaculate Heart. . . ."

These were the motives which transformed the dreaded
hospital into a consolation. There would be more suffering
than at home and, above all, the absence of her beloved
Lucia. This thought was like a sword in Jacinta's heart.

" Your mother will take you to the hospital," Our Lady
had declared, " and then you will stay there alone. . . ."

To suffer, yes, to suffer always, but to have the support
of a friend! Was not Our Lord's agony made doubly bitter
on this account? " *Could you not watch an hour with
me . . . ?* "

Can we wonder that in Jacinta's childish heart we find
the same sensitiveness, the same weakness?

" Lucia, if only you could come! How dreadful it is to
go without you! Perhaps the hospital will be all dark so
that you can't see, and I shall have to suffer there alone!"

It had to be, however, and at the beginning of July Ti
Marto lifted the thin little body out of bed, placed it tenderly
upon the humble ass and set out for Vila Nova de Ourem.

The treatment was severe, but availed nothing. For
Jacinta these two months were a martyrdom except the two
days when her cousin visited her. When she came Jacinta
threw her arms about her and asked her mother to leave
them alone.

> I found her as happy as ever (Lucia tells us), suffering for
> the love of God and the Immaculate Heart of Mary, for sinners
> and the Holy Father. She was living her ideal and it was of
> this that she spoke.

The hospital, fortunately, was neither dark nor gloomy but
a spotless whitewashed building. The ward where Jacinta
lay was light and cheerful and, in fact, she did not suffer
there alone. Lucia was not there, it was true, but Our Lady
did not abandon her for an instant.

" Do you suffer much, Jacinta?" asked Lucia.

" Yes, but I offer it all for the conversion of sinners and
the Holy Father. I love to suffer for the love of Jesus and

Mary. *They* love people who suffer for the conversion of sinners. . . ."

However, Lucia was Lucia and nothing could take her place. The visit passed in a flash, for the way back to Fatima was long and departure could not be long delayed. Lucia and Olimpia climbed the winding road up the *serra* to Fatima, while Jacinta was left again in the painful loneliness which was her " ideal."

CHAPTER XXXIX

JACINTA'S PASSION

AT the end of August, as the treatment was ineffective and the expense involved beyond the means of the Marto family, it was decided that Jacinta should return home. She had an open wound in the side which had to be dressed daily, not so much with the object of curing her as of prolonging her life.

As can easily be understood, the primitive surroundings of Aljustrel and the Marto cottage in particular, were totally unsuitable for the nursing of such a case. The wound became infected, pus formed, and the child wasted day by day. At about this time Dr. Formigão came to see her and found her in a deplorable condition.

> Jacinta is like a skeleton and her arms are shockingly thin. Since she left the local hospital where she underwent two months' useless treatment, the fever has never left her. She looks pathetic. Tuberculosis, after an attack of bronchial pneumonia and purulent pleurisy, is undermining her enfeebled constitution. Only careful treatment in a good sanatorium can save her. But her parents cannot undertake the expense which such a treatment involves. Bernadette, the peasant girl of Lourdes, heard from the mouth of the Immaculate Virgin in the cave of Massabielle, a promise of happiness not in this world but in the next. Has Our Lady made an identical promise to the little shepherdess of Fatima, to whom she confided an inviolable secret?

As Dr. Formigão noted, the Koch bacillus was eating away Jacinta's body, now little more than bone and skin. She must have suffered horribly, yet her thirst for sacrifice did not abate and she carried her efforts at mortification to the extreme. Only when she could do no more did she relax her continual asceticism.

"When I am alone," she confided to Lucia, "I get out of bed to say the prayer of the angel. But I can't get my head on to the ground any more because I fall, but I say it on my knees."

Lucia said nothing at the time, but on the first occasion that she saw Fr. Ferreira she revealed this fact to him. He at once told her that Jacinta must not attempt to get out of bed but was to pray lying down.

"Will Our Lord mind?" she asked anxiously when she heard.

"No," her cousin assured her. "He wants us to do what Fr. Ferreira says."

"Then I won't get out of bed again."

In the cold windy days of winter Jacinta's parents no longer allowed her to go to the Cova da Iria but permitted an occasional weekday Mass in Fatima, which is considerably nearer to Aljustrel.

"Don't come to-day, Jacinta," urged Lucia, "you're not strong enough and it's not Sunday."

"Never mind," said the younger girl, who felt "hidden Jesus" as a magnet drawing her, "I can go for sinners who don't even go on Sundays."

On returning from church she felt a great weakness sweeping over her and went to rest on the bed. The winter days prevented her from spending any time out of doors and Lucia passed long hours in her company. The two had no secrets; they talked of their sacrifices and their mortifications which always seemed so few to console the Hearts of Jesus and Mary.

"Do you know why Our Lord is so sad? Because Our Lady said that He was so much offended and no one minds; they go on doing the same sins."

Jacinta then passed in review the various occasions during the preceding day and night which had been used to repair such outrages.

"I was thirsty and I didn't drink and I offered it to Jesus for sinners. In the night I had pains and I offered Our Lord the sacrifice of not turning over in bed and so I didn't sleep at all. Lucia, what sacrifices have you made?"

Great little apostle! How perfectly she understood the mystery of the Redemption through the sufferings of God made man!

Sometimes, however, human nature rebelled against the bitter chalice of suffering.

Lucia tells us the story:

> One day her mother brought her a milk pudding and told her to take it.
>
> "I don't want it, mother," she said, pushing it away.
>
> My aunt tried to persuade her but finally went away, saying: "I don't know how to get her to take anything. . . ."
>
> When we were alone I asked her:
>
> "Well! You disobeyed your mother and didn't offer the sacrifice to Our Lord!"
>
> When Jacinta heard this she dissolved into tears, which I had the happiness of wiping away, and said:
>
> "I forgot that time!"
>
> Then she called her mother and asked her pardon and said that she would take whatever she gave her. The milk pudding was brought back and Jacinta took it without any sign of repugnance. Afterwards she said to me:
>
> "You don't know how hard it was to take!"
>
> Her will, or rather her love for the Heart of Mary and for sinners, triumphed.

Jacinta never forgot this lesson and although she found it increasingly difficult to take the milk puddings and soups she offered them all for her well-known and loved intentions. And when her mother brought with the hated milk a beautiful bunch of grapes it was to the milk that her preference was given.

Lucia received Holy Communion, if not every day, at least frequently, and on returning from church never failed to pay a visit to her cousin's bedside. Jacinta asked her gently:

"Lucia, have you been to Holy Communion to-day? Then come close to me because you have hidden Jesus in your heart. I don't know how it is, but I feel Our Lord inside me and I understand what He says though I can't see Him or hear Him, but I love to be with Him."

Then Lucia took out of her prayer book a picture of the Chalice and the Host, which Jacinta kissed passionately.

"It's hidden Jesus, *how* I love Him. If only I could receive Him in the church. Can you go to Holy Communion in Heaven? If so, I shall go every day. If the angel could go to the hospital and take me Holy Communion how happy I should be. . . ."

On another occasion Lucia gave her a little picture of the Sacred Heart and although she did not think it beautiful enough to be Our Lord she always kept it with her and at night hid it under the pillow and kissed it frequently.

"I kiss His Heart," she said. "It's what I like best. I

wish I had one of the Immaculate Heart of Mary. Haven't you got one, Lucia? I should like to keep the two together."

Indeed the Immaculate Heart of Mary was the particular passion of this little apostle.

" I shall go to Heaven very soon," she said one day about this time. " You must stay to tell people that God wants to establish in the world devotion to the Immaculate Heart of Mary. When you have to say this don't hide, but tell everybody that God gives us His grace through the Immaculate Heart and that people must ask it through her and that the Sacred Heart of Jesus wants the Immaculate Heart of Mary by His side. They must ask peace through the Immaculate Heart because God has given it to her. I wish I could put into everybody the fire that I have here in my heart which makes me love the Sacred Heart of Jesus and the Immaculate Heart of Mary so much!"

It was not the fever which consumed Jacinta so much as the fire of love and reparation.

CHAPTER XL

LISBON

IT must have been about the end of December when Our Lady came again to tell Jacinta that she would soon come to take her to Heaven, not there, but in a hospital in Lisbon.

Lisbon . . . so far!

At the first opportunity she told Lucia the good but sad news.

" Our Lady told me that I was to go to Lisbon, to another hospital, and that I shall never see you again, nor father and mother; that I shall have to suffer much and die alone, but that I must not be afraid, because she will come and take me to Heaven. I shall never see you again!" she sobbed, throwing her arms round Lucia's neck. " You won't even be able to come and visit me. But pray for me very much . . . because I have to die alone."

This thought of dying alone tortured Jacinta's heart and one day Lucia found her kissing a picture of Our Lady and saying:

" Darling Mother in Heaven, must I die alone?"

The cup was almost too bitter and, like Our Lord before His passion and death, she prayed that it might be taken away. *Father, if it be possible let this cup pass.*

Lucia tried in every way to comfort her:

" What does it matter if you die alone, if Our Lady is coming to fetch you?"

" That's true, it doesn't really matter, but sometimes, I don't know how it is, I can hardly remember that she is coming to fetch me."

" Be brave, Jacinta! You will be going so soon to Heaven but I. . . ."

This time it was Jacinta's turn to delight anew in the idea of Heaven and to encourage her cousin.

" Poor Lucia, don't cry. I shall pray so much for you. You must stay, but Our Lady wants it like that."

" What will you do in Heaven, Jacinta?" asked Lucia.

" I shall love Jesus and the Immaculate Heart of Mary very much and I shall pray for you, and for sinners, and the Holy Father, and for father and mother and the others, and everyone who has asked me to pray for them. I love to suffer for Our Lord and Our Lady because they love people who suffer for the conversion of sinners."

In the Marto family Jacinta's assertions that she would go to Lisbon were considered nonsense. Lisbon? Why should she go there? The treatment in Ourem had been useless, what then would be the point of going to another hospital, even in Lisbon? And then there was the question of expense, for the great hospitals of the capital would not be content with the small fees which St. Augustine's Hospital in the Vila had charged.

Providence, however, had decided otherwise. One day a motor car arrived in Aljustrel and from it descended Dr. Formigão—by now an intimate friend of the family—and Dr. Eurico Lisboa and his wife, who had come to visit the sick child. This doctor has left us a document on the illness and death of Jacinta and we will allow him to tell his story:

In the middle of January, 1920, we went for a run to the Cova da Iria in order to try out the new motor car which we had recently bought. On our way through Santarem we went to pay our respects to Dr. Formigão, who we knew could tell us all about Fatima and the events of which he had been a witness. Dr. Formigão, whom we had not known personally before, but who has been our intimate friend ever since, had the kindness to accompany us to Fatima on that occasion and it was through him that we came to know the seers, Jacinta and Lucia.

After a visit to the Cova with Lucia, in whose company we prayed the Rosary with unforgettable faith and devotion, we returned to Fatima, where we spoke to Jacinta and the mothers of the two seers. They told us about Francisco, who had been a victim of the widespread epidemic of pneumonia influenza which had swept with such tragic results through Europe. He had, we learned, realised his only wish since the Apparitions, which was to go to Our Lady. He refused all help and advice from the people who knew him in his life and only desired death, with the least possible delay.

Little Jacinta was very pale and thin and walked with great difficulty. The family told me she was very ill, which they hardly regretted, because Jacintha's only ambition also was to go to Our Lady, whose will it was that she should die in the same way as Francisco.

When I censured them for their lack of effort to save their daughter, they told me that it was not worth while because Our Lady wished to take her, and that she had been interned for two months in the local hospital without any improvement in her condition.

I replied that Our Lady's will was certainly more powerful than any human efforts and that in order to be certain that she really wished to take Jacinta, they must not neglect any of the normal aids of science to save her life.

Impressed by my words they went to ask the advice of Dr. Formigão, who supported my opinion in every respect. It was therefore arranged on the spot that Jacinta should be sent to Lisbon and treated by the best doctors in one of the hospitals of the capital.

And in fact, some days later, on *2nd February* 1920, Jacinta was interned in Ward No. 1, bed No. 38, of the Estafânia Hospital, under the care of Dr. Castro Freire, then, and now, one of the most famous children's specialists in Lisbon. The diagnosis was as follows: Purulent pleurisy, osteitis of the 7th and 8th left ribs.

How extraordinary are the ways of Providence, and how unexpectedly was Our Lady's prediction realised!

The Martos consented to this reluctantly, convinced as they were that their daughter's illness could have but one end. Ti Marto told Jacinta of the decision in the following words, which he repeated to us:

"Jacinta, we are going to arrange for you to go to Lisbon, to a hospital."

"Yes, father," was the reply, between sobs. "I'm in a fine way to go to Lisbon!"

"It has to be, dear. Otherwise everyone will say that we have neglected to have treatment. Perhaps after all you'll be all right."

Then (continues her father) she said the following words to me as if quite resigned:

" Father, dear, even if I recover from this illness, I should get another straightaway. If I go to Lisbon it means good-bye."

Indeed she was a sorry sight. Her heart was enlarged and her digestive organs were ruined. It seemed as if she could not recover.

In the middle of January the decision was taken, but before leaving Fatima Jacinta asked her mother to take her to the Cova da Iria.

I arranged (says Olimpia) to take her on a friend's donkey because Jacinta could not have managed the walk. When we arrived at the Carreira pool, Jacinta got off the donkey and began to say the Rosary alone. She picked a few flowers for the chapel. When we arrived we knelt down and prayed a little in her own way.

" Mother," she said when she got up, " when Our Lady went away she passed over those trees, and afterwards she went into Heaven so quickly that I thought she would get her feet caught! "

Meanwhile, Ti Marto had arranged everything in the best way possible for the forthcoming journey to Lisbon. Senhora Olimpia, who had never been in a train, was to accompany Jacinta to the capital.

I went to see Baron Alvaiázere (says the old man) and I said: " I think the journey will be all right, sir, they will go in such-and-such a train and Antonio will tie a white handker-chief to his wrist so that the ladies who are coming to meet them at the station will be able to recognise them."

Then I went back to Fatima and registered the letter.

" Oh, Senhor Marto," they said in the post office, " what a lot of money you're spending! "

" Never mind," I replied, " they'll be sure of getting it, any-way."

That night I gave my wife the last instructions for the follow-ing day.

" When you get into the train you must ask the other people to excuse you because your little girl is very ill, and it is because of this that she has an unpleasant smell. Be very careful that she doesn't lean out of the window when another train is passing. When you are going through the Rossio tunnel (the approach to Lisbon) don't forget to tie on the white handkerchief and don't worry."

The next day saw the heartbreaking separation from Lucia, who recalls it as follows:

It nearly broke my heart. She stayed a long time in my arms and then said, sobbing:

"We shall never see each other again! But pray for me very much till I go to Heaven and then I will pray very much for you. Don't ever tell the secret to anyone even if they kill you. Love Jesus very much and the Immaculate Heart, and make many sacrifices for sinners."

These were the last words, the testament of Jacinta, to her inseparable companion:

> We went to the station in a mule cart (recalls Olimpia) with my eldest son, Antonio. During the journey Jacinta stood nearly all the time by the window looking through the glass. In Santarem a lady came to the train and gave her some sweetmeats but Jacinta wouldn't eat anything.
>
> We knew nobody in Lisbon and it was for this reason that Baron Alvaiázere and my husband had arranged for some ladies to meet us. They were to recognise us by the white handkerchiefs tied to our arms. But when we got out of the train, Antonio, who knew how to read, went off to see something outside the station and I lost sight of him.
>
> "Antonio, Antonio," I shouted out. . . ."
>
> And then a few moments later he appeared again with the three ladies, who came up to us. They took us out of the station and we went to various houses but nobody would take us in. When we were nearly tired out from walking we came to the house of a good woman who opened her doors to us and could not have given us a better welcome. I stayed there with Jacinta for over a week and then went back to Fatima.[1]

Soon after Jacinta's entrance into this orphanage, for orphanage it was, arrangements were put in hand for her internment in the Estafânia Hospital. Various difficulties arose, however, chief among them the reluctance of the mother to allow her daughter to undergo an operation in the lamentable state she was in. In order that the question might be settled, it was imperative that Olimpia should return to Fatima to ask the advice of Ti Marto.

---

[1] While mother and daughter were in the waiting-room a certain Dona Maria de Castro, who was a patient of Dr. Lisboa, came to see Jacinta. This lady was a believer in the Apparitions of Fatima and held Jacinta in great esteem and she at once asked her to pray to Our Lady for her. But Jacinta gave no reply and looked at her so sadly that Dona Maria went away disheartened. She left a fifty escudo bank note with the little girl, who at once handed it over to the Superior of the house, Mother Godinho, who, in her turn, did not wish to accept it.

"Give it to your mother," she advised Jacinta.

"No, it's for you because I shall give you a lot of trouble."

Later the nun asked Jacinta why she had not replied to D. Maria when she asked for prayers.

"I did pray," was the answer, "but I didn't say so that day because I was afraid of forgetting. I was in such pain."

CHAPTER XLI

FORETASTE OF HEAVEN

JACINTA at once began to feel at home in the orphanage. It was run like a large family and the children called the Superior " Madrinha " or godmother, a term which Jacinta adopted without delay.

The house, which adjoins the Chapel of Milagres, has a choir from which one can see the Tabernacle and assist at Mass, which was daily celebrated in those days by a very deaf old priest.

Jacinta's delight, when they took her here a short time after her arrival, was indescribable. To live under the same roof as Jesus in the Blessed Sacrament was a privilege of which she had never dreamed and to be able to receive Him each day was a foretaste of Heaven.

While she was in this orphanage in the Rua da Estrela, Jacinta received Holy Communion daily, while during her internment in the hospital she never once had this happiness.

> She went to the altar (says Senhora Olimpia) either in my arms or carried by the Superior. I remember that she said to me before I left for home:
> "Oh, mother, I want to go to confession."
> We went very early to the Estrela church and when we came out Jacinta seemed very happy and said to me:
> "What a good priest that was. He asked me so many things!"
> I would have given anything to know what the good Father had asked her but one can't ask about confessions.

Jacinta passed all the time that she was allowed in the tribune of the church. Sitting on her little chair, for she was not allowed to kneel, she remained with eyes fixed on the Tabernacle, praying and meditating, but if she saw people in the church below talking or behaving otherwise than respectfully she would complain to Madre Godinho, saying that Our Lady was displeased if people did not show proper respect to the Blessed Sacrament.

In order that Jacinta might benefit as much as possible from the sun and air, Mother Godinho made her sit at the open window, which looked out over the Estrela Gardens. There, homesick for the *serras,* she would enjoy the sight of the green trees and the song of the birds. She felt the absence of Lucia even more than her separation from her family.

> I soon began to realise that a little angel had come into my house (says Mother Godinho). Although I had long wanted to see the privileged children of Fatima I never imagined that I would have the good fortune to shelter one under my roof.
>
> We had some twenty to twenty-five children in the asylum. Jacinta was friendly with them all but she preferred the company of a little girl about her own age to whom she would give little sermons. It was delightful to hear them, and hidden behind the half-open door I assisted at many of these conversations.
>
> "You mustn't lie, or be lazy or disobedient, and you must bear everything with patience for love of Our Lord if you want to go to Heaven." She spoke with such authority; hardly like a child.
>
> During the time she was in my house she must have received a visit from Our Lady more than once. I remember on one occasion she said:
>
> "Please move, dear mother, I am waiting for Our Lady," and her face took on a radiant expression.
>
> It seems that it was not always Our Lady in person who appeared but a globe of light such as had been seen in Fatima, because we once heard her say:
>
> "This time it wasn't like it was in Fatima, but I knew it was she."

*   *   *   *

That these visions were not simple hallucinations is proved by the fact that Jacinta's conversation during this time showed a wisdom which would be impossible in an unlettered ten-year-old child with only the most rudimentary religious instruction, unless directly infused. Let us take as examples the following sentences which Mother Godinho has carefully noted, clothing them in her own words:

On sin:

> "The sins which cause most souls to go to hell are the sins of the flesh."[1]
>
> "Fashions will much offend Our Lord. People who serve God should not follow the fashions. The Church has no fashions; Our Lord is always the same."
>
> "The sins of the world are very great."
>
> "If men knew what eternity is they would do everything to change their lives."

---

[1] It was not the first time that Our Lady referred to the sin of impurity. Senhora Olimpia recalls that one night in Aljustrel, her daughter said to her: "Mother, you must never eat flesh (meat) on Fridays, nor give it to us because Our Lady said that sins of the flesh brought many people to hell."

" People are lost because they do not think of the death of Our Lord and do not do penance."

" Many marriages are not of God and do not please Our Lord."

On the war:

" Our Lady said that the world is full of war and discords."

" Wars are the punishments for sin."

" Our Lady cannot at present avert the justice of her Son from the world."

" Penance is necessary. If people amend their lives, Our Lord will even yet save the world but if not punishment will come."

Referring to these words, Mother Godinho wrote:

The reference is to a great punishment which she spoke of in secret and was revealed in her last days. There is nothing to prevent its revelation now.

Jacinta said that Our Lord was profoundly outraged by the sins and crimes which were committed in Portugal and for this reason a terrible social cataclysm threatened our country and particularly the city of Lisbon. A civil war or Communist revolution would be unchained which would be accompanied by sacking and violence and devastation of all kinds. The capital would be converted into an image of hell. This threatened punishment should be revealed little by little and with due discretion.[2]

On priests and rulers:

" You must pray much for sinners and for priests and religious. Priests should concern themselves only with the things of the Church."

" Priests must be very, very pure."

" Disobedience of priests and religious to their superiors displeases Our Lord very much."

" Pray, mother, for rulers."

" Heaven forgive those who persecute the Church of Christ."

" If the Government would leave the Church in peace and give liberty to religion it would have God's blessing."

---

[2] Is not this an allusion to the Communist invasion (at the time of the Spanish war) by which we were menaced; and which the Portuguese Episcopate implored Our Lady to avert from their country?
A question: Has the necessary reparation been performed? We may note in the first place the intensification of religious life in Portugal and the characteristic note of penance which marks the Fatima Pilgrimages. We may also cite the walking pilgrimage of 10,000 young men from Lisbon and the triumphal reception of the statue of Our Lady in the capital (from Dr. Galamba's *Jacinta*). It will be remembered that the Portuguese Bishops led a great National Pilgrimage to Fatima to thank Our Lady for deliverance from the Communism which threatened at the time of the Spanish Civil War.

On Christian virtues:

" Mother, fly from riches and luxury."
" Love poverty and silence."
" Have charity even for bad people."
" Do not speak evil of people and fly from evil speakers."
" Mortification and sacrifice please Our Lord very much."
" Confession is a sacrament of mercy and we must confess with joy and trust. There can be no salvation without confession."
" The Mother of God wants more virgin souls bound by a vow of chastity."
" I would gladly go to a convent but I would rather go to Heaven."
" To be a religious one must be very pure in body and mind."
" Do you know what it means to be pure?" I asked her.
" Yes, yes, I know. To be pure in body means to be chaste, and to be pure in mind means not to commit sins; not to look at what one should not see, not to steal or lie and always to speak the truth even if it is hard."
" Doctors do not know how to cure people properly because they have not the love of God."
" Who taught you these things?" I asked her.
" Our Lady, but some of them I thought myself. I love to think."

Our Lady, however, did not content herself with teaching Jacinta the maxims of wisdom only, but sometimes revealed the future to her. One day Mother Godinho asked Olimpia, who had come to visit her daughter:

" Would you like your daughters Florinda and Teresa to enter the religious life?"

" Heavens no!" exclaimed the good woman with natural feelings.

A few moments later Jacinta, who had not heard this conversation, said very seriously to Mother Godinho:

" Our Lady would like my sisters to be nuns although mother wouldn't like it, and so she will take them to Heaven before long."

And so it was. Shortly after Jacinta's death, the two girls, Florinda, aged 17, and Teresa, aged 16, also died.

Jacinta also told Mother Godinho, who had long wished to visit the Cova da Iria without having the opportunity to do so, that she would, in fact, do so after her (Jacinta's) death. And so it fell out. Unforeseen circumstances having prevented the burial in Lisbon, Jacinta's body was taken to the family vault of Baron Alvaiázere in Vila Nova de Ourem. It fell to Mother Godinho to accompany the body of her protégée and she was able to visit Fatima on the

same day and make a visit to the Cova in the company of
Lucia.

On another occasion one of the two doctors who treated
her asked her to pray for him in Heaven and Jacinta replied
that she would, but soon afterwards looked at him with a
serious expression and said:

" You, too, will be going before long."

An identical scene occurred with the other doctor, whose
death, and that of his daughter, she also predicted.

Once she heard an excellent sermon from a priest who
was considered exemplary in every way.   Jacinta, however,
expressed her disapproval to Mother Godinho in explicit
terms:

" That priest will turn out badly though you wouldn't
think it now."

She was right.   Shortly afterwards the unfortunate man
abandoned the priesthood and lived in open scandal.

With regard to the operation which it was hoped would
save her life, she wrote to Lucia (a dictated letter) saying
that Our Lady had appeared to her and had revealed the
day and hour of her death.

CHAPTER XLII

CALVARY

JACINTA was so happy at the orphanage that she seemed
almost to forget her home and family and might even have
come to forget Lucia.   But the little girl had not yet
ascended the summit of her calvary nor drunk the last bitter
drops of her cup of suffering.

Our Lord, in order to complete His work would demand
of her yet further separations; separations from the much-
loved Mother Godinho and from Himself in the Chapel of
Milagres.

Dr. Lisboa in a vain hope that he could save her life
succeeded in having her interned in the Estafânia Hospital,
and on 2nd February, Mother Godinho accompanied
Jacinta there and saw her installed in bed No. 38 in the
children's ward.

There Jacinta was one of many.   Both doctors and nurses
severely censured Mother Godinho for having accepted a

tuberculous patient in the orphanage thereby running serious risks of infection for the other children. The observation was perhaps justified, but Mother Godinho was the only person who had acted with charity towards the homeless shepherdess of Aljustrel.

Now the surroundings were cold and lonely. What a difference between that desolate ward and Jacinta's simple little room in the Rua da Estrela! When the good Superior left her Jacinta suffered terribly from loneliness. There was no one in whom she could confide, and above all, there was no hidden Jesus.

Among the visitors and nurses (not the modern professional nurse) were many who offended Jacinta by their over-decorative dress, often immodest as well.

" What is it all for," she observed, " if they only knew what eternity was!"

Of some doctors whom she knew to be unbelievers:

" Poor things! If they knew what awaited them!"

She revealed also that Our Lady had again appeared to her, speaking of the prevalence of the sins of luxury and the flesh which caused the loss of so many souls, and of the necessity of penance.

Mother Godinho with Dona Maria Castro and other friends, visited her every day and for Jacinta these were times when she could pour out her confidences to sympathetic ears. Ti Marto also paid one fleeting visit, fleeting because the illness of his other children in Fatima obliged him to return there without delay.

On 10th February Jacinta's operation took place at the hands of Dr. Castro Freire. She suffered greatly because her condition only allowed her to have a local anæsthetic. The result was satisfactory and two ribs were extracted from her left side, leaving a wound in which the hand could be inserted. The daily dressings were excruciating agony, but Jacinta's only cries were repetitions of Our Lady's name when the pains were worst. She bore her sufferings with the resignation of a saint and no one ever heard her complain.

" We must suffer if we want to go to Heaven," she said. For her the sufferings were the means of converting many sinners.

Our Lady did not forget her, and occasionally appeared to her as she confided to Mother Godinho:

" Now I'm much better. Our Lady said that she would soon come to fetch me and that she would take away the pain."

> And in fact (Dr. Lisboa affirms) with the Apparition, there in the middle of the ward, her pain completely disappeared and she began to be able to play and enjoy certain distractions. She liked to look at holy pictures one among them in particular—given me later as a souvenir—of Our Lady of Sameiro which she said most closely resembled the Lady of the Apparitions. I was told several times that Jacinta wished to see me but as my professional duties were heavy and Jacinta was apparently better I, unfortunately, put off my visit until too late.

When Mother Godinho sat at the bedside in the place where Our Lady appeared Jacinta would protest at once: " Not there, Mother, that's where Our Lady stood."[1]

February twentieth was the Friday of Carnival (that is the Friday before Ash Wednesday) and the day on which Our Lady was to fulfil her promise to fetch Jacinta.

Dr. Lisboa's deposition is as follows:

> On the evening of that 20th of February, at about 6 o'clock, Jacinta said that she felt worse and wished to receive the Sacraments. The parish priest (Dr. Pereira dos Reis) was called and he heard her Confession about 8 o'clock that night. I was told that Jacinta had insisted that the Blessed Sacrament be brought to her as Viaticum but that Dr. Reis had not concurred because she seemed fairly well. He promised to bring her Holy Communion in the morning. Jacinta again asked for Viaticum saying that she would shortly die and, indeed, she died that night, peacefully, but without having received Holy Communion.

A young nurse, Aurora Gomes, was the only person present at her death.

---

[1] One of the nurses who looked after her and to whom we spoke told us that she purposely stood in the place where Our Lady said to appear and at which Jacinta constantly looked. " She did not say anything," said the nurse, " but her face took on such an expression of pain that I felt I could not remain there."

CHAPTER XLIII

Incorrupt Flesh

Silently, on the night of 20th February, Our Lady came for the last time to visit the patient in bed No. 60 of the children's ward.[1] This time she took a soul to Heaven, leaving the virginal dress behind.

The other patients slept on as usual while Nurse Aurora kept watch by the little corpse. First thing in the morning the sensational news became known in Lisbon. Jacinta, one of the privileged children of Fatima, had died that night.

Her body, wasted by three years of penance and a year and a half of sickness, was clothed in a white dress with a blue sash—Our Lady's colours. But here we will let Dr. Lisboa speak once more:

When I was told what had occurred during the night I spoke to Dona Amelia Castro, who came every day to my consulting room for treatment to her eyes, and she obtained from certain members of her family a white First Communion dress used by poor children, and money to buy a blue silk sash. Jacinta was thus laid out in Our Lady's colours according to her wish.

As soon as her death became known various people sent money for the expenses of the funeral which was fixed for the following day, Sunday, at noon, the body to be taken to one of the cemeteries of Lisbon.

When the coffin left the hospital mortuary, it occurred to me that it might be wiser to have the body deposited in some special place, in case the Apparitions should later be confirmed by the Ecclesiastical Authorities or the general incredulity on the subject be overcome. I, therefore, proposed to have the coffin containing Jacinta's body deposited in the Church of the Holy Angels until its removal to some vault could be arranged.

I then went to see my good friend, Dr. Reis, the parish priest, who however demurred at the idea of the body remaining in his church owing to certain difficulties. However, with the help of the Confraternity of the Blessed Sacrament some of whose members happened to be in the sacristy at the time, Dr. Reis was persuaded to give his permission to let the body remain there. Soon afterwards it arrived and was placed humbly on two stools in a corner of the sacristy.

The news spread rapidly and soon a sort of pilgrimage of believers in Fatima began, the faithful bringing their rosaries and statues to touch Jacinta's dress and to pray by her side. All this profoundly disturbed Dr. Reis who was averse to his church being used for what might well be a false devotion

---

[1] Her bed was changed after the operation.

and he protested energetically by both word and action, thereby surprising those who knew him as a most kind and courteous priest.

It had finally been decided that the body should be taken to a vault in Vila Nova de Ourem and matters were accordingly arranged though this involved a delay of two days, the funeral being fixed for Tuesday at 4 o'clock from the Holy Angels Church to the Rossio Station and from thence by train to Vila Nova de Ourem.

Meanwhile the body remained in the open coffin which again caused serious anxiety to Dr. Reis who feared an intervention on the part of the sanitary authorities[2] and he continued to be worried by the stream of visitors, which he only avoided by locking the coffin in an office.

At last Dr. Reis, in order to avoid the responsibility of the open coffin and the pilgrims, deposited the body in the confraternity room above the sacristy and handed the key to the firm of undertakers, Antonio Almeida and Co., who had been engaged for the funeral. Senhor Almeida remembers to this day, and in great detail, what passed on that occasion.

In order to satisfy the innumerable requests to visit the body he remained during the whole of 23rd February in the church accompanying each group of pilgrims—whose numbers were strictly limited—to the room above, in order to avoid any unseemliness which might occur.

He was deeply impressed by the respect and devotion with which the people approached and kissed the little corpse on the face and the hands and he remembers very clearly the live pinkness of the cheeks and the beautiful aroma which the body exhaled.[3]

At last, on 24th February at 11 in the morning, the body was placed in a leaden coffin which was then sealed. Present at this act were Senhor Almeida, the authorities, and several ladies, among them Senhora Maria Pena (who died recently), who declared in the presence of various people who can testify to it to-day, that the body exhaled a beautiful aroma of flowers as the coffin was being sealed. Owing to the purulent nature of the disease and the length of time that the body remained unburied, this fact is remarkable.

In the afternoon, which was wet, the funeral took place on foot, in the company of a large crowd. The coffin was finally laid in the vault of Baron Alvaiázere in Villa Nova de Ourem.

---

[2] In Portugal not more than twenty-four hours may elapse between death and burial.

[3] Senhor Almeida later wrote: " I seem to see Jacinta still, looking like a little angel. In her coffin she seemed to be alive; her lips and cheeks were a beautiful pink. I have seen many corpses, large and small, but I have never seen anything like that. The beautiful perfume which the body exhaled could not be explained naturally and the hardest sceptic could not doubt it. One remembers the smell which so often makes it repugnant to remain near a corpse and yet this child had been dead three days and a half and the smell of her body was like a bouquet of flowers. . . ."

I remember that on that day the General Annual Conference of St. Vincent de Paul took place and that I excused my late arrival on account of the work of mercy which had claimed my attention, namely, the burial of one of the seers of Fatima. These words provoked an outburst of mirth on the part of the assembly, composed, as may be imagined, of some of the most prominent Catholics of the capital, among them the Cardinal Patriarch[4] himself, who joined in the laugh at my expense. Later he became a great admirer of Fatima and declared that his great desire was to celebrate Mass in the Cova da Iria before he died.

It is interesting to record these curious facts, showing as they do the great reluctance on the part of the great majority of clergy and certain of the laity in Portugal to believe in the events of Fatima. There were a few believers, among them Dr. Formigão, who assisted at the Apparitions and bore witness to them by means of the written and the spoken word; also holy old Fr. Cruz whom I have seen in Fatima ever since my first visits there and who was the first priest I heard in a Lisbon church publicly exhorting the people to pray to Our Lady of the Rosary at Fatima at a time when the general run of the clergy were afraid to give public utterance to any shred of belief they might have in the revelations.

After all these years it is a great consolation to me to have been instrumental in arranging that Jacinta, in her last illness, should have been under the care of the best doctors and nurses in a Lisbon hospital where the odious calumny, which has been spread abroad, namely, that the Catholics brought about the deaths of the two younger children in order that they should not be able to contradict Lucia's affirmations, can be most emphatically repudiated.

Thus ends Dr. Lisboa's invaluable document on the illness and death of Jacinta. Meanwhile the sad news reached Fatima.

After the operation (says Ti Marto) they wrote and told us that Jacinta was all right. I immediately had a letter written to Baron Alvaiázere telling him of this and thanking him and all the good people who had helped to arrange it. The Baron had also received a letter telling him the same news but about ten days later another letter arrived from him telling me to go and see him at once. I set off for the town and when I arrived the Baron told the servants to get me something to eat and then pulled out a letter and read it to me:

"Jacinta stood the operation well but they did something and she died."

"Is there anything I must do?"

"Nothing, Senhor Marto, nothing."

I went home after that and told the family about the death of our Jacinta.

[4] At that time, D. Antonio Mendes Belo.

A few more days passed and I received another letter from the Baron saying that I was to go to Vila Nova de Ourem to meet the train which was bringing Jacinta's body to be buried in his family vault.

When I arrived in the town and saw that group of people round the coffin of my Jacinta . . . I broke down and cried like a child. I felt heartbroken and have never cried so much . . . I felt it had all been no good, all useless; she had been in the hospital here two months and then gone to Lisbon and in the end she died all alone. . . !

" I shall go back to Fatima but only after my death," Jacinta had told Mother Godinho in the last days of her exile. The prediction was realised on 12th September, 1935, when the Bishop of Leiria decided to translate the mortal remains of the seer to the cemetery of Fatima to a new tomb specially built for her and for Francisco.

Before the departure, however, the coffin was opened, and to the astonishment of the onlookers, Jacinta's face was seen to be perfectly incorrupt. Our Lady had not allowed the decay of that innocent flesh, made sublime by a life of love and penance.

A photograph was taken and a copy sent to Lucia (then a Dorothea lay-sister) who in her letter of thanks to the Bishop wrote as follows:

I thank you for the photographs with all my heart. It is impossible to express how much I value them. From Jacinta's I almost wanted to tear off that shroud and see the whole of her. I was so anxious to see the rest of the body that I forgot it was a photograph at which I was looking; such was my happiness at seeing again the most intimate friend of my childhood.

I have a great hope that Our Lord may concede her the halo of sanctity for the honour of Our Blessed Lady. She was a child only in years and already knew how to show God and Our Lady her love by means of sacrifice. . . .

It was with great regret that Baron Alviázere gave up the precious relic which brought, as he says, so many graces to him and his family.

At half-past three in the afternoon. a motor car bore the body, covered now with a rich silken pall, to the Chapel of Penance in the Sanctuary, where the Archbishop of Evora celebrated Mass. Afterwards both bodies were taken to the cemetery of Fatima where they lie in a tomb on which are inscribed the simple words:

Here lie the mortal remains
of
Francisco and Jacinta
to whom Our Lady appeared.

How long will they remain there? Perhaps one day they will return again to the Cova da Iria, where Francisco's dust and Jacinta's incorrupt flesh will receive the supreme homage which the Church reserves for her heroes.

May these humble pages contribute not only to the honour of the most Blessed Virgin but also to the beatification of her two beloved children.

CHAPTER XLIV

GOOD-BYE TO FATIMA

WHEN, at the second Apparition, Lucia asked Our Lady to take her to Heaven with her cousins, she was told:

" I will take Jacinta and Francisco before long. But you must stay here for some time. Jesus has need of you to make me known and loved, for He wishes to establish in the world devotion to my Immaculate Heart."

" Shall I stay alone?"

" No, my daughter. Does this thought disturb you? Take courage, I will never desert you. My Immaculate Heart will be your refuge and the way which will lead you to God."

By now Our Lady had begun to fulfil her promises. Jacinta and Francisco were already in Heaven and Lucia was left alone. In spite of Our Lady's promise not to abandon her, the loss of her two beloved companions left a gap in Lucia's life, brought a loneliness and solitude which nothing could fill.

> How sad I felt when I was left alone! (she later wrote). Within a short time I lost my dear father and then Francisco and Jacinta. Whenever I could I went to the Cabeço and hiding behind the rocks alone with God, I poured out my heart in tears.

Everything reminded Lucia of the little friends whom Our Lady had taken away. There were the same sheep

grazing on the *serra;* the spring flowers waving to the
breeze; the oak trees which Francisco had climbed for the
acorns of mortification; and above all the Cova da Iria
with its tiny white chapel marking the spot where on that
lovely May day the Queen of Angels came to earth for the
first time. Everything spoke of Jacinta and Francisco,
and were so many swords in Lucia's heart.

Years passed and in the cemetery of Fatima new graves
were opened. After Jacinta and Francisco and Lucia's
father, it was the turn of Florinda and Teresa, Ti Marto's
daughters. The immensity of Heaven . . . the Lady bathed
in light . . . Jesus Who had fleetingly shown Himself near
the sun on that 13th of October; indeed it must be good to
die!

But Lucia had to live. The designs of the Mother of
God were not yet complete, and her mission on earth was
not yet fulfilled.

*   *   *   *

The Church, after the first years of indifference if not of
distrust in face of the progressive developments in the Cova
da Iria, began to watch events there more closely.

The Diocese of Leiria was restored in 1918, and the
Bishop appointed was his Excellency D. José Alves
Correia da Silva, consecrated on 15th May, 1920, who took
up office on 5th August of that same year.

Dom José saw at once that prudence demanded the
removal of the only remaining seer, Lucia, from Aljustrel.
This for two motives: first, in order that a careful exam-
ination of the extraordinary events of which she was the
centre might be made; and secondly, to spare the poor
child the continual questions to which she was still submitted.

This measure would also test the continuation of pilgrimages to the Cova da Iria without the presence of Lucia,
to whose prestige exclusively, many people attributed the
ever-increasing flow of pilgrims. Should the events be of
merely human origin, or even of the powers of darkness,
the absence of Lucia would be one of the best means to
test results. If her mother should consent, nothing could
be more opportune than to place the girl as a boarder in
some college away from her home where no one would
know her or speak to her of Fatima.

Maria Rosa welcomed this suggestion with alacrity and

took her daughter—who was no less jubilant in spite of certain misgivings—to the Bishop's house in Leiria to interview Dom José.

" You must not tell anyone where you are going," he told Lucia with the utmost seriousness.

" No, my lord," she replied.

" In the college you must not tell anyone who you are."

" No, my lord."

" And you must not speak again about the Apparitions of Fatima."

" No, my lord," said Lucia for the third time.

It was June 13th. On the way back from Leiria, they met groups of pilgrims returning from their devotions in the Cova da Iria. Drawing her kerchief closely round her face Lucia bent her head to hide the tears which were pouring down her face.

The departure was arranged for the 18th. No one was to know where she was going and no farewells were to be said.

" When you go away you must come and say good-bye to me," Maria da Capela (now her greatest friend) had told her a fortnight before.

" Of course," Lucia assured her.

But the Bishop's command had to be rigorously obeyed. She must not say a word to anybody, not even to relations and friends. No one must know that she was leaving Aljustrel perhaps for ever, and was going to disappear into the College of the Dorotheas in Vilar, near Oporto.

The days seemed to pass in a flash. The little trousseau was prepared, but as the day of departure approached Lucia's heart filled with a heaviness and sadness which nearly overwhelmed her.

Her last day in her home was spent, not in taking leave of people, but of the places which had played such a great part in her life.

She went first to the Cabeço. The shadows in the rocks contrasted strongly with the light tones of the sunlit olives and oak trees on the slopes. The heat was oppressive and the crickets set up their deafening song. Bees hummed in the rock roses in full flower. Lucia saw none of these things. She ran straight to the place where she and her cousins had spent so many hours in prayer and contemplation. Prostrating herself on the ground she poured out

the angel's prayer, more fervently, more deeply than ever
before.

She stayed there for the greater part of an hour.   All
sound, all movement, ceased around her.   The silence was
broken only by her whispers sometimes breaking into sobs,
repeating over and over again:

" My God, I believe, I adore, I hope, and I love You.
I ask pardon for those who do not believe, do not adore,
do not hope, and do not love You "—and the prayer of
the angel to the Holy Trinity for the reparation of sin and
the conversion of sinners.

At Valinhos, Lucia stopped for a few moments to kneel
by the oak tree and remember with gratitude Our Lady's
unexpected visit in reward for the children's constancy in
the prison at Vila Nova de Ourem.   Running through the
trees by stony paths that she knew well, she came to the
Carreira pool where she stopped again.   The June sun had
reduced it to a muddy basin in the ground where a few sheep
paddled in the dregs of stagnant water which Jacinta, in her
thirst for mortification, had wanted to drink.

But Lucia's heart was running before her to the Cova da
Iria.   She sped to the simple white chapel which at this
hour was deserted.   Kneeling devoutly, she relived the
almost unbelievable moments of the Apparitions and from
time to time lifted her eyes to the smiling statue which
seemed to say:

" Do not be afraid . . . I will not desert you. . . . My
Immaculate Heart will be your refuge and the way which
will lead you to God. . . ."

When the sun began to descend over the horizon, Lucia
rose from her knees, tenderly kissed the threshold of the
chapel and took the road which led to the Church of
Fatima.   This also was one of the stations on her way of
the cross.

Here, as a new-born baby, she had been made a child of
God; six years later she had received the body of her Lord;
and with Jacinta and Francisco what happy times she had
spent with hidden Jesus!   We may divine what passed in
Lucia's homely but sensitive heart during those agonizing
moments.

And now it was time to go.   Her mother would be getting anxious and would send someone to find her.   She made
a last round of the church to say good-bye to the saints she
had known all her life: Our Lady of the Rosary, St.

Anthony, St. Sylvester, who was carried in the ox-cart procession, and St. Quiteria.

Yet one more station must be passed on the dolorous way.
In the cemetery she knelt at her father's graveside and by
the plot of land which held the mortal remains of Francisco.
It was over. She ran quickly back to Aljustrel, and as
darkness fell opened the cottage gate and went in. Supper
was not yet ready, and in the few moments left she went
out again under the stars to the well at the bottom of the
garden where she spent a few moments in converse with
Jacinta and Francisco. The moon—" Our Lady's lantern "
shone above, and the millions of stars—" the angels' lamps "
—sprinkled the great vault of the heavens with their golden
dust. And now her mother was calling her to supper—
the last supper in her home.

Lucia's sleep was short that night. At two o'clock in
the morning, with her small bundle of belongings, she set
off with her mother into what was for her the unknown.
The stars, in their changed positions, still shone brilliantly
in the summer night. As they passed the Cova da Iria,
Lucia begged Maria Rosa to go with her and say the Rosary.
They made their way down the slope to the chapel where
they knelt together on the dewy ground. The Ave Marias
came tenderly from Lucia's lips, for it was a conversation
not between two friends, but between a beloved mother and
devoted daughter who understood each other perfectly.
What is for us a matter of faith was for Lucia an object of
clear vision.

After the Rosary, Maria Rosa and Senhor Carreira who
was accompanying them, rose from their knees but Lucia
could not get up; an unseen force seemed to nail her there.
Her last tears fell over the mutilated trunk of the miraculous tree.

" Good-bye, dearest Mother, good-bye! "

But a well-known voice seemed to answer:

" It is not good-bye, for I shall always be with you."

CHAPTER XLV

OFFICIAL INTRUSION

So closed the first chapter in Lucia's life. Another was to open in the college in Vilar. There, however, we will leave her and pass on to a rapid survey of the events which followed her departure from the place of the Apparitions. We cannot do better than allow Maria da Capela to tell the story as she saw it:

> Hardly a month had passed since the completion of the chapel (she says) when a man from Torres Novas called Gilbert appeared and asked me who had built the chapel, etc. I told him how it had happened. He looked upset and went on:
> " I had made a promise to make a large contribution to the first building here and would have spent a great deal of money on a chapel. I came on the 13th of last month and there wasn't a stone out of place, and now I find a chapel already complete."
> I told him that it was a pity but that he could fulfil his promise by contributing towards the statue. This seemed to please him and he said he would speak to his parish priest and if he agreed, would arrange to have a statue made. It was not long before he came back with the answer that the parish priest had consented and that he was going to arrange everything. He returned several times to Fatima with the sculptor to question the children, and sometimes came with Dr. Formigão, who was a great friend of Ti Marto and Maria Rosa. Jacinta had not yet left for the hospital in Lisbon. However, it all took a very long time and one day some people from the Quinta da Cardiga came and offered an image of Our Lady of the Rosary which they had at home. I told them that we must wait for the other and that if it did not arrive we might use theirs. But at last the statue was finished and by the beginning of May was in Senhor Gilbert's house. It was arranged that it should be brought here on the 13th but when it arrived at Fatima it was prevented from going on to the Cova for some reason. Fr. Antonio Reis (who was taking Fr. Ferreira's place) blessed it and it stayed for some time hidden in the sacristy because rumours had been spread about that the Freemasons were planning to blow up the chapel and kill us all.

These fears were not unjustified, for hostility to the Apparitions had in no way diminished. On the contrary, in proportion to the peaceful increase of devotion, so did the hate of its opponents gather like a storm round what they called " this despicable reactionary superstition ".

In Lisbon, towards the middle of April, 1920, a frantic effort to discredit Fatima burst into the open. It appeared that a great pilgrimage was being organised in Torres Novas for Ascension Day, to accompany the new commemorative statue. People were going in hundreds of motor cars from Lisbon and many more on horseback and on foot; multitudes of priests and the inevitable Jesuits were to take part in it; crowds of children dressed as angels, etc., etc. There was to be a parade of the forces of reaction, the like of which had not been seen before.

This called forth a letter addressed to the Mayor of Vila Nova de Ourem, dated 24th April, 1920.

> Sir,
>
> Through our mutal friend, Senhor de Sousa, it has come to our knowledge that reactionary elements in your county are preparing to canonise the deceased seer of Fatima and so continue the disgusting religious exploitation of the people which has been set in motion. We beg you, therefore, to inform us as to what stage these manœuvres have reached in order that we, the Government, and your good self may take such precautions as seem advisable to neutralise this shameless Jesuitical trick.
>
> Certain that we may rely on your valuable help in this matter, we are, dear Sir,
>
> > Yours fraternally,
> >
> > Secretary for the Exterior,
> >
> > JULIO BENTO FERREIRA.

The Mayor's help could obviously be relied on.[1] On the 30th of the month all the *regedors* of the county received the following circular:

> For reasons of public security, you are asked to appear in the County Hall on Thursday next, May 6th.

The meeting took place as arranged, and after full discussion the Mayor was satisfied. On the next day, the 7th,

---

[1] Senhor Julio Lopes, who was at that time secretary to Arthur Santos, told us the following: " As the rumour of the proposed pilgrimage began to be spread abroad, Arthur exclaimed: ' I must put a stop to this ridiculous fairy tale!' I replied: ' You won't be able to do anything!' He then said: ' Not a soul shall get in there; they can't do anything against brute force!' "

Arthur Santos received a telegram from the Civil Governor of Santarem, Dr. José Dantas Baracho:

To the Mayor of Vila Nova de Ourem.

His Excellency, Minister Interior, decided repetition Fatima arranged for this month must be prevented. Notify organisers of procession or other religious manifestation under law which will be applied in case of non-co-operation. Disobedience to be answered for in court, after legal notice given. His Excellency determines this matter to be brought directly my attention without intermediary.

Civil Governor.

The zealous Mayor, of course, lost no time in the matter, and on that same day sent instructions to his *regedors*:

By order H.E. Minister Interior, Fatima repetition arranged for 13th inst. to be prevented. Kindly supply at once names organisers and propagandists in your district in order that law may be applied in case of disobedience.

Suspecting, however, that his orders might not be fulfilled with much zeal by these functionaries, Arthur Santos decided to ask for troops from Santarem.

The answer was not long in coming:

To the Mayor of Vila Nova de Ourem.

Armed Municipal Guard will be placed at your disposal, occupy strategic points, prevent transit Fatima procession.

JOSE DANTAS BARACHO.
Civil Governor.

And on the 12th, another telegram:

To the Mayor of Vila Nova de Ourem.

According agreement made here yesterday force commandant will only prohibit religious manifestation on the spot. Strong armed guard despatched locality.

JOSE DANTAS BARACHO.
Civil Governor.

Let us now consider the effect of these diligent arrangements as seen through the eyes of Dr. Formigão and related
in the first book published on the Apparitions, *Os Episódios
Maravilhosos de Fátima* (1921):

> I arrived at Vila Nova de Ourem early in the morning on
> 13th May last. It was pouring with rain and a thunderstorm
> was in progress at the same time.
>
> When I left Lisbon there were alarming rumours about
> Fatima, and people said that it was useless to attempt to go
> there because there were official orders to prevent transit
> through Vila Nova de Ourem.
>
> For this reason, many people who had arranged to come
> with me did not in fact leave Lisbon but I took a chance
> on it and came to see for myself how much truth there was
> in the reports.
>
> On arrival I saw two ladies, one young and attractive and
> the other older but distinguished looking, both of whom I
> knew slightly.   Poor things!   In that torrential rain I was
> reminded of the verse of Genesis: *Et apertae sunt cataractarum
> aquarum et fontes abyssi magni.* But they did not complain
> and were full of faith and enthusiasm.   Their only fear seemed
> to be that they might be prevented from arriving at the place
> of the Apparitions.
>
> With great difficulty we made our way to a little inn in
> front of the church, and there we rested until daybreak because
> it was quite impossible to get rooms.
>
> Very early in the morning we heard a troop of horses pass-
> ing, and ran to the window where we saw a squadron of
> Cavalry of the Republican Guard which was proceeding at
> a gallop in the direction of Fatima.   The rumours were not,
> then, without foundation.   We asked a servant what was in
> the air but received the same reply.   Nothing but rumours . . .
> rumours.   That there were infantry, cavalry, machine-guns
> and I know not what besides.   A general offensive seemed to
> be in progress, but against what, in the name of God!   No one
> knew, said the woman.   One thing was certain; from Ourem
> no one could go to Fatima.   Transport was available and in
> great demand at $40.00 a cart, but all were eventually dispensed
> with to the intense annoyance of the owners, good Republicans
> all, but unable to see why peaceful citizens should be pro-
> hibited from an excursion which suited them so well.
>
> In Tomar, it seemed, the same prohibition was in force,
> also in several other districts whose authorities had forbidden
> the departure of vehicles.
>
> While we were talking, a young man, owner of a printing press
> in Lisbon, and shortly afterwards Dr. da Fonseca, a lawyer,
> who was defending a client in the local court, came up to us.
> We asked them if they knew anything.   No more than we
> did apparently.   People were being allowed to go as far as
> Fatima but no further.   At about that time the rain stopped
> and I went out into the road where I watched the passage

of carts and cars, lorries, footfolk and horsemen—a regular excursion!

I wondered to what purpose all the prohibitions had been. I had expected to see nobody and yet here was this constant stream of men, women and children.

There were huge char-a-bancs drawn by mules, filled with people roaring with laughter, laughing apparently at the Mayor whom I could see in the middle of the road looking uncomfortable in a straw hat with a forced smile on his lips.   There were carts decorated with flowers . . . motor cars blowing their horns, grand looking carriages, modest dog carts . . . men and women on foot, soaked to the skin and covered with mud, dripping with water but happy, smiling.   All this unfolded before me like a long cinema film.   Where did all these people come from?   From all parts but mostly from Torres Novas I was told.   And what was the Mayor doing flitting about in his straw hat?   What new development was about to unfold?   It was all most entertaining!

I wanted to go to Fatima with all speed but there was Mass to be thought of.   I asked what time it was said in the church and was told at eleven.   I heard Mass, lunched in great haste and set off on the steep road which winds uphill from Ourem to Fatima.

Coming the other way was a car travelling at speed in which I caught a glimpse of rifles, fanning out menacingly.   It was the Mayor and his escort!   "He's up to no good," observed a lad pedalling uphill on a bicycle.   After climbing for an hour and a half we neared Fatima and the rain began to fall again.   At last we entered the little square facing the church.   Everywhere we saw carts, carriages and cars parked. A great crowd of people, numbering thousands, was blocking the square and the church.   In the middle of the road a force of infantry and cavalry of the Republican Guard was preventing the people from passing and completing the remaining three kilometres which separate Fatima from the Cova.   I asked some bystanders whether anyone had in fact passed. Until midday, I was told, everyone had gone through but then the Mayor had arrived and forbidden it.   I asked the commandant whether one might go through but he informed me politely that he had allowed people to pass until the Mayor had given orders to the contrary.   He was very sorry but he had to obey orders.   I went back and mingled with the enormous crowd which was gathered inside the church and in the porch sadly commenting on the affair and unable to understand what threat to public order could possibly exist in the Cova da Iria and not in Fatima since the people were the same.   It was perfectly ridiculous everyone agreed.

Many people tried to get through the fields without being seen, climbing walls and other obstacles, and managed to arrive at the place of the Apparitions, counting themselves fortunate to kneel there and say the Rosary.   Perhaps it was this which put the Government in peril!

Inside the church at Fatima, Fr. Cruz was delivering sermons

and leading the Rosary, while many people were going to
Confession. A blind woman who had come at the cost of
much sacrifice from Aveiro was leaning on the arm of a
friend in the pouring rain which had begun again. She
made no complaint, but on the contrary entrusted herself with
great faith to God and began walking towards the church. A
bearded individual, who told me he was a doctor, was explain-
ing the providential reasons for the prohibition to a crowd
which had gathered round him. According to him, people
had begun to turn the place into a sort of fair with music,
etc., and obviously Our Lady did not want this. She had
appeared in a deserted place precisely because she wanted to
be loved and venerated in spirit and truth, without accompani-
ments more reminiscent of the less edifying *festas,* etc., etc.
Prayer and penance, this and this alone was what she wanted,
therefore by this prohibition the authorities were all uncon-
sciously satisfying the desires of Our Lady!

The rain began to fall torrentially again and everyone tried
to find shelter underneath carts or in the porch of the church
which was already crammed to capacity.

At this moment I saw a Republican Guard dealing out
blows right and left on some peaceful peasants who were sadly
surveying the scene from under their umbrellas. Surprised
by the entirely unexpected attack they fled without knowing
why they had been set upon. Somebody went up to the
guards to ask the reason for this. They complained that a
man had tried to force a way through and that when they
prevented him he threatened them and in the confusion that
followed the innocent suffered with the guilty as is the way of
the world.

After this explanation, and order having been restored, I
began to talk to some peasants and prudently advised them not
to make any attempt to pass, adding that there would be great
merit in obeying orders however unjust, provided there was
nothing against conscience in doing so. Then one of the
guards said to me with the utmost sincerity:

"If you only knew, sir, how I dislike this duty. I obey
orders because I have to, but believe me, I hate it in my heart.
I am religious myself and I cannot understand why these
poor people should be prevented from going to the Cova to
pray. It's enough to upset a man. I have a sister whose
life was saved by Our Lady of Fatima!"

As he said this a drop of water rolled down his cheek, most
certainly not from the rain which poured and dripped from
his waterproof hood.

After this I went to the presbytery whose veranda, designed
in the old Portuguese style, was being assaulted by those
trying to find shelter from the weather. Here I saw one of
the ladies who had been my companions in the morning, and
she confided to me in a whisper that she was going to find
her way to the Cova by a secret path through the fields. I saw
her set off in the soaking rain and mud, delighted at the idea
that she was going to get the better of the modern Herods
in the Government.

At last our coachman warned us that the road was bad and that we ought to leave soon. We performed our last devotions, said our farewells and returned to Ourem and thence to our home.

At the station, while we were waiting for the train, we met many people from different parts of the country who were returning home as we were. We saw the blind lady from Aveiro with a companion from Oporto, both of whom, in spite of being soaked to the skin, and in poor health, were none the less in splendid spirits. I saw a friend who was a jeweller in Lisbon and many other people from the capital. . . .

A respectable business man, apparently a Republican, poured forth his invective upon the Mayor of Ourem because he prevented the progress of the countryside and obstructed legitimate trade.

" He's a fool," he exclaimed. " Just think of how much the cabmen of Tomar and Torres Novas must have lost to-day!"

CHAPTER XLVI

DEVOTION

THE authorities of the district were entirely satisfied with the result of the Mayor's work, and two days later he received the following communication:

Sir,
The Portuguese Federation of Freethought tenders you its profound sympathy in the action, so well in accord with Republican sentiments and freethought, which you have taken with regard to the pretended miracle of Fatima whereby Jesuit and clerical reaction are trying to exploit popular ignorance. Certain that you will appreciate the extent of our admiration for your manner of procedure, we remain,
Most faithfully yours, etc.

To this complimentary epistle, Arthur Santos replied on 5th June, 1920:

To the Portuguese Federation of Freethought.
Largo do Intendente, 45. Lisbon.

I acknowledge the receipt of your letter of the 15th ult. and thank you for your congratulations which are however unmerited.

On 13th May, thanks to the foresight of the Republican Government, under that great patriot and illustrious citizen, Antonio Maria Baptista, reaction suffered a complete reverse, while the projected parade, whereby the ignorance of illiterate people was to be exploited once again, was brought to nothing, together with the new attack which was being prepared against the Republic.

However, these authentic enemies of the Republic and promoters of Fatima are not yet entirely disarmed for they propose to transfer with all their pomps, the body of an unfortunate child and pretended intermediary of the Virgin, who died in Lisbon, to another tomb. They also still make use of a so-called seer, Lucia, an ailing child of thirteen years, in order further to exploit the ignorance of the people.

But such absurd projects can have no effect while a Government such as we have at present, and Associations such as the Federation of Freethought, fulfil their august mission, which is to combat lies and defend liberty.

At the same time the Mayor wrote to the *regedor* of Fatima:

I beg to inform you that in future no religious parade *of any kind* may take place in your parish without the knowledge of my Administration. Kindly notify the parish priest and the promoters of any religious manifestation of my orders and inform me personally of any incident of a superstitious nature which may occur in connection with the so-called miracle of Fatima.

Although as we have seen, events moved favourably up to a certain point, it was still deemed prudent not to bring the statue immediately to the Cova da Iria. Several months passed and the niche designed for it still remained empty.

We were so afraid of some profanation (says Maria da Capela) but at the same time we were longing to be able to venerate a statue of Our Lady in the very place where she had appeared. One day Gilberto came and said that he thought it would be a good idea to veil over the niche so that people would think that the statue was already there. Then we could see if anything untoward happened. So I put a towel over the niche and everyone thought that Our Lady was behind it. Nothing at all happened. So Gilberto brought the statue and put it in the niche. Months passed and there began to be new rumours that the statue was to be stolen and the chapel burned down. So we thought it would be better to take the statue to my home and bring it to the chapel every morning. It must have been about the end of October when my husband brought Our Lady to our home in Moita. We arranged a little altar in the sitting-room and put the statue on it with two oil lamps burning.

We were perfectly right to be afraid, for on 6th March in the next year (1922) we heard a terrible explosion during the night. The freemasons had placed four bombs in the chapel and a fifth by the tree where Our Lady appeared. The roof was blown off but the bomb by the tree did not explode.

We wanted to repair the chapel at once but the Bishop said we were not to do so till he gave permission. This made us very sad. It depressed us very much to see the chapel in such a state and we didn't like to stay by it. We used to go there, say our prayers, and come away again. The people used to come to our house instead and pray by the statue. Among them were Dr. Marques and Dr. Formigão. People used to kneel by the door and pray. There were always people there and Our Lady answered them just the same so that people should have more faith. I was very happy to have Our Lady in my house. But now, Father, it upsets me to see people getting worse and worse.

On the 13th a great many people gathered to take the statue in procession to the Cova da Iria. We had no bier but every-one wanted a turn at carrying it. There were many promises to do this, and so each one carried it a little way. We sang and prayed as we went and when we arrived there we spent the afternoon at our devotions and had a procession; then we returned to my house. Oh, what happy times those were! As Our Lady passed, the people knelt in the road as they do for the Blessed Sacrament. It was beautiful in those days to see so many people thinking only of holy things. There was so much prayer, in fact we would spend a whole day from early morn-ing onwards in Our Lady's company.

Many came to fulfil their promises and light candles; others came to ask for certain graces, but everyone went away happy.

A poor woman from Tomar took earth away from here to make infusions and cure sick people because in those days there was no water. They dug up the earth near the tree and rubbed the sick with it. Some people ate it and were better afterwards. Sometimes, even ladies would rub it on their well-dressed little children without minding the dirt!

In Alqueidão there was a girl who had been paralysed for seven months. Her parents did not have her treated and she was very poor. One day Our Lady of Fatima appeared to her and told her that she would cure her if her mother would go to the Cova and take some earth from under the oak tree and eat some of it during a novena. It all happened as Our Lady had said and the girl was perfectly cured.

Another time I saw a man from Torres Novas in tears near the big oak tree. I went and asked him what was the matter and he told me his story. He had had an open wound in the leg for twenty-four years which was always full of pus and prevented him from working or even moving. The wound absolutely refused to heal, and he said to me:

" My wife came to Fatima and took away some earth to make an infusion to wash my wound with. I did not want her to do this because the wound needed cleanliness and the mud would certainly make it worse. But my wife, who had great faith, said that many people had been cured with the earth, and although I had no faith at all in God nor any religion, she insisted so much that at last I let her have her way. Every day for nine days she washed the wound with that mud and each

day it healed a little more until at the end of the novena it was
perfectly cured. I burst into tears, took off the bandages and
came here on foot although I couldn't move before!"

Another time it was a consumptive from Tomar, also an
unbeliever. His wife told him that they would go to Fatima
or at least make a novena with an infusion of the earth under
the tree where Our Lady had appeared. But he wouldn't hear
of anything of the kind. His wife insisted so much that in the
end he consented to drink the infusion though without faith or
devotion. In spite of this Our Lady cured him and in a few
days he was strong and healthy again.

From this time people came every day to get the earth for
their sick. We dug it up in spoonfuls and the people took it
away in their handkerchiefs or in paper bags. On the 13th
we would give out two or three sackfuls of earth from an open
trench by the tree of the Apparitions. At night we filled up
the trench again with earth from somewhere else.

CHAPTER XLVII

THE SPRING

THE miracles operated by means of the infusions of earth
from the site of the Apparitions did much to spread devotion to Our Lady of Fatima.

They came from everywhere (continues Maria da Capela)
with their afflictions and their miseries. At the time of the
pneumonic " flu ", before the chapel was built, Friar David,
from Sta. Caterina, gave the first sermon here. People came
from the three parishes of Fatima, Santa Caterina and
S. Mamede. We took our own saints in the procession, St.
Lucy, Our Lady of the Rosary and others.

" This is all very fine, my children," said Friar David, " but it
is worth nothing without amendment of life."

Jacinta was there on that day, very weak with pneumonia.
The people wept in their affliction because of this epidemic
and Our Lady heard them because from that day we had no
more cases in our district. From then the devotion increased
even more, and after the chapel was built thousands of people
came. And there was not one spring or well for them all.

When on 12th October, 1926, the Bishop of Leiria made
his first visit to the Cova da Iria he saw at once the urgent
necessity for water, and set Senhor Carreira the task of
opening a well.

At first (says his wife) we thought of opening it about eighty
yards from the chapel near a fig tree, but in the end it was José
Alves whose idea won the day. Dr. Marques dos Santos (at

present Vicar-General of the diocese), the Prior of St. Caterina and the Vicar of Olival were also present.

"I am sure it's no good digging a well here," said José Alves.

"Well, what do you suggest?" asked the vicar of Olival.

"There," replied José, pointing to the place where the Cova was deepest. Even after a month without rain there is always a little moisture and some reeds there."

"And there we dug, to my delight ever afterwards!" he used to say. However, we had hardly worked half a day when we hit rock.

"What happens now?" asked their reverences.

"Now we blast the rock," was our reply, and we went to get the necessary tools. Afterwards the water came up abundantly though we didn't finish the well. It remained like that until the following year.

Did the water appear miraculously? The people of the *serra* and pilgrims from everywhere took it to be so, and an increasing number came to fill their vessels from the ever-running fountain.

They came here (recalls José Alves) with their bottles and their pitchers which they filled and took home for their sick to drink and wash their wounds in. Everyone had the greatest faith in Our Lady's water and she used it to cure their pain and wounds. Never did Our Lady do so many miracles as at that time. I saw people with terrible legs, running with pus, but they washed them there and left their bandages behind because Our Lady cured them. Others knelt and drank that earthy water and were cured of internal diseases.

Our Lady, tender Mother that she is, seems to play a joke on mankind and to laugh at the hygienic fears of the well-to-do, working miracles with elements which, humanly speaking, could only cause infection and worse complications! And, in fact, those responsible for public health began to grow alarmed.

On 15th July, 1927, the Mayor of Ourem (Antonio Pavilon) sent the following official note to the *regedor* of the parish of Fatima:

My attention has been called by the Sub-delegate of Public Health in this county, to an open ditch of water which Manuel Carreira of Moita has dug in the Cova da Iria. This water is used by persons suffering from exterior and interior diseases in such a manner that I have resolved to call the said Carreira, with yourself as intermediary, before the Administration of this county and call upon him to cover this ditch which

*is an immediate danger to public hygiene. Will you
kindly inform me without delay as to what can be
done in this case?*

(*Signed*) PAVILON.

This functionary knew, however, that little or no help
could be expected from the *regedor,* so he went personally
to Fatima with the Sub-delegate of Public Health, Dr.
Joaquim Francisco Alves.   They visited the locality in
question, and on the way had an interview with the parish
priest, Father Ferreira, who recalls the conversation:

" The place is disgusting," declared Dr. Alves. " It must be
covered over at once. It's a disgrace to the parish."
" Faith never hurt anyone yet," replied I.   " It's a miracle
already that such dirty, impure water does no harm to those
who drink it, apart from the fact that people declare miracles
to have occurred in the place."

Taking leave of the priest, the two officials at the same
time intimated that he must see to the covering of the well,
otherwise he would be held responsible for anything that
might subsequently occur.

If the *regedor* did not dare to offend the susceptibilities
of the people how was their parish priest to proceed?

In the following year, on 13th August, the Mayor sent
yet another official note to the Sub-delegate of Public
Health:

*It appears that the well in the Cova da Iria con-
tinues to remain open, constituting a menace to public
health and sanitation, in view of the fact that the said
water is full of dirt and microbes. I, therefore, request
your advice on the matter and await your suggestions
for the destruction of this ditch, which I am determined
to effect as soon as possible.*

This sudden preoccupation on the part of the authorities
seems strange when so many other water supplies of the
same kind exist in the county.   However, the Bishop
ordered that the well should be deepened and covered, and
this work was carried out under the supervision of the
Mayor, the parish priest and the Sub-delegate, who had been
alarmed at rumours that the water had been poisoned.

Dr. Alves finally declared the water to be drinkable, and
after the Chapel of the Apparitions, the fountain was the

first of the buildings which we now see within the Sanctuary.

Slowly but surely, as is the way with all the works of God, the tiny seed which had been sown was to grow until it became a tree, with branches spreading out over the whole earth. Such is the grain of mustard seed in the Gospel parable.

CHAPTER XLVIII

THE CHURCH SPEAKS

DURING the five years which followed the Apparitions the ecclesiastical authorities maintained the most prudent reserve.

On 3rd May, 1922, two years after the restoration of the Diocese of Leiria, Dom José Alves Correia published a Pastoral Letter from which we extract the following passages:

In this Diocese of Leiria, there can be no fact connected with our Holy Religion to which our pastoral action is or could be indifferent.

Practically every day, but more especially on the 13th of each month, great numbers of people go to Fatima. These people are drawn from every social category and they go there to thank Our Lady of the Rosary for the benefits they have received through her mediation.

It is well known that in 1917 a series of phenomena occurred there, witnessed by thousands of people of all kinds and foretold by some unlettered children to whom, it was affirmed, Our Lady had appeared and made certain recommendations. From that time there has never ceased to be a flow of pilgrims to the place.

Of the three children who said they were favoured by the Apparitions, two died before our appointment to this diocese. We have questioned the remaining seer several times.

Her story and her replies are always simple and sincere; in them we can find nothing contrary to faith or morals. We ask, could this child, now 14 years old, exercise an influence which could explain such a continuous concourse of people? Could her personal prestige alone draw such

multitudes of human beings? Could any precocious quali-
ties in her attract vast crowds to herself alone? It is most
improbable that such could be the case since we are dealing
with a child of most rudimentary education, and without
instruction of any kind.

Moreover, this child has now left her native place and
has not been seen there again; yet the people go in ever-
increasing numbers to the Cova da Iria.

Could one explain it perhaps by the natural beauty or
picturesqueness of the place? On the contrary, it is a
lonely and deserted spot, without trees or water, far from the
railway, almost lost in the serra and destitute of scenic
beauties.

Do the people go there because of the chapel perhaps?
The faithful have constructed a tiny cell, so small that it is
impossible to celebrate Holy Mass inside, and in the month
of February of this year some unfortunate people—may Our
Lady forgive them—destroyed the chapel with explosives
during the night and set fire to it.

We have advised against its reconstruction for the
moment, not only with the idea of further attacks in mind
but also to test the motives which draw so many people to
the place.

And yet, far from diminishing in numbers, the crowds
are ever greater.

The Ecclesiastical Authority has delayed its decision and
the clergy have abstained from taking part in any manifesta-
tion. Only lately have we permitted Low Mass to be cele-
brated and sermons to be given on the occasions of the great
popular pilgrimages.

The Civil Authorities have employed every means in their
power, not excluding persecution, imprisonment, and threats
of all kinds, to stop the religious movement in the place.
But all their efforts were in vain and no one can say that the
Church Authorities have in any way encouraged faith in the
Apparitions; the exact contrary is the case.

In answer to the demand implied in this letter, the Bishop
nominated a commission to study the case and set up the
canonical inquiry, among whose members were the Revs.
Dr. Formigão and Dr. Marques dos Santos.

In October, 1926, the Diocese of Leiria commemorated
the seventh centenary of St. Francis of Assisi. The
Apostolic Nuncio, who was present at the ceremonies, visited

Batalha and later the place of the Apparitions in company with the Bishop. The first impressions of Mons. Nicotra communicated to the Holy See, are not on record, but what is certain is that three months later, on the 21st January, 1927, the privilege of a Votive Mass was conceded to Fatima.

On the 26th of July of the same year, ten years, that is, after the Apparitions, the Bishop presided for the first time at an official ceremony in the Cova da Iria after the erection of the Stations of the Cross on the road from Leiria to Fatima.

Before the visit of the Nuncio, two prelates had visited the Cova da Iria, among them the Archbishop of Evora and the Primate of Braga. Later, came all the Bishops of the Mother Country and her Islands and Colonies, among them the Bishop of Portalegre, who was the first to allow Our Lady to be invoked under her new title in his diocese. When in Rome he had verified the fact that Our Lady of Fatima was venerated there, and that the Holy Father had distributed holy pictures of her to the students of the Portuguese College. He returned full of zeal for Our Lady's new Apparitions in his country and said: " I must not be more papist than the Pope!" He thereupon organised an imposing pilgrimage and was the first Bishop to celebrate Pontifical High Mass in the Cova da Iria.

So time passed until the commission set up by Dom José Alves Correia announced the results of its work. The Bishop then published a new Pastoral Letter in October, 1930, on the Apparitions, which contained the following memorable paragraphs:

In virtue of considerations made known, and others which for reason of brevity we omit; humbly invoking the Divine Spirit and placing ourselves under the protection of the most Holy Virgin, and after hearing the opinions of our Rev. Advisers in this diocese, we hereby:—

1° Declare worthy of belief, the visions of the shepherd children in the Cova da Iria, parish of Fatima, in this diocese, from the 13th May to 13th October, 1917.

2° Permit officially the cult of Our Lady of Fatima.

Nothing further was needed. The Pilgrimages to the Cova da Iria grew to immense proportions not only from Portugal but from both hemispheres and almost every corner of the earth. Fatima was to call down upon

Portugal an immensity of grace and for Christendom at large has come to symbolise the spiritual war against Communism and to be the focal point of the new Crusade.

The Apostolic Nuncio presided at the first Portuguese National Pilgrimage on the 13th May, 1937, at which it is calculated some half million pilgrims were present. The second National Pilgrimage took place on the 13th May, 1938, and was the fulfilment of a promise made by the Portuguese Episcopate if Our Lady should deliver Portugal from the Communist menace which caused the terrible civil war in Spain and which was waged in places only a few yards from her soil.

The 13th October, 1939, marked one of the most glorious pages in the history of the great new Marian Shrine. The Cardinal Patriarch of Lisbon presided at the Pilgrimage to implore peace for Portugal.

From the 8th-13th April, 1942, on the occasion of their Second National Congress, the *Juventude Catolica Feminina* (Girls' Catholic Youth Movement) organised the triumphal journey of the Statue from the Chapel of the Apparitions to Lisbon and back again to the Cova da Iria by the 13th of May, where another notable National Pilgrimage took place to celebrate the Silver Jubilee of Fatima. In October of the same year the Holy Father, Pius XII, broadcast in Portuguese his famous Consecration of the human race to the Immaculate Heart of Mary.

*   *   *   *

Consecration of Humanity to the Immaculate Heart of Mary.

Venerable Brethren and Beloved Children: *Benedicite Deo Caeli et coram omnibus viventibus confitemini ei, quia fecit vobiscum misericordiam suam.* Bless the God of Heaven and glorify Him before all the living because He has shown you His mercies. Once again, in this year of grace, you climbed the holy mountain of Fatima, taking with you the heart of all Christian Portugal. There in that oasis fragrant with faith and piety, you laid at the feet of your Virgin Protectress the tribute of your love, your homage and your gratitude for the immense benefits which you have lately received; you also made your humble supplication that she would continue her protection of your country at home and overseas and defend it from the great tribulation by which the world is tormented.

We, who as common Father of the faithful, make Our Own the sorrows as well as the joys of Our children, unite Ourselves with all the affection of Our heart with you to praise and exalt the Lord, giver of all good; to thank Him for the graces of her by whose hands you receive the divine munificence and this torrent of grace. We do this with the greater pleasure, because you with filial affection have desired to associate the Jubilee of Our Lady of Fatima and Our Own Episcopal consecration in the same Eucharistic solemnities. The Blessed Virgin Mary and the Vicar of Christ on earth are two devotions profoundly dear to the Portuguese. They have had a place in the heart of Portugal Fidelissimo from the dawn of her nationhood; from the time when the first reconquered lands, nucleus of the future Nation, were consecrated to the Mother of God as the *Terra de Santa Maria* and the newly-constituted kingdom was placed under the protection of St. Peter.

The first and greatest duty of man is gratitude.

There is nothing so pleasing to God as a soul grateful for the graces and benefits received and in this you have a great debt towards the Virgin Mother and Patron of your country.

In a tragic hour of darkness and distress, when the ship of the State of Portugal, having lost the guide of her most glorious traditions and driven off her course by anti-Christian and anti-national currents, seemed to be running for certain shipwreck, unconscious of present or future dangers whose gravity no one could humanly foretell; in that hour, Heaven, which foresaw these dangers, intervened, and in the darkness light shone; out of chaos order reigned; the tempest abated and Portugal the Faithful can pick up her glorious part as a crusading and missionary nation. All honour to those who have been the instruments of Providence in this glorious enterprise!

But glory and thanksgiving first and foremost to the Blessed Virgin, Queen and Mother of this land, which she always aided in its hours of tragedy, and in this most tragic of all made her protection so manifest, that in 1934, Our Predecessor, Pius XI (of immortal memory), attested in an apostolic letter " Ex officiosis Litteris " to the extraordinary benefits which the Mother of God had recently accorded to Portugal.

At that time the promise of May, 1936, against the Communist peril had not yet been made. This peril came so fearfully close, loomed up so unexpectedly that no one could have affirmed with certainty that the marvellous peace which Portugal has enjoyed, and which in spite of everything is immeasurably less ruinous than the present war of extermination, could be maintained. To-day further benefits can be added to those mentioned. The atmosphere of miracle in which Portugal is enveloped has been transformed into innumerable prodigies, many physical, and those yet more marvellous miracles of grace and conversion which flower in this springtime of Catholic life, and which promise to bear abundant fruit. To-day with even greater reason we must confess that the Mother of God has accorded you the most real and extraordinary blessings. The sacred duty of thanksgiving is all the more incumbent upon you.

That you have done this during the present year we are well aware. The official homage must have been agreeable to Heaven and also the sacrifices of children, the prayer and penance of the lowly and humble. The welcome given to Our Lady during her pilgrimage to the Capital of the Empire during the memorable days of last April was perhaps the greatest demonstration of faith in the eight centuries of your history as a Nation. Also the National Pilgrimage of the 13th of May, Heroic day of sacrifice, when in cold and rain hundreds of thousands of pilgrims came to Fatima on foot to pray and give thanks and make reparation. Among these the youth, enterprise, and vigorous example, of Catholic Youth were apparent; there were the Eucharistic Crusades of children who told the Mother of God that they had done what she desired—prayers, sacrifices, Communions in thousands—and therefore prayed: *Our Lady of Fatima, it now rests with you. Say but one word to your divine Son and the world will be saved and Portugal delivered from the scourge of war.* The precious crown of gold and jewels, and more important, of pure love and sacrifice which you offered to your august Protectress as a symbol and sign of your eternal gratitude; this and other most beautiful demonstrations of piety which, with the zealous help of the Episcopate, have been so fertile in all parishes and dioceses in this Jubilee Year, show the gratitude of the faithful Portuguese people and satisfy the debt which they owe to their heavenly Queen and Mother.

Gratitude for the past is a pledge of confidence for the future. God demands our gratitude for His benefits not because He needs our thanks but because these provoke Him to further generosity. For this reason it is right to trust that the Mother of God, in accepting your thanksgiving, will not leave her works incomplete and will faithfully continue to be your protectress as in days past and preserve you from greater calamities.

But, in order not to presume upon her goodness, it is necessary that each one, conscious of his responsibilities, should make every effort to be worthy of the singular favour of the Virgin Mother and as grateful and loving children, deserve her maternal protection more and more.

We must obey her maternal counsel as given at the Cana wedding and do all that Jesus desires us to do. And she has told everyone to do penance and turn away from sin, which is the principal cause of the great chastisements which Eternal Justice sends upon the world; that in the midst of this materialised and pagan world, in which the way of all flesh is corrupted, they must be the salt of the earth and the light, preserving and illuminating; they must carefully cultivate purity and reflect the holy austerity of the Gospels in their lives; and, at all costs, as the gathering of Catholic Youth affirmed in Fatima, openly live as sincere and convinced Catholics. More yet; filled with Christ, they must diffuse around them the sweet fragrance of Christ and by assiduous prayer, particularly the daily Rosary, and by the sacrifices with which God inspires them, obtain for sinners the life of grace and eternal salvation.

You will then most confidently invoke the Lord and He will hear you; you will call on the Mother of God and she will answer: " I am here." Then the watchman of the city will not keep watch in vain, because the Lord will keep guard and defence, while the house, which is built upon a secure foundation, will be fortified by the Lord. Happy are the people whose King is God and whose Queen is the Mother of God. She will intercede with God and bless her people with peace, which is the compendium of all good: *Dominus benedicet populum suum in pace.*

But you cannot be indifferent (indeed who could be so?) to the vast tragedy which torments the world. Rather, the more you are privileged by her mercies for which you give thanks to-day, the more securely will you place your confidence in the future under her protection, the more tragic will seem to you the fate of so many nations torn by the greatest calamity of history.

Terrible manifestation of Divine Justice! Let us adore

its greatness! Yet we must not doubt the divine mercy because Our Father in Heaven does not forget us, even in the days of His wrath: *Cum iratus fueris, misericordia recordaveris.*

Now that the fourth year of war has dawned more threateningly than ever with the spread of the conflict, now more than ever can our trust rest only in God; and, as mediator by the throne, in her name whom one of our predecessors in the First World War ordered to be invoked as Queen of Peace, let us invoke her again, for only she can help us. She whose maternal heart was moved by the ruin of your country and so wonderfully came to its aid; she, saddened by her foreknowledge of this terrible tragedy by which God's justice punishes the world, had already indicated in prayer and penance the road to salvation. She will not now deny us her maternal tenderness nor her most efficacious protection.

Queen of the most Holy Rosary, help of Christians, and Refuge of the human race, conqueror in all the great battles of God, we humbly prostrate ourselves, certain of obtaining mercy and finding grace and opportune help in the present calamity. We do not presume on our merits but only on the immense bounty of your maternal Heart. To You, to your Immaculate Heart, We as common father of the great Christian family, as Vicar of Him to Whom was given all power in Heaven and earth and from Whom we receive the charge of so many souls redeemed by His Precious Blood and which people the whole earth; to You, to Your Immaculate Heart in this tragic hour of human history, we confide, we consecrate, we deliver, not only Holy Church the Mystical Body of your Jesus which bleeds and suffers in so many parts and is in so much tribulation, but also the whole world, torn by discord, burning in the fires of hate, victim of its own iniquity. May You be moved by so much ruin, material and moral, so much sorrow, so much agony of fathers, mothers, wives, brothers and sisters, of innocent children, cut off in the flower of their lives, so many bodies destroyed in the horrible carnage, so many souls tortured and agonised, so many in danger of eternal loss.

Mother of Mercy, obtain from God both peace, and above all those graces which can convert evil hearts in a moment of time and which prepare, conciliate, assure true peace. Queen of Peace, pray for us and give peace to the world at war, that peace for which the peoples sigh, peace in the truth, the justice, the charity of Christ! Give peace from armed warfare and in souls, so that the Kingdom of God may develop in tranquillity and order.

Extend your protection to unbelievers and those who still lie in the shadow of death; give them peace and let the sunlight shine upon them so that they may repeat before the one Saviour of the World: Glory to God in the Highest and on earth peace to men of goodwill!

To peoples separated by error and discord, namely, those who profess You singular devotion where there was no house that did not display your holy icon, to-day hidden perhaps until better days, give them peace, and lead them again to the only flock of Christ under the true and only Shepherd. Obtain peace and complete liberty for the Holy Church of God. Stem the flooding waves of paganism and materialism, and kindle in the faithful love of purity, the practice of a Christian life, and apostolic zeal, that the people who serve God may increase in merit and in numbers.

Finally, as the Church and the whole human race were consecrated to the Sacred Heart of Jesus, so that placing in Him all its hopes it might have a pledge of victory and salvation, thus from to-day may they be perpetually consecrated to your Immaculate Heart, Oh Mother and Queen of the world, that your love and protection may hasten the triumph of the Kingdom of God and that all generations of mankind, at peace with themselves and with God, may proclaim you Blessed and with you may intone, from pole to pole, the eternal Magnificat of glory, love and thanksgiving to the Heart of Jesus where alone may be found Truth, Life and Peace.

In the hope that these our supplications and prayers may be favourably heard by the Divine Bounty; to you, beloved Cardinal Patriarch, venerable Brethren and clergy, that grace from on high may ever render your zeal more fertile; to the President of the Republic; to the illustrious Head of the Government and his Ministers and authorities, that in this singularly grave and difficult hour Heaven may continue to assist them in their activities in favour of peace and the common good; to all our beloved children in Portuguese territory at home and overseas, that the Blessed Virgin may confirm what she has deigned to operate in you; to all and each of the Portuguese as a pledge of celestial grace, we

bestow with all our paternal love and affection Our
Apostolic Benediction.

*   *   *   *

Rome had recognised and blessed the Apparitions to the
shepherd children of Aljustrel.   Henceforth Fatima was to
spread throughout the world.

CHAPTER XLIX

CORONATION

SOME four years passed and the World War came to an end.
Portugal, which had been visibly protected by the Blessed
Virgin and saved almost miraculously from the horrors
which almost every other European nation suffered, sought
to give public expression to the generally felt gratitude.

The women of Portugal contributed precious stones from
among their jewels to make a crown for the Statue which
had been venerated in the Chapel of the Apparitions since
the beginning.

Knowing that Pope Pius XII had followed with the
greatest interest and approval the resurgence of religion
in Portugal—a resurgence so obviously connected with the
Apparitions of Fatima—the Episcopate decided to ask the
Holy Father to send a Legate to the solemn Coronation
ceremony.

On the 10th May Cardinal Aloisi Masella arrived and
was received with all the honour due to a Pontifical Legate.
His first words were broadcast throughout the country:

*The great and sincere friend of Portugal, speaking to you
at this moment, experiences great satisfaction in returning to
this country after many years.   He is the Holy Father Pius
XII, gloriously reigning, who loves this country and is deeply
interested in its affairs.   He sends me to you, beloved
Portuguese children, with the most worthy mission of crowning Our Lady of Fatima, our Mother and Our Queen.*

*It is a Pontifical Legate who has come to tell you that the
Holy Father Pope Pius XII unites with you in the impressive
homage which you will pay to the Blessed Virgin during
these days.*

The ceremony, which will take place next Monday, will

certainly draw down upon your beloved country the choicest blessings of God.

It is for me an immense satisfaction to see the affection and regard with which you have received the Legate of the Supreme Pontiff. I will, as is my duty, make known to His Holiness the noble sentiments with which you have received me accompanied by such a great manifestation. I am sure that the Holy Father will feel the deepest satisfaction.

At this moment I would like to express my most sincere and profound gratitude to His Excellency the President of the Republic present in his representative, to His Eminence the Cardinal Patriarch, to the Bishops here present, the Ministers of State, the civil and military authorities and to all of you, together with my warmest wishes for the prosperity of your beloved country.

On the 12th of May about 800,000 people awaited the Cardinal Legate in the Cova da Iria. He arrived in company with all the Bishops of the Metropole and other eminent persons.

We find it impossible adequately to describe what we can justly call the most memorable day in the history of Christianity in Portugal. *Fatima was not only the altar of Portugal, it was the altar of the world.*

We shall now quote—and thus close this volume—the words of the Pope which he spoke to the pilgrims of Fatima and the Portuguese at home and overseas, directly after the Coronation Ceremony. Our last words shall be those of the Vicar of Christ on earth:

" Venerable Brethren and Beloved Sons and Daughters:

Blessed be the Lord God, Father of Our Lord Jesus Christ, Father of Mercies and God of all consolation, Who comforts us in all our tribulations. Blessed also she whom He appointed Mother of Mercy, Our Queen and our beloved Advocate, Mediatrix of all graces and dispenser of all His treasures.

When, four years ago, amid the turmoil of the most deadly war history has yet seen, we ascended this Holy Mountain in spirit with you for the first time, to join our thanks with yours for the immense benefits accorded you by Our Lady of Fatima, it was a magnificent occasion to mingle our prayers of filial confidence to the Immaculate Queen and Protector of Portugal and pray that she would complete that which she had so marvellously begun.

Your presence to-day in this Sanctuary in such immense numbers that they can hardly be calculated, is an affirmation that the Immaculate Virgin Queen, whose maternal and compassionate Heart conceived the prodigy of Fatima, has superabundantly heard your prayers.

Ardent grateful love has brought you here and, wishing to present her with a concrete expression of it, you symbolised and condensed the same into a precious crown —fruit of so much generosity and sacrifices—which by the hand of Our Cardinal Legate we have just placed upon the head of the miraculous Statue. It is a symbol to attest your love and gratitude to your Heavenly Queen and brings to your minds the love and benefits without number which the Virgin Mother has accorded to her *Terra de Santa Maria*. Eight are the centuries of benefits. The first five under the emblems of Santa Maria de Alcobaça, Santa Maria da Vitoria and Santa Maria de Belem, in the epic struggles for nationhood against the Crescent, and in the discovery of new islands and continents where your great men planted the Cross of Christ side by side with the national flag. The last three centuries came under the special protection of the Immaculate One Whom the Monarch of the Restoration, united in assembly with the whole nation, acclaimed Patron of his realms and possessions, offering her his crown as an especial tribute of vassalage with an oath to defend even to the death the privilege of her Immaculate Conception. He trusted, according to his own words, *with great confidence in the infinite mercy of Our Lord, and through Our Lady, Patron and Protectress of our realms and possessions, of Whom by our honour we confess ourselves to be vassals and servants, may we be defended and guarded from our enemies, with great increase of these realms to the glory of Christ our God, and to the exaltation of our Holy Catholic Roman Faith, the conversion of the heathen and the downfall of heretics.*

The Virgin most Faithful did not betray the trust which had been placed in her. It is enough to reflect on these last decades, on the crises surmounted and the benefits received. Enough to lift up the eyes and see the Cova da Iria transformed into a fountain flowing with supernatural grace; to see the physical prodigies and the even greater moral miracles, the torrents which flow from here over all Portugal and then, bursting all frontiers, spread to the whole Church and the world. How is it possible not to give thanks—or, rather, how is it possible to give thanks worthily?

Three hundred years ago, the Monarch of the Restoration laid his royal crown at the feet of the Immaculate Virgin, proclaiming her Queen and Patron. To-day it is all of you who act, the people of the *Terra de Santa Maria,* together with the shepherds of your souls and with your Government.

To the ardent prayers, to the generous sacrifices, to the Eucharistic solemnities, to the thousand acts of homage which your filial love has suggested to you, you have added the precious crown and with it have girded the brow of Our Lady of Fatima, here in this blessed oasis impregnated with the supernatural, where in a concrete manner you experience her marvellous protection and where you all feel nearer her Immaculate Heart filled with immense tenderness and maternal solicitude for you and for the world. Most precious crown, symbol of love and gratitude! This great concourse, the fervour of your prayers, the thunder of your acclamations, the holy enthusiasm which vibrates in your hearts; and, finally, the sacred rite which in this moment of incomparable triumph has just been performed, call to Our mind another multitude innumerable, other cries of homage yet more ardent, another solemn and eternal hour, the endless day of eternity when the glorious Virgin, triumphantly entering the Heavenly Homeland, through the nine choirs of angels, was raised even to the throne of the most Holy Trinity, Who placed upon her brow the triple diadem of glory. There she was presented to the court of Heaven, seated at the right hand of the Immortal King of Ages and crowned Queen of the Universe. And the King saw that she was truly worthy of such honour, glory and empire, because she was more filled with grace, more holy, more beautiful, nearer to the divine, incomparably more so than the greatest saints and sublimest angels separately or together. This because she is mysteriously related in the order of the Hypostatic Union with the Blessed Trinity, with Him Who is in essence the Infinite Majesty, King of Kings and Lord of Lords. She is the first-born Daughter of the Father and pure Mother of the Word, beloved Bride of the Holy Ghost, because Mother of the Divine King, of Him to Whom from her maternal womb the Lord God gave the throne of David and everlasting Kingship in the House of Jacob. He alone, proclaimed to have received all power in Heaven and earth, He the Son of God, decrees for His Mother all the glory, power and majesty of His Kingdom.

Because she is associated as Mother and Helper of the King of Martyrs in the ineffable work of human redemption, she is also for ever most powerfully associated in the distribution of grace and divine redemption. Jesus is King of the eternal ages by nature and by conquest. By Him, with Him, and under Him, Mary is Queen by grace, by her divine relationship, by conquest and by singular election. And her kingdom is vast, vast as that of her divine Son, because from her dominion none is excluded. So the Church salutes her as Lady and Queen of Apostles and Martyrs, of Confessors and Virgins, acclaims her Queen of Heaven and earth, most glorious and worthy Queen of the Universe— " Regina Cælorum ": most worthy Queen of the world— " Regina mundi ": the light shining amid the tears of this exile. " Hail, Holy Queen! Mother of Mercy, Hail! Our life, our sweetness and our hope." It is precisely this royalty that you have known not only in the more obvious benefits but also in the innumerable blessings of that maternal Heart which you praise and proclaim to-day.

The most terrible war which the world has seen, threatened for four long years to cross your frontiers, but thanks to Our Lady in her throne and heavenly watch-tower, here in the centre of your country, you were protected; the war was not allowed to touch you except in such ways as might the better cause you to realise the calamities from which you were preserved.

You have crowned her Queen of Peace and of the world which may thus be helped to find peace and to rise again from the ruins. And so this crown, symbol of love and gratitude for the past, as of faith and loyalty for the present, becomes also a message of hope for the future.

By crowning the Statue of Our Lady of Fatima you signed as it were a document of faith in her supremacy, a loyal submission to her authority, a filial and constant correspondence to her love. You did yet more; you enlisted as Crusaders in the conquest and reconquest of her Kingdom which is the Kingdom of God; that is to say, you bound yourselves before Heaven and earth to love her, to venerate her, to serve her, to imitate her in order that you might better serve the Divine King; and, at the same time, you bound yourselves to labour that she might be loved and venerated and served all around you, in the family, in society, in the world.

In this decisive hour of history in which the kingdom of evil employs all its forces with devilish cruelty to destroy faith and morals and the Kingdom of God, the children of Light and children of God must employ every means and unite wholeheartedly to defend them, that they may not be lost in a ruin incomparably greater and more disastrous than all the material ruin caused by the war.

In this struggle there must be no neutrals, no indecisive ones. There must be an enlightened, convinced and fearless Catholicism in its faith and works, in private as in public, 100 *per cent. Catholic,* in the words of the great gathering of Catholic Youth in Fatima four years ago.

In the hope that our prayers will be favourably heard by the Immaculate Heart of Mary and that the hour of her triumph and the triumph of the Kingdom of God may be hastened; as a pledge of celestial grace, to you Venerable Brethren and to all your clergy, to the President of the Republic and the illustrious head of the Government and his Ministers, to all the civil and military authorities and to all of you beloved sons and daughters, pilgrims of Our Lady of Fatima, with as many as are united to you in spirit in Portugal, at home and overseas, we bestow, with all paternal affection and love Our Apostolic Blessing.

CHAPTER L

«WE HAVE COME AS A HUMBLE AND FAITHFUL PILGRIM TO THIS HOLY SANCTUARY...» (PAUL VI)

On the 13th of May, 1967, the Holy Father, Pope Paul VI, made a pilgrimage to Fatima to celebrate the 50th anniversary of the first apparition of Our Lady to the three little shepherds.

The two-fold purpose of that journey was well understood by the immense crowd. As the Pope himself had announced, he wished to pay homage to the Mother of God and to implore from her Peace for the Church and for the world.

At Fatima, the Pope wanted Sister Lucia of the Immaculate Heart at his side, and he presented her to the crowd. His visit lasted only for a few hours, yet nevertheless it aroused great enthusiasm among the pilgrims, who had come from every corner of Portugal and from various parts of the world. It spurred them on, above all, to renew their Christian life and to live it according to the Gospel, so that the Lord might grant, through the intercession

of Mary, peace to souls, to families, to the nations and to the whole
of society.

Meaningfully linked with the Papal Pilgrimage was the apostolic exhortation "Signum Magnum" on devotion to Mary, which
bore the date of May 13th. It ended with the invitation to all to
renew personally their consecration to the Immaculate Heart of
Mary, in memory of the consecration of the Church and of mankind to that same Immaculate Heart, and to honour this most noble
act of veneration through a life ever more in keeping with the will
of God and in devout imitation of their Heavenly Queen.

As a way of concluding this book, we would like to give here
a summary of the homily delivered by the Pope during the celebration
of the Eucharist.

So great is Our desire to honor the Holy Virgin Mary, Mother
of Christ and therefore Mother of God and our Mother, so great
the faith in her Divine Son, that We have come as a humble and
a faithful pilgrim to this Holy Sanctuary, where the 50th anniversary
of the apparitions of Fatima is being celebrated today and where
the 25th anniversary of the consecration of the world to the
Immaculate Heart of Mary is being commemorated.

We are happy to meet with you, dear brethren and children,
and to include you all in the profession of our devotion to Mary and
in our prayer in order to give strength and filial love to our common
veneration and to make our invocation more fervent and acceptable.
We greet you, brethren and children, here present, and in a special
way the citizens of this illustrious nation, which in its long history
has given to the Church holy and great men and an industrious and
Christian people; you pilgrims who have come from all parts of the
country and from abroad; and you faithful of the Holy Catholic
Church, who from Rome, from distant lands and from your homes
scattered around the world are now spiritually facing this altar.
We greet all of you!

We celebrate now with you and for you the Holy Sacrifice of
the Mass and together we stand as children of one great family near
the Celestial Mother in order to be included in the celebration of
the Holy Sacrifice in a closer communion with Christ Our Lord and
Saviour. We would like to include everyone in this spiritual remembrance, because we want all to share the graces, which we now here
entreat from Heaven. The Holy Father then fondly recalled the
Bishops, Priests, Religious, the dear laymen who so desire to
collaborate with the clergy in order to increase the kingdom of God;
you young people, whom we so desire to have around us and all who
labor and suffer, who are sick and troubled, who certainly remember
that Christ calls upon you to partake in the suffering of His
redemption. The Holy Father also remembered all non-catholic
Christians "brothers in Baptism" for whom his memento in prayer

is that perfect unity desired by Jesus Christ. He included the whole world "so that our charity has no bounds" and all people and all governments would be included. Then the Holy Father recalled his special intentions "the Church One, Holy, Catholic and Apostolic. We want to pray for its internal peace. The Ecumenical Council has vitalized the heart of the Church, has opened up new vistas in the field of doctrine, has called all her children to a greater awareness, to a more intimate collaboration, to a more fervent apostolate. We desire that these be preserved and extended. What terrible damage could be caused by arbitrary interpretations not authorized by the Church, disrupting its traditional and constitutional structure, re-placing the theology of the great Fathers of the Church by new and peculiar ideologies, stripping the norms of faith of all that which modern thought, often lacking rational judgement, does not under-stand and does not like. Such interpretations change the apostolic fervor of redeeming charity to the negative structure of a profane mentality and mundane customs. What a delusion our efforts to arrive at universal unity would suffer if we failed to offer to our christian brethren divided from us and to the rest of humanity, which lacks our Faith, its clearcut authenticity and its original beauty, the patrimony of truth and charity, of which the Church is the guardian and the dispensor!   •

We want to ask from Mary a living Church, a united Church, a holy Church. We want to pray together with you, that the fruits of the Holy Spirit, the font of true christian life, whose feast — Pente-cost — we are celebrating tomorrow, the aspirations and efforts of the Council may find fulfillment. According to Saint Paul the fruits are: love, faithfulness, joy, peace, patience, kindness, goodness, gentleness and self-control. We want to pray that the love of God reign now and for ever in the world, that His law guide the conscience and customs of modern men. Faith in God is the supreme light of humanity and this light not only must never be extinguished in the hearts of men, but must be renewed through the stimulus of science and progress." The Holy Father then spoke of "those nations, in which religious liberty is almost totally suppressed and where the negation of God is proclaimed as representing the truth of these times and the liberty of the people, whereas this is not the case. We pray for the faithful of these nations, that God's strength may uphold them and that true civil liberty may once more be conceded to them.

"The second intention of our pilgrimage which fills our heart, is the world, peace in the world! You all know how the realization of the mission of the Church in the world, a mission of love and service, has been turned more alive and active after the Council. You know how the world is in a phase of great transformation due to the enormous and marvelous progress in the knowledge and in the conquest of the resources of the earth and of the universe. But you can also see very easily that the world is not happy, not tranquil; that the first cause of its uneasiness is the difficulty it has to enter into harmonious relationships, its difficulty to follow the path of peace. Everything seems to lead to a world of brotherhood and unity, but instead the heart of mankind still bursts with continuous and tremendous conflicts. Two conditions render this historic moment of mankind difficult. One, the world is full of terrifying and deadly arms, while it has not progressed morally as much as it has scientifically and technically. Two, humanity suffers under a state of need and hunger. While it has been awakened to the disturbing consciousness of its need it is aware of the wellbeing which surrounds it. Therefore we say, the world is in danger. For this reason We come to the feet of the Queen of Peace to ask from her the gift of peace. Yes peace, a gift from God, which needs His intervention, gracious, divine, merciful and mysterious. But it is not always a miraculous gift; it is a gift that works its wonders in the depth of the hearts of men; a gift therefore which has need of our free acceptance and our free collaboration. Our prayer therefore after having been directed towards heaven, is now directed towards all men in the whole world.

I call upon all men to strive to be worthy of the divine gift of peace! Men be true men, be good, wise seeking the common good of the world. Men be magnanimous! Men, try to see your dignity and the interest of others. Men, do not contemplate projects of destruction and of death, of revolutions and of suppression, but think rather of projects of mutual help and of solid collaboration. Men, think of the gravity and of the magnificence of this hour, which can be decisive for the history of the present and of future generations; begin to approach one another with the intention of building a new world, yes a world of true men, a world which can never be achieved without the light of God on the horizon. Men, listen to our humble and trembling voice, which echoes the powerful words of Christ "Blessed are the meek for they will possess the earth; blessed are the peaceful for they shall be called the children of God."

Behold my brothers and children, who listen to us here, behold, the immense and dramatic aspects which the world and its destinies present to us. It is the vista which our Lady opens before our eyes, a condition which we contemplate with frightened eyes, but ever confident; a condition to which we are drawing ever closer, to which we pledge ourselves, following the counsel which our Lady herself gave to us, that of prayer and penance, since, God willing, the world shall never again have to face wars, tragedies and catastrophies, but rather see the conquests of love and the victory of peace.

CHAPTER LI

«MARY'S APPEAL IS NOT FOR JUST ONCE» **(JOHN PAUL II)**

Pope John Paul II was in Portugal from the 12th to 15th May, 1982.
He came especially as a pilgrim to Fatima, in thanksgiving.
From his homily to the vast assembly during the Eucharistic concelebration of May 13th, we quote:

«And so I come here today because on this very day last year, in Saint Peter's Square in Rome, the attempt on the Pope's life was made, in mysterious coincidence with the anniversary of the first apparition at Fatima, which occurred on 13 May 1917.

I seemed to recognize in the coincidence of the dates a special call to come to this place. And so, today I am here. I have come in order to thank Divine Providence in this place which the Mother of God seems to have chosen in a particular way. «*Misericordiae Domini, quia non sumus consumpti*» (Lam. 3:22), I repeat once more with the people: Through God's mercy we were spared.

And further:

Today John Paul II, successor of Peter, continuer of the work of Pius, John, and Paul, and particular *heir of the Second Vatican Council,* presents himself before the Mother of the Son of God in her Shrine at Fatima. In what way does he come?

He presents himself, reading again with trepidation the motherly call to penance, to conversion, the ardent appeal of the Heart of Mary that resounded at Fatima sixty-five years ago. Yes, he reads it again with *trepidation in his heart,* because he sees how many people and societies — how many Christians — have gone in *the opposite direction* to the one indicated in the message of Fatima. Sin has thus made itself firmly at home in the world, and denial of God has become widespread in the ideologies, ideas and plans of human beings.

But for this very reason the evangelical call to repentance and conversion, uttered in the Mother's message, remains ever relevant. It is still more urgent. And so it is to be the subject of next year's *Synod of Bishops,* which we are already preparing for.

The successor of Peter presents himself here also as *a witness to the immensity of human suffering,* a witness to the almost apocalyptic menaces looming over the nations and mankind as a whole. He is trying to embrace these sufferings with his own weak human heart, as he places himself before the mystery of the Heart of the Mother, the Immaculate Heart of Mary.

In the name of these sufferings and with awareness of the evil that is spreading throughout the world and menacing the individual human being, the nations, and mankind as a whole, Peter's successor presents himself here with greater *faith in the redemption of the world,* in the saving Love that is always stronger, always more powerful than any evil.

My heart is oppressed when I see the sin of the world and the whole range of menaces gathering like a dark cloud over mankind, but it also *rejoices with hope* as I *once more* do what has been done by my Predecessors: namely, I entrust the world to the Heart of the Mother, I entrust especially to that Heart those peoples which need particularly to be entrusted. By doing this, I am entrusting the world to Him who is infinite Holiness. This Holiness means redemption. It means a love more powerful than evil. No «sin of the world» can ever overcome this Love.

Once more this act is being done. *Mary's appeal is not for just once.* Her appeal must be taken up by generation after generation, in accordance with the ever new «signs of the times». It must be unceasingly returned to. It must ever be taken up *anew.*»

APPENDIX I.

A letter from Dr. Carlos Mendes to his fiancée, written in September, 1917.

DEAREST ———

When I arrived at Aljustrel, at the house of Francisco's parents, I asked to speak to the children. Jacinta appeared and came up to me at once. She is very tiny, very babyish. I sat down so as to be able to see her better and sat her down on a chest near me. Thus I was able to observe her at will. I must tell you at once that she is a darling—a little angel! She had a red handkerchief on her head, the points tied behind. It was rather torn and old and her coat was not particularly clean. Her skirt was full and wide in the local manner. I wish I could describe her face to you but I fear I cannot do so adequately. I will try to do the best I can.

The kerchief served to emphasise her features. Her eyes are very dark and enchantingly vivacious, while her expression is really angelic, so extraordinarily sweet and kind that one is attracted in spite of oneself. She was so shy and timid that it was only with the greatest difficulty that I could make out her answers to my questions. After chatting for a while (I can imagine how you would have enjoyed it!) Francisco arrived. He carried his cap in his hand and wore a very short jacket, the waistcoat open and showing his shirt, narrow trousers—in fact he is a little man in miniature. He has a splendid boyish face and his expression is both lively and manly. He answered my questions with confidence, and then Jacinta, too, began to gain courage. Shortly afterwards Lucia arrived. You cannot imagine Jacinta's joy when she saw her! She seemed to dissolve into laughter and ran to her cousin, never leaving her side again. It was a charming sight to see Lucia in the middle with Francisco on one side and Jacinta on the other, very close with her head against her cousin's side.

Lucia is not very impressive to look at. I should say that she is very typical of the region. Her expression is lively but for the rest she is ordinary-looking. She, too, was shy to begin with, but I soon put her at her ease and she began to reply without any embarrassment. As I told you, I questioned the three of them separately. They all say the same thing without any alteration of the story. The principal thing which emerges, according to my own analysis, is that the Lady wishes the spread of devotion to the Rosary. All three children say that a Lady appeared to them but they do not know who she is. After six appearances, on 13th October she will say who she is and what she wants. The naturalness and simplicity with which they tell one all this is extraordinary and impressive. Lucia sees the Lady, speaks to her and hears her. Jacinta sees and hears but does not address her. Francisco neither hears nor speaks but sees her. The difference is very interesting, is it not?

To hear these children, to see their candour and to observe them in general makes such a remarkable impression on one that one is led to conclude that there is something in what they say. To be with them is an intensely moving experience. It is now my con-

viction that we are confronted with something outside mere reason.
I await the next 13th (October) with growing impatience. I repeat
that, near these children, one has a sense of goodness and loses
one's sense of time. There is an attraction which I cannot explain.
The chief impression of the children seems to be of the Lady's
beauty. The boy, to express his admiration, said that she was
" perfectly sweet ". I showed him your photograph and asked him
if she were prettier than you. " Much more," he said, " and the
Lady was all dressed in white and gold."

After this the parents offered me some refreshments and during
that time I questioned them closely, too. They only know what
the children tell them and I don't think their knowledge goes further
than mine at present. Senhora Olimpia told me of her apprehen-
sions because of the excitement which has been caused, and added :
" If we were worthy of such a thing it might be all right, but just
think, sir, my brother (Lucia's father) is a tippler!" Then she told
me all about the imprisonment of the children.

Later, we went with the children to the place of the Apparitions
in the Cova da Iria. The little tree has been reduced almost to
nothing. Round what remains there is a stone wall and over it an
arch made of greenery. On the wall are pots of sweet basil and
other flowers.

When we arrived, the three children knelt down and Lucia, who
was in the middle, began to recite the Rosary. The recollection
and devotion with which she prayed made a profound impression
on us. The " offering " of the Rosary was interesting—" for the
soldiers at the war ". When it was finished I asked the children if
I could take a little piece of sweet basil as a souvenir and was presented with some by each of them. The prayer which they say the
Lady taught them is simple, and is as follows : " O Jesus, forgive
me and deliver me from the fire of hell. Take all souls to Heaven,
especially those who are most in need."

APPENDIX II.

A Masonic Pamphlet.

To all Liberal Portuguese. Reaction let loose! ! The Association
    for Civil Registration and the Portuguese Federation of Free-
    thinkers energetically protest against the ridiculous comedy
    of Fatima.

CITIZENS!

As if the pernicious propaganda of reactionaries were not enough,
we now see a *miracle* trotted out in order further to degrade the
people into fanaticism and supersitition. There has been staged . . .
an indecorous comedy in Fatima at which thousands of people
have assisted, a ridiculous spectacle in which the simple people
have been ingeniously deceived by means of collective suggestion
into a belief in a supposed Apparition of the Mother of Jesus of

Nazareth to three children jockeyed into this shameful spectacle for the commercial purposes of clerical reaction!

As if, however, the declarations of these poor little dupes who affirm they have seen a " Virgin " which, however, nobody else can see and hear, were not sufficient, it is affirmed, or rather invented, that the sun, at a certain hour on 13th October, 1917, (on the eighth anniversary of the assassination of Francisco Ferrer) and in the height of the 20th century, was seen to dance a fandango in the clouds!

This, citizens, is a miserable and retrograde attempt to plunge the Portuguese people once more into the dense darkness of past times which have departed never to return. The Republic and those citizens who are charged with the noble and thankless task of guiding it in the glorious paths of Civilisation and Progress cannot consent to the degradation of the people into fanaticism and credulity, for this would be an unpardonable failing in their primal duty, not only towards their country but to Humanity as a whole. It is therefore our duty to demand from the public authorities the most energetic and immediate precautions against this shameless plan by which reaction seeks to plunge the people once more into mediævalism. . . .

What shall be our means of co-operation with those from whom we claim the action necessary for the end we envisage? An intensive and tenacious propaganda, which will raise the mentality of our co-citizens to the realms of Truth, Reason and Science, convincing them that nothing can alter the laws of Nature and that the pretended miracles are nothing but miserable tricks to abuse the credulity which is the child of ignorance. . . .

Let professors in the schools and colleges educate their pupils in a rational manner, liberating them from religious preconceptions as from all others, and we shall have prepared a generation for the morrow, happier because more worthy of happiness.

Let us, then, liberate ourselves and cleanse our minds, not only from foolish beliefs in such gross and laughable tricks as Fatima but more especially from any credence in the supernatural and a pretended *Deus Omnipotente,* omniscient and omni-everything, instrument of the subtle imaginations of rogues who wish to capture popular credulity for their purposes.

Citizens!

LONG LIVE THE REPUBLIC!
DOWN WITH REACTION!
LONG LIVE LIBERTY!

APPENDIX III.

The following letter, dated 24th July, 1927, was received a few days later by Senhora Maria Rosa : —

MY DEAREST MOTHER,

As I know that it is a great consolation to you to receive a letter from me I am sending you this to encourage you and help you to offer the sacrifice of my absence to God. I understand very well how much this separation must mean to you, but I think that if we had not submitted to it voluntarily, God Himself would have done it for us. Do you remember how Uncle Manuel would not let his children go out of the house and in the end God took them all? For this reason, dear mother, offer this generously to the Blessed Virgin in reparation for the offences of her ungrateful children; I would also like to ask you to give me the consolation of embracing a devotion which I know is very pleasing to God and was asked for by our beloved Mother in Heaven. As soon as I knew about it I wanted to practise it and get everyone else to do it, too. I hope, dear mother, that you will be able to tell me that you are practising it and also as many people as possible as well. You could never give me greater happiness than this. It consists only in doing what is written on this little holy picture: the confession can be made on another day but I think the fifteen minutes (meditation) is what will worry you the most although it is really very easy. Who cannot think about the Mysteries of the Rosary? The Annunciation of Our Lady and her humility at her great exaltation, calling herself a slave; the Passion of Our Lord Who suffered so much for love of us, and Our Lady near Jesus on Calvary? Who could not pass fifteen minutes with Our dear Lady thinking about these holy things?

Good-bye, dearest mother. Try to console Our Lady in this way and get many others to do the same. This would give me a happiness that I could not explain.

I kiss your hand and am your most loving daughter,

LUCIA DE JESUS.

APPENDIX IV.

THE SECRET.

During the July Apparition Our Lady confided a secret to the seers, the two first parts of which were only divulged after the second World War has broken out. The third part, written in Lucia's own hand, is in the possession of the Pope, who has declined to reveal it.

The first part of the secret concerns the vision of hell; the second part is of universal value and interest. In it Our Lady predicted the second World War, which was to be preceded by a sign which Lucia recognised in the aurora borealis of the night of 25th-26th January, 1938. This phenomenon was witnessed in nearly all the nations of Europe and was largely referred to in the Press.

In order to prevent this terrible scourge, Our Lady would come (she said) to ask for the consecration of Russia to her Immaculate Heart and for the reparatory Communion of the First Saturdays. The consequence would be the conversion of Russia and peace among the nations. If her desires were not complied with " Russia would spread her errors throughout the world, causing wars and persecutions of the Church; the good will be martyred and the Holy Father will have much to suffer. Various nations will be annihilated. . . ." The fulfilment of this prophecy is the sad reality through which humanity is living at present and the subject is of the utmost importance and merits our close attention.

Now a question: Why did Lucia wait so long before making the prophecy known?

From the interrogations and depositions of Lucia we may deduce the following: On 10th December, 1925, Our Lady appeared to her in her room with the Child Jesus and said: " Look, my daughter, at my Heart, encircled with thorns, with which ungrateful men pierce it at every instant with their blasphemy and ingratitude. You at least try to console me with the practice of the First Saturdays."

Lucia immediately began to make this devotion known around her. There is a letter extant* (dated 24th July, 1927), written to her mother, Maria Rosa, in which Lucia urges the practice of the devotion that Our Lady made known to her. Lucia also declares: " From 1925, I asked that the devotion of the reparatory Communion might be propagated, together with confession, the Rosary and a quarter of an hour's meditation, for five consecutive Saturdays. In order to realise this desire of Our Lady I requested the help of my confessor, then Fr. Lino, and the Rev. Mother Superior, Mother Maria das Dores Magalhães. By order of Rev. Mother I wrote to my former confessor in Oporto, Mons. Pereira Lopes. As he did not reply, I spoke of Our Lady's wish (again by order of Rev. Mother) to a Jesuit Father who was then living in Pontevedra (at present in the " Broteria " in Lisbon), Rev. Fr. Francisco Rodrigues.

In 1926, when I came from Tuy, I made Our Lady's request known to my confessor at that time, Rev. Father José da Silva Aparicio, Superior of the Jesuits in that city (at present in Brazil, where he is Rector of the Jesuit House in Ceará Baturitá). At that time Our Lady had not yet made her demand about Russia. It was two years later (1929), in the chapel of the Dorotheas, in Tuy, that Our Lady came to request this consecration which was to be made by the Holy Father in union with all the Bishops of the world.

In 1929, as Fr. Aparicio had relinquished his post of confessor to the community, I made Our Lady's desire about the consecration of Russia known to Fr. Francisco Rodrigues, who came to Tuy frequently on his way to Portugal. I also told Fr. Gonçalves, who came to replace Fr. Aparicio. (He is at present Superior of the Zambesi Mission in the Mission of Lifiége, Mozambique.) His Reverence made me write it down and promised to work for the realisation of Our Lady's wishes. He also informed the Bishop of Leiria and arranged that the matter should come to the knowledge of His Holiness the Pope (Pius XI).[1]

*Appendix III.

[1] Lucia does not remember the exact date on which this message was delivered to the Holy Father but recalls that her confessor told her that it had been graciously received and would be taken into consideration.

As we see, therefore, Lucia had repeatedly spoken of the second World War a long time before it broke out although her requests went unheeded.

When Pius XII took the helm of the Church the world was already on the eve of the terrible conflagration. Lucia insisted once more, not on the consecration of Russia alone but of all the world, with an especial mention of Russia. " In 1940 I wrote to the Bishop referring to the failure to fulfil Our Lady's wishes. I wrote: ' If the world only knew the moment of grace which is conceded and would do penance. . . .' In the letter which, by order of my spiritual directors, I wrote to the Holy Father in 1940, I exposed the exact request of Our Lady and asked for the consecration of the world with especial mention of Russia."

From all this the following facts emerge. Pius XI did not make the consecration which our Lady had asked Lucia to make known. Pius XII, in his turn, did not consecrate Russia in the original form whioh had been indicated, but as Lucia asked him in the direct letter of 1940. That is to say, he consecrated the whole world to the Immaculate Heart of Mary with an especial mention of Russia. " Especially those who profess singular devotion to You, where there is hardly a house that did not display Your holy icon, to-day hidden perhaps, in expectation of better days."

All the peoples of the earth form, as it were, one great family which has God for its invisible Father and Mary as its Mother. The Holy Father in his turn is the Vicar of Christ on earth—the visible Father of the family. The different nations are his children. Among these children are some who have openly broken away from the family and the common Father. Such a child is the Russian nation, which in its ideology and its institutions, in its manner of life, is the absolute negation of Christianity. Like a gangrene this militant atheism tends to spread throughout the whole world. Our Lady, a watchful Mother, wishes to save all her children but in particular those most in need of salvation, just as an earthly mother pre-occupies herself first and foremost with those of her children who are sick. Such is the case with Russia. Our Lady asked for the consecration of Russia but she did not exclude the other nations, her other children. We can go further: the consecration of the whole great human family was certainly in the heart and mind of the Blessed Virgin, and the Holy Father could not consecrate Russia to her Heart in a better way nor correspond more closely with the desires of Mother of Mercy than by consecrating the entire world to her.

The common Father in a moment of sorrow, seeing some of his children far from home and tragically separated from God, does everything possible to reunite them round himself, the faithful ones sharing in his sorrow and the others, though separated of their own free will, nevertheless remaining in his paternal heart notwithstanding their evil-doing.

The common Father of the Christian family confides, hands over, " not only Holy Church, the Mystical Body of Christ which bleeds and suffers in so many parts of the world and is in so much tribulation but also the whole world lacerated by discord, burning in great fires of hate, victim of its own iniquity ".[1]

No, Pius XII could not have better interpreted the desires of Our Lady and we, children of the Church, must unite in a crusade of prayer and penance, that, in the Holy Father's own words, we may " hasten the triumph of the Kingdom of God so that all generations at peace among themselves and with God, may proclaim the blessedness of the most Holy Virgin and with her intone from pole to pole the eternal Magnificat of glory and love and thanksgiving to the Heart of Jesus where alone may be found truth, peace and life ".

APPENDIX V.

" THE MIRACLE OF THE SUN."

A Critical Note by Pio Scatizzi, S.J.

In world history, outside ordinary eclipses, nothing prodigious has been recorded of the sun, with the single exception of the Biblical miracle of Josua—the day's standstill of sun and moon. This fact and no other marks Fatima with a stupendous singularity quite apart from the rest of the story.

The thousands of pilgrims, as we know, were caught in pouring rain, while gusts of wind swept the rocky hillsides. Suddenly, at midday, the heavens opened and the clouds drew back to the

[1] It is only in this order of ideas that the consecration of individuals, families or dioceses can contribute to and hasten the conversion of Russia and the world.

horizon leaving the air pure and clear as a mirror. Such would be the case after prolonged and copious rain, when the air becomes more transparent than usual and appears to have been washed. At this moment the sun begins to pale and it may be argued that the diminution of light could have been caused by mist or flakes of mist suspended in the air. After all those hours of rain and all that humidity, it would be logical to suspect that at least some fragments of mist would remain in the atmosphere. At first sight such doubts might be justified, since many witnesses describe the sun's disc as being opaque, silvered, or like mother-of-pearl.

Yet we can admit without hesitation that the sun looked opaque, with a well-defined rim, and at the same time prove that there was no intervening mist. In fact we can postulate this alternative: either the mist was light or it was dense. I define a "light" mist that which exists between zero and the extreme point at which the eye cannot with impunity be fixed on the sun. I call a "dense" mist that which exists from this point until there is complete occultation. Now it is certain that the first alternative must be excluded, for the sun appeared like mother-of-pearl on which the vision could easily be fixed. There remains, therefore, the second alternative. But if the mist were dense the sun's disc would not have been clearly defined. For, in fact, when a dense damp fog veils it there is formed in the surrounding atmosphere a kind of aureole or crown (not in the technical and astronomical sense of the word) which, so to speak, confirms the presence of mist. Yet all affirm that the sky behind the sun was perfectly clear. Now between this and a mist capable of dominating solar light there would seem to be an excessive difference, one may say a contradiction: the sky a clean background and at the same time a mist obscuring the sun. . . .

This opaqueness of the sun in a clear sky was but the beginning of events, for immediately there began to radiate from its centre thousands upon thousands of coloured monochromatic lights in sectors, which, in the form of spirals, began to whirl around the centre of the solar disc in such a manner that the sun itself seemed to turn on itself rather like a catherine wheel, while the coloured rays spread out in a centrifrugal movement covering the sky as far as the curtain of clouds and turning everything various colours as if by magic. Such a spectacle of red, yellow, green and violet rays from the sun, spreading and sweeping over the sky, cannot be explained by any known laws, nor has such a thing been seen before.

Could it have been a rainbow? Obviously not, for the simple reason that a rainbow is a stationary object. Further, the rainbow is drawn on a vertical plane opposite the sun and does not originate in the solar disc itself but in the opposite line of vision. The eye rests on the summit of a cone on whose base rests the plane of the arch. The solar rays, which are parallel and horizontal, radiate from behind the observer, not from the front, and with a penetrating action reflect themselves once or twice in the falling drops of water, returning to the eye with the dispersion of the iris. In the case under review, on the contrary, the phenomenon is one of radiation over the whole circle of the horizen with uniform and continuous movement. Certainly there can occur other prismatic effects in the atmosphere but they are seen, as is well known, at dawn or sunset. The air then operates as a prism, dispersing the light in various coloured beams—those of the spectrum.

In the case of Fatima, it is extremely difficult to place such a phenomenon within a known framework when outside the solar disc there was only limpid air without any reflecting agent, as with a rainbow, when along each monochromatic ray numberless drops of water renew the prismatic effect. In Fatima, as seen by motionless observers, the monochromatic sectors appeared to revolve and to subsist without any support. We must conclude that each coloured ray was maintained autonomously, with its origin in the solar body, the air providing no means of transmission. At an altitude of 42° 44′—that of the sun at midday in October—clear air, in some measure disturbed by wind, could not of itself cause a phenomenon of spectral dispersion of autonomous rotating rays.

The only comparable phenomenon is, perhaps the aurora borealis. Professor Vercelli, in his book, *The Air*, quotes a description by Mr. Herdel of an exceptional aurora which was seen in the State of Iowa (U.S.A.) on the night of 14th May, 1921. Taking this account as a base for comparison, I note a great divergence between the two events. In Fatima, stable, compact, above all homogeneous. The aurora was variable, disordered, unstable. Further, it is proved that the zone of maximum occurrence of the aurora borealis is limited by a quasi-parallel running through North Cape-Northern Siberia-coast of Alaska-Hudson Bay-Labrador-Iceland and back to North Cape in Norway. We can then be nearly certain that on the 50th parallel the aurora cannot be seen—at least according to current theory.

The aurora borealis is caused by trajectories of electrons, or better, according to Vegard, by particles thrown off by the sun and diverted to the magnetic field of the earth. Then, coming in contact with the air, they give origin to the variegated lights which can be observed. The quasi-parallel trajectories which pass through the magnetic north are seen by us converging and diverging only by an effect of perspective. In substance, the aurora boreales are inherent in the terrestial magnetic poles and thence to the *hyperboreal* regions—hence their name.

In spite of all this, one cannot absolutely exclude the possibility of the aurora borealis being seen in low latitudes. In fact one was observed in Rome in 1938. But one fact alone distinguishes the Fatima phenomenon from this and other appearances of the aurora. The origin of the lights in Fatima was in the sun, from whence they sprang, whereas during the true aurora the sun is always invisible. Apart from this the latitude of Fatima (39°-36) is even lower than that of Rome. Also the synchronising, revolving movement of the sectors and their three stops at regular intervals (according to witnesses) is far from the irregular, disordered movements, the disappearance and reappearance of light as described in Mr. Herdel's account. Lastly, if there had been a true aurora borealis it would have been observed in some European observatory.

It now remains to examine the third phase of the phenomenon, that is to say the movement of the sun, which appeared to detach itself from the sky and to fall on the earth in a zigzag path. It can be affirmed that such a phenomenon is outside and against all natural and astronomical laws. It appears that with this final occurrence, all doubts as to the natural origin of the events, all scepticism on our part, must be laid aside.

At this point it would be well to refresh our motives for belief in such an unheard of incident. The number and nature of the witnesses exceed all requirements for verification. With twelve such, the law justifies the execution of a man. In this case eye-witnesses numbered some 70,000.

To resume our study: First, we have the rotation of the sun and the various colours; secondly, a movement outside the normal daily path of the sun in the heavens. In the first case there would be a normal admiration such as would be excited by a first view of an aurora borealis. There would be no cause for terror. Yet, suddenly, without the intervention of any new factor, the multitude is seized with terror as if menaced by a cataclysm. Everyone feels threatened by imminent catastrophe. There is a sensation that the sun is about to fall on the earth; that it is being torn from the cosmic laws of its eternal path. Hence the invocations, the prayers, the cries of affliction as in a universal cataclysm.

Observe well the second phase. It is not religious hysteria nor a species of pentecostal fervour. It is sheer panic in the presence of Him Who alone can dominate the forces of the universe. Contemporary accounts will show that it was not a case of suggestion but that an objective vision was the cause of the panic which, when it had passed, left everyone perfectly calm, contented even, at having witnessed a prodigy which had been exactly foretold and anxiously awaited. How also could everyone have seen the danger pass at one and the same moment?

Of the historical reality of this event there can be no doubt whatever. That it was outside and against known laws can be proved by certain simple scientific considerations.

The " movement " of the sun is relative to the earth's own. The orbit of the latter is nearly an ellipse of extremely small ex-centricity. The daily transitional movement of the earth—even with its velocity of thirty kilometres per second—is projectively imperceptible. Much less would it be so during the ten minutes' duration of the phenomena. If ten minutes are sufficient, as was the case in Fatima, for a generic qualitative observation, they would not suffice for the observation with the naked eye of a solar dislocation which can be known only in relation to the distances of the zodiac constellations.

Conclusion: The above-mentioned solar phenomena were not noted in any observatory. Impossible that they should escape the notice of so many astronomers and indeed the other inhabitants of the hemisphere. It must then be admitted that there is no question of an astronomical or meteorological phenomenon as we have already said. We are thus confronted with an inescapable dilemma. Either all the observers in Fatima were collectively deceived and erred in their testimony or we must suppose an extra-natural intervention. Given the indubitable reference to God, and the general context of the story, it seems that we must attribute to Him alone the most obvious and colossal miracle of history.

APPENDIX VI.

A detailed account of Lucia's First Communion appears in her memoirs. It took place when she was six years old, three years after the Decree of Pope Pius X admitting small children to Holy Communion, and seems to have been attended by certain supernatural features and a promise of future sanctity. It is also interesting in the light of later events that the first confession of the seer was made to Father Cruz, S.J., who later became renowned for his sanctity and was to be one of the most celebrated personages in Portugal, like Lucia herself.

The parish priest had decided that Lucia was too young to receive Holy Communion although she had responded well to the Catechism. Father Cruz, who happened to be giving a triduum, saw her in tears and, after examining her, personally intervened and secured a reversal of the decision of the parish priest, expressing his opinion that the little girl was perfectly ready and able to receive Our Lord. After her confession she prayed before Our Lady's statue and (instructed perhaps by her confessor) prayed earnestly: " Please keep my poor heart for God." It seemed to her at that moment that the statue smiled upon her and gave her a visible sign of assent. Again, before the Mass on the following day, she knelt before the statue and prayed: " Make me a saint." Once again she seemed to have a supernatural sign and certainty that her prayer had been heard. " I do not know," she writes, " whether the facts I have written about my First Communion were a reality or a little girl's illusion. All I know is that they had a great influence in uniting me to God all my life." When she received Our Lord she felt an " unalterable serenity and peace " and kept saying in her heart " Lord, make me a saint. Keep my heart always pure—for You alone." And she heard distinctly the reply: " The grace that I grant thee to-day will remain living in thy soul producing fruits of eternal life." Although the Mass was very late in finishing Lucia could not eat when she arrived home. Her spiritual experience had almost abstracted her from her senses and those around her noticed her recollection and absorption.

THE END

BIBLIOGRAPHY

Ir. Lúcia do Coração Imaculado, *Memória e escritos*, Fátima, 1978.

Visconde de Montelo (pseud.) Manuel Nunes Formigão, *Os Episódios maravilhosos de Fátima*, Guarda, 1921.

Idem, *As grandes maravilhas de Fátima*, Guarda, 1927.

L. Gonzaga da Fonseca, *Nossa Senhora de Fátima*, 1934.

Idem in italiano, *Le meraviglie di Fatima*, Casale Monferrato, 1942, IV ediz.

Antero de Figueiredo, *Fátima, Graças, Segredo, Mistérios*, Lisboa, 1936.

J. De Marchi, *Era uma Senhora mais brilhante que o sol*, Fátima, 1946, III ediz.

Costa Brochado, *Fátima à luz da História*, Lisboa, 1948.

S. Martins dos Reis, *Fátima, as suas provas e os seus problemas*, Lisboa, 1953.

L. M. Fisher, *Fatima, das portugiesische Lourdes*, Baden, 1930.

Idem, *Fatima im Lichte der kirchlichen Autoritat*, Bamberg, 1931.

Ch. Barthas, *Fatima merveille du XXe siecle*, Toulouse, 1953.

António M. Martins, *Documentos de Fátima*, Porto, 1976.

Finbar Ryan, *Our Lady of Fatima*, Dublin, 1939.

José Galamba de Oliveira, *Jacinta of Fatima*, Sydney, 1945.

W. T. Walsh, *Our Lady of Fatima*, New York, 1947.

T. McGlynn, *Vision of Fatima*, Boston, 1948.

Joseph Cacella, *The Wonders of Fatima*, New York, 1948.

M. Norton, *Eyewitness at Fatima*, Dublin, 1950.

C. C. Martindale, *The Message of Fatima*, London, 1950.

G. L. Baker, *The Finger of God is Here*, St. Paul's, 1961.

J. M. Haffert, *Meet the Witnesses*, Washington, N. J., 1961.